JCMS Annual Review of the European Union in 2017

Edited by

Theofanis Exadaktylos,
Roberta Guerrina
and
Emanuele Massetti

General Editors: Toni Haastrup and Richard Whitman

WILEY

This edition first published 2018

© 2018 John Wiley & Sons Ltd except for editorial material and organization

Registered Office
John Wiley & Sons Ltd, The Atrium, Southern Gate, Chichester, West Sussex, PO19 8SQ, UK

Editorial Offices
350 Main Street, Malden, MA 02148--5020, USA
9600 Garsington Road, Oxford, OX4 2DQ, UK
The Atrium, Southern Gate, Chichester, West Sussex, PO19 8SQ, UK

For details of our global editorial offices, for customer services, and for information about how to apply for permission to reuse the copyright material in this book please see our website at www.wiley.com/wiley-blackwell.

Library of Congress Cataloging-in-Publication Data
Library of Congress Cataloging-in-Publication data is available for this book

ISBN 978-1-119-48905-4
ISSN 0021-9886 (print) 1468-5965 (online)

A catalogue record for this book is available from the British Library.

Set in 11/12.5 pt Times by Toppan Best-set Premedia Limited
Printed in Singapore

1   2018

CONTENTS

JCMS 2018 Volume 56. Annual Review pp. 5–10   DOI: 10.1111/jcms.12775

Editorial: 2017 – A Year in Review

THEOFANIS EXADAKTYLOS, ROBERTA GUERRINA and EMANUELE MASSETTI
University of Surrey

It is with great pleasure that we write our first editorial note for the *JCMS Annual Review*. When we applied for the position in 2017, we were cognisant of the challenge facing us as incoming editors and the discipline of EU studies more broadly. We welcome the opportunity to stand on the shoulders of the previous editors and the legacy of the *Journal of Common Market Studies* as we strive to open the journal to new voices and fields of research. We would like to collectively thank all those who have contributed to the success of the *Annual Review* with their articles and ideas, and to welcome this year's contributors. We would like to formally thank the previous editors, Nathaniel Copsey and Tim Haughton, whose achievements will be a source of inspiration for us. Finally, we would like to thank the outgoing president of UACES, Helen Drake, and the chief *JCMS* editors, Toni Haastrup and Richard Whitman, for trusting us with such an impactful journal. We hope that we will not let you and the community of readers down with our work.

The 2016 *Annual Review* touched on the many and varied challenges facing the EU, its institutions and Member States. It was certainly an eventful year on all aspects of politics, economics and society that largely set the tone for 2017. We believe that this is indeed a very critical moment for all of us studying the EU and its politics. It is both an exciting and equally daunting juncture in European Union history, not least because of the complexity of global challenges, be those addressed at the national, European or transnational levels.

The 2017 *Annual Review* touches on a number of key debates: from the future of European integration as a process such as the triple challenge of economic governance, migration and representation in Europe, foreign affairs and external action, through to the impact of electoral behaviour and civic engagement on shaping the future direction for the Union and its members. We are delighted that we have managed to open the journal to critical voices at this particular moment, thus providing a forum for an open and robust discussion about the future of the discipline, social inclusion, social cohesion and different manifestations of power. We strongly encourage you to have a look at the *Annual Review* as a whole rather than individual stand-alone contributions.

I. Our Vision

We aim to enhance the role of the *Annual Review* as a forum of analysis, reflection and deliberation, inviting key academic researchers across disciplines. We take a holistic and interdisciplinary view of EU studies to include political, economic, social and legal issues affecting the European Union and the wider continent, as well as the international context in which Europe operates. At the same time, we also aim to include articles from emerging researchers whose work has been already recognized as having an impact on our subfields of study or in the practitioners' community. In this way, we aim to increase participation, access and visibility of the *Annual Review* to a wider set of readers. Finally, we appreciate the input of the policy-making and practitioner communities in our scholarly work and we would like to make the *Annual Review* a forum for some key stakeholders to be able to present their views, evidence and analysis. Our ultimate goal is to maintain the status of the *Annual Review* as a truly reliable and informed source of information and a point of reference, not only for educators and researchers in the academic world, but also for wider audiences of key policy stakeholders.

As mentioned before, and underscored by many of this issue's contributions, the coming years represent a 'juncture' for the EU, its members and the peoples of Europe. There are three possible scenarios or outcomes: (a) there is a breakthrough in the development of European public sphere, and there will be significant advances in co-operation, growth, inclusion and democratization; (b) key decisions are perennially postponed, thus reifying the dominant paradigms of integration; or (c) the future takes us back to past political paradigms through the retrenchment of integration. We as editors, believe in the reflexive and co-constitutive nature of academic work. Therefore, the role of academic outlets, such as the *JCMS Annual Review,* is to capture the complexity and diversity of the challenges facing the 'Union'.

Mapping the issues of salience for 2017 is a productive process, insofar as it highlights key preoccupations for the discipline and points to the direction of travel. However, this requires the opening up of access to and the creation of lateral mechanisms of dialogue. And within this novel paradigm we will strongly underpin the contributions on the focal points of innovation, originality, audience outreach, theoretical and empirical advances in the field and of course evidenced-based arguments. This space is aimed to inform and engage with the wider public and the practitioner community to the largest possible extent. At the same time, it needs to be informed by that audience. Therefore, beyond our public lecture and keynote articles, we will look out for contributors outside academic circles for a dynamic dialogue.

II. How We Want the *Annual Review* to Look

Among the key priorities for our editorial team are the development of a balance between established academics and emerging scholars, a wider coverage of contributors' country bases and gender balance. These we see as the benchmark requirements for the development of a more inclusive and diverse canon. As elsewhere in academia and in the editorial world, contributors have been predominantly male and the geographical coverage of where contributors are based was leaning to the West. While the geographical coverage is expected given the nature of the field of study, we will aim to widen the spectrum of countries. At the same time, achieving balance between male and female contributors is imperative.

Looking at the *Annual Review's* fabric of contributors, the majority in the past were based in the UK and Western Europe, predominantly from the UK. Considering the rapid developments across all social, political and economic fronts within Europe in the past few years, and the likely trajectory of the European Union in the years to come in the domain of the future of the euro and the EU itself as a set of institutional arrangements; the continuous growth of socio-economic inequality in most EU countries; the perseverance

of high levels of unemployment in peripheral Member States; the rise of right-wing extremism across Europe; the process of departure of the UK from the EU; the securitization
of policy and the accommodation of refugees; the dynamics developing between the US
and Russia; and the continuous international narratives of post-truth politics, we envisage
further challenges to emerge on democratic guarantees, social welfare, strong checks and
balances and the further demise of scientific expertise in policy-making. It is, therefore,
imperative for publications such as the *Annual Review* to safeguard the space for deliberation beyond academic silos and include the segments of academia that are directly exposed to political attacks or silenced by social practice and, by creating a mini-forum
within a future issue of the *Annual Review*, to foster dialogue and constructive debate.

Given the fast-moving nature of political developments and the main priority of the
Annual Review to 'review' the year before, we aim to follow rapidly evolving events,
such as electoral contests, public debates and protest, with commentaries or shorter
pieces. Although this was not possible this year, we would like our readers to look
forward to its launch with the 2018 *Annual Review*.

In conclusion, we envisage the future development of the *Annual Review* to provide a
platform for a range of different voices and scholars to reflect the impact of a particular
year on the future trajectory of the Union, its members and, ultimately the people of
Europe. Looking at 2016 and 2017 together, what is clear is the need to reach beyond
the narrowly defined boundaries of our discipline in order to understand the relationship
between high and low politics, the impact of citizens' engagement and new forms of politics on the very nature of the beast we need to study. Closer links between the academic
and practitioners' community draws attention to the nature and thrust of the scholarship
and increasing need for our work to be 'relevant'. In doing so, we also need to consider
our positionality and that of our 'research objects', which voices have historically been
favoured and, which ones have been silenced. Ultimately, our aim here is to augment
the development of EU studies through a dialogue between different camps and
approaches.

III. The Content of the 2017 *Annual Review*

The contributions of this year's *Annual Review* should not be read only as individual
pieces but with a holistic view of the state of affairs in the European Union. Providing empirical findings and new evidence, all articles aim at highlighting key developments
through a critical lens of true expertise. We focus on Brexit as a process and the UK
elections; different visions of Europe; the German and French elections in comparative
perspective; the wave of right-wing populism; the state of the economy and the euro;
regulation and good governance; the (un)intended consequences of austerity; security
and migration; external affairs and the Presidencies.

We invited Simon Hix to deliver the Annual Lecture which formed the foundation of
his contribution to this issue. The Annual Lecture is the hallmark of our public engagement activities and took place at Portcullis House in the heart of Westminster. Hix focused on the future of the relations of the EU and the UK after the negotiations for
withdrawal from the EU are concluded. More than a year after Article 50 was formally
triggered by Theresa May, Hix offers a game-theoretical approach to the outcomes of
the negotiations and how these are likely to evolve given the state of affairs and the

political sensitivities in the process. He argues that the most likely outcome based on the state of negotiations is a basic free trade agreement mainly regarding trade in goods but not extending to other areas.

Following the vision set out in this editorial note, Ian Manners and Ben Rosamond looked at the state of the discipline in light of the 60 years from the Treaty of Rome, helping us to set the tone for all other contributions in this issue. They argue that a different Europe is possible if the scholarly field of EU studies manages to redefine its scope and object of study to include a historical context, the EU's neoliberal preferences and the EU's public interest not only in terms of democratic sovereignty but also in terms of transnational solidarity. They call for increased diversity in our disciplinary and theoretical perspectives and, of course, methodological pluralism to capture the complexities, logics and structures of European integration as a living process.

Brexit as an unfolding event was at the spotlight throughout 2017, not least because it resulted in the reconfiguration of the political spectrum in the UK. The focus on the UK concludes with the contribution by Sara Hobolt on the 2017 general election. Hobolt argues that the electoral outcome revealed a highly polarized electorate, particularly on the key socio-economic dimension. Yet, her analysis also shows the persistent effects of voters' positions on Brexit. The election outcome weakened the position of the UK prime minister in terms of setting the agenda for the future of the UK outside the EU, making it difficult for a united and coherent position to emerge.

In many ways, 2017 was the year of elections. We thus turn our focus to the two electoral contests in France and Germany that created ripple effects across the EU. Hanspeter Kriesi proposes an interpretation of the election results that stresses similarities over differences, starting with the breakthrough of the radical-right in Germany. By giving prominence to the socio-cultural dimension of politics, Kriesi shows how the party systems in the two countries are *de facto* bipolar. In terms of governments, it is all about centre-ground politics and that leaves the losers from the margins of the political spectrum, especially the New Right, to handle their position in opposition. Kriesi concludes, however, that these new governments are not as stable as they appear, albeit providing an opportunity for the 'cosmopolitan forces' to regroup.

Such electoral outcomes were not unique to France and Germany. Daphne Halikiopoulou takes on the task of reviewing electoral contests across the EU in a comparative perspective, looking at the rise of right-wing populism. Halikiopoulou argues that right-wing populism is not a uniform phenomenon in terms of rhetoric and agendas. It is also not new: it is a trend that has held in Europe for the past 30 years and does vary across time and country, with very evident differences between Western and Central-Eastern Europe. It does, however, pose a series of common challenges in terms of electoral expansion and contagion effect *vis-à-vis* the mainstream political forces.

No issue of the *Annual Review* would be complete without some considerations on economics and governance. In reviewing economic developments in the EU for 2017, Amy Verdun takes a closer look at the institutional architecture of the euro. While 2017 was characterized by an improvement in the economic indicators of the eurozone, discussions took place about the future of EMU in light of the financial and debt crises in many euro member states. Discussing economic developments through the electoral lens, Verdun focuses on two policy documents that introduced small and incremental changes that point to deeper integration in economic and monetary affairs.

Here is where the importance of regulation and governance tools come into play. Claudio Radaelli reviews the 'Better Regulation' strategy that the Juncker Commission introduced, as a set of tools and guidelines for regulatory management. He takes stock of the period 2015–17 to look at inter-institutional relationships and the way policy and politics intersect, among the Parliament, the Council and the Commission. Radaelli argues that better regulation is an exercise in controlling institutional job descriptions and it is an area that will most likely dominate the new Commission's agenda.

This discussion leads into the contribution by Rosalind Cavaghan and Muireann O'Dwyer reviewing socio-economic power structures and narrative of exclusion in the EU. They focus on the economic policy of the Union through an intersectional lens to analyze the narrative of growth and recovery that the Commission put forward in 2017. The argument becomes that EU economic policy is quintessential in establishing gendered and racialized hierarchies in the EU and in the process of European integration.

Taking this argument a step further, there is a story to be told on the 'politics of becoming' and the ways in which austerity measures generate unexpected consequences with a bias towards women and minority groups. Akwugo Emejulu and Leah Bassel tackle precisely this problem: privatization of care, the rolling back of the social welfare state and the impact this had on women of colour activism. It turns from the macro politics of the EU to the lived micro-level experiences offering a unique reframing of austerity politics and the narrative of economic crisis. It maps the disproportionality of austerity measures with special reference to Britain and explores how this state of affairs obstructs and facilitates new public politics. Lessons drawn become quite relevant for many EU Member States where narratives of austerity are dominating the public policy space.

Similarly, on the effects of crisis, migration management was prominent in the EU in 2017. The refugee crisis challenged and put additional strains on the EU migration governance system. Andrew Geddes takes up the challenge to review developments in the drivers of migration to Europe, the migration and asylum policies and the participants in its governance mechanisms, as well as the politics of migration including mobilization and public attitudes. In his article, Geddes explores the way the wider politics of EU migration governance impact upon the allocation of resources and values, as well as the consequences on intra- and cross-member state dynamics and beyond.

Taken together these trends pose a challenge for the EU as a global actor. In 2016, Federica Mogherini presented the EU Global Strategy setting out a new agenda in light of an integration crisis as the UK decided to leave the EU. Nathalie Tocci takes stock of the goals set out in 2016 and how these were implemented in 2017 leading to significant activism in the area of security and defence. These two areas experienced increased attention by EU leaders. Tocci argues that for long time the EU has been underperforming in the external dimension. However, the implementation of a European Security and Defence Union is a start but political will and developments in other internal policy areas have to encircle this momentum if it is to succeed. Tocci's contribution also shows awareness of the challenges associated with pursuing integration in 'high politics' areas without deeper political integration to provide the foundation for this process.

The Review then examines the Council in light of the Presidencies of two small Member States. In January 2017, Malta took over and following the decision of the UK to leave the EU, Estonia moved up a semester, taking up the Presidency in July 2017. Panke and Gurol review the objectives and visions of the two Presidencies comparing the way in which small Member States who have limited resources and human capital can handle the task and set the tone of the EU agenda. They argue that despite similarities, there were differences between the two states in the scale and number of priorities. It seems that smaller states are more successful concentrating their efforts on a limited number of priorities and overarching themes.

Finally, as it is customary for the *Annual Review*, we provide a Chronology of events. Nikolaos Gkotsis Papaioannou has taken on this herculean task of collecting the most important developments and recreating a calendar of events that defined the politics, policies and public opinion in the EU for 2017. From this year onward, the Chronology will be published online only, recognizing the need for it to be open to amendments and addendums.

From all of us at the editorial team, we truly hope you enjoy the new *Annual Review* and the insights it provides on the multifaceted debates that took place regarding the state and the future of the European Union in 2017.

JCMS 2018 Volume 56. Annual Review pp. 11–27   DOI: 10.1111/jcms.12766

Brexit: Where is the EU–UK Relationship Heading?*

SIMON HIX
London School of Economics and Political Science

Introduction

I am delivering this lecture almost two-thirds of the way between the June 2016 EU referendum and the day the UK is scheduled to leave the EU, yet the long-term relationship between the UK and the EU still remains unclear. The basic elements of the Article 50 Withdrawal Agreement and the transition arrangements seem to be in place (except for the issue of the Northern Ireland–Ireland border), but there has been far less discussion of the post-transition 'future relationship' between the UK and EU27. The basic options for the future relationship have been known for some time: such as a 'soft' form of Brexit represented by the UK remaining in the European Economic Area (EEA); a 'hard' form of Brexit represented by the UK leaving the EU's single market and signing a free trade agreement similar to the EU's agreements with Canada or South Korea; or 'no deal' and the UK trading with the EU as a member of the World Trade Organization (WTO). The British government has started to clarify its preferred outcome: what the Secretary of State for Leaving the EU described in December 2017 as a 'Canada plus plus plus' agreement.[1] Only the basic features of the future relationship need to be agreed before March 2019, and the final agreement and ratification will only take place after the UK has become a third country. Hence, the final settlement is unlikely to be known before late 2020 at the earliest.

So, I focus my lecture today on precisely this: where the UK's relationship with the EU is heading in the medium-term. You might reasonably say that only a fool would try to predict this future, especially with so many uncertain moving parts. So, to simplify the considerations I focus my analysis on the economic and political interests of the UK government and the EU27 as a bloc, and how these interests are likely to shape the bargaining strategies. My analysis leads me to conclude that the most likely outcome – the equilibrium in the bargaining game between the UK and the EU27 – is a basic free trade agreement, mainly covering trade in goods with not much on trade in services. Of course, the outcome might be very different from a basic trade agreement, but the aim of my analysis is to help us think about what would need to change on either side for a different/better outcome to emerge. Having solved the bargaining 'game', I will then briefly discuss what a basic FTA might mean for ongoing relations between the UK and the EU27. Let me start, though, by briefly reviewing the main options for the future relationship.

*I would like to thank Angus Armstrong, Catherine Barnard, Theofanis Exadaktylos, Anand Menon, Jonathan Portes, Brendan O'Leary and Simon Usherwood for their helpful comments on an earlier version.
[1] BBC News (2017).

I. Options for the Future Relationship

Although 'hard' or 'soft' Brexit sound like discrete choices, the possible terms of a future relationship between the UK and EU27 are better characterized as a continuum of five 'harder' or 'softer' variants, as Figure 1 shows.

First, at the 'hard Brexit' end of the continuum is the UK leaving the EU without an agreement and trading with the EU as a normal WTO member. There are two possible scenarios of this **No Deal (or 'WTO') outcome**: 1) the UK and EU fail to agree or ratify a Withdrawal Agreement (which requires a qualified-majority vote in the EU Council, and majorities in the European Parliament and UK Parliament) and the EU fails (by unanimity) to extend the 29 March 2019 deadline; or 2) a Withdrawal Agreement is agreed and ratified, with a transition period included, but the UK and EU then fail to agree or ratify the future relationship before the end of the transition period, and the transition period is not extended. Either way, the UK would leave without any new agreement on the terms of trade with the EU27. Such a No Deal outcome could have significant economic costs for both sides, but particularly for the UK. On the other hand, the UK would be free to set its own regulatory standards and customs rules, within WTO rules, and would probably not have any financial liabilities owed to the EU, although it would have to contribute during a transition period, the EU may pursue a claim through international courts, and there would be diplomatic costs for not honouring liabilities.

Second, at the 'soft Brexit' end of the continuum is the **EEA (or 'Norway') option**. Here, the UK would leave the EU institutions but would re-join the European Free Trade Area (EFTA) and apply to become a member of the EEA, like Norway, Liechtenstein and Iceland. Joining the EEA would mean a continuation of the free movement of goods, services, capital and persons between the UK and the EU27 and other EEA states, applying EU single market rules (with some derogations), and largely accepting the jurisprudence of the Court of Justice of the EU (ECJ), although via the fig leaf of the EFTA Court. The UK would also have to make a contribution to the EU's finances. Nevertheless, the UK could leave the EU customs union (although a customs agreement could be agreed), and so sign its own trade agreements with third countries, and the UK would regain sovereignty in some policy areas, including fisheries, agriculture and home affairs.

Between these two extremes are several 'bespoke' options. Third, at the 'harder' end is a basic **FTA (or 'Canada') option**: a free trade agreement similar to the EU agreements with Canada, South Korea, and now Japan. These FTAs mainly cover trade in goods, with some limited regulatory equivalence and mutual recognition. However, these agreements do not cover trade in services in any comprehensive way, for example with the ability of service providers who are registered in one market to be established in or to trade freely in the other market.

Figure 1: The Brexit Continuum.

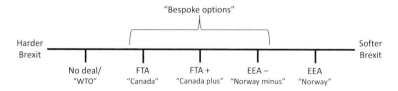

Fourth, a slightly 'softer' version of an FTA would be what has become known as the **FTA+ (or 'Canada Plus') option**. Although the UK government has talked about various aspects of co-operation with the EU that go beyond a basic FTA – such as security co-operation, data sharing, and defence co-operation – the 'plus' here mainly refers to an agreement which includes financial services. Financial services is the UK's largest economic sector, constituting 3.1 per cent of total UK employment for example (Taylor, 2017). From the EU's side, Sapir *et al.* (2017) estimate that approximately 90 per cent of the European financial services wholesale market is located in the UK, and 92 per cent of the total European revenue of the top five US investment banks is generated in the UK. Hence, financial services is the key industry both sides will focus on, in terms of how to include financial services in an FTA.

There are various options here (see, for example, Kern *et al.*, 2018). The most liberal version would be the continuation of 'passporting', whereby banks and insurance companies registered in the UK would continue to sell their services in the single market. Even if passporting is discontinued, there could be continued free trade in financial services via 'mutual recognition' of the regulatory standards of the two jurisdictions. Alternatively, there could be some rules on what would constitute 'regulatory equivalence' and a joint mechanism for policing equivalence and for adjudicating disputes – although market access could be unilaterally withdrawn by either side. And, at the more restricted end, there could be an agreement that UK financial services firms gain access to the EU single market if the UK applies all EU financial services regulations and is subject to the jurisdiction of the ECJ.

Fifth, and finally, an even 'softer' option would be what has become known as **EEA– (or 'Norway Minus')**. Here, the UK would remain a member of the EEA, as described above. However, there would be some specific opt-outs for the UK. In particular, there would be special derogations on the free movement of people, such as allowing the UK to cap the number of EU migrants registering to work each month or applying an 'emergency brake' if the number of EU migrants exceeded a certain amount in a particular period, region or sector (*cf.* Pisani-Ferry *et al.*, 2016; Portes, 2017). A Norway minus outcome would hence be 'softer' than an FTA+ outcome because it would mean the UK applying all EU single market rules, but it would be 'harder' than an EEA option, as it would mean the UK having more freedom in a highly-salient area of public policy.

There are, of course, other variants: such as the 'Swiss model', of a series of bilateral agreements covering sector-specific access to the EU single market; or the 'Turkish model', of a customs agreement with the EU but remaining outside the single market; or the 'Ukrainian model', of an Association Agreement with the EU covering some access to the single market as well as co-operation on economic and other policies. Nevertheless, the main elements of these other models are largely subsumed within the five basic choices.

To help think about which of these outcomes is most likely, I now consider the economic and political interests of the UK and the EU27, which will determine how the UK and EU27 rank these options.

II. The Economics of Brexit

In terms of the economic impacts of the various options, there is remarkable consistency in the research. Put simply, the 'harder' the Brexit, the bigger the likely economic impact to both the UK and the EU27. The main reason for this, of course, is the assumption that the more physical, fiscal or regulatory barriers to the current complete free movement of goods, services, capital and labour between the UK market and the EU27, the greater the costs to businesses and consumers, and the greater the impact on employment and public tax revenues. The UK would save in terms of its contributions into the EU budget, and the UK could claim back some of the losses in EU trade with new trade agreements with countries the UK does not currently have trade agreements with via its EU membership. But, standard trade 'gravity' models suggest that agreements with countries that are further away are unlikely to compensate for any loss of trade with the UK's closest and largest external market.

For example, one of the most comprehensive analyses of the likely economic impact of Brexit is by Dhingra *et al.* (2017). Using a standard, and empirically robust, general equilibrium trade model, Dhingra and her colleagues estimate that the EEA option would immediately cost the UK 1.3 per cent of GDP, whereas trading under a no deal/WTO outcome would cost 2.7 per cent of GDP, with presumably the intermediate options falling somewhere between these extremes. However, when modelling the dynamic effects of Brexit on trade, productivity and investment, the estimated losses of a 'hard Brexit' are much higher: 6.3 per cent to 9.4 per cent of GDP.

These estimates are consistent with the calculations in the UK government's leaked cross-Whitehall report on Brexit. In the report, the UK Treasury estimated that a no deal/WTO outcome would reduce UK GDP by 8 per cent over 15 years (relative to current trend growth), a free trade agreement along the lines of the EU–Canada agreement would reduce GDP by 5 per cent over the same period, and the EEA option would lower GDP by 2 per cent (House of Commons Exiting the European Union Committee, 2018).

There would also be an economic cost if there is a significant reduction in EU immigration to the UK, as a result of the replacement of the free movement of people from the EU27 with a restrictive immigration regime. For example, using existing patterns of migration to the UK and models of the relationship between migration and economic performance, Portes and Forte (2016) estimate that the likely reduction in immigration to the UK resulting from Brexit could cost between 2.7 per cent and 8.2 per cent of UK GDP by 2030. Hence, 'frictionless migration' between the EU27 and the UK, for both high-skilled and low-skilled labour – for example in the EEA scenario – would minimize further economic welfare losses.

Migration from the UK to the EU27 is less of an issue for the EU side, except perhaps in some high-skilled sectors. Similarly, the broad economic interests of the two sides are not symmetric. After Brexit, the EU27 and the UK will continue to be critical export markets for each other: the EU27 will be the UK's largest export market, while the UK will be the EU27's second largest export market outside the EU, after the United States. However, the proportional size of trade between the two economies is asymmetric. In 2016, the EU27 constituted 43 per cent of UK exports in goods and services,[2] while the UK constituted only 16 per cent of EU exports in goods and services.[3] Also, a far larger percentage of the UK's goods exports go to the EU27 than the other way around: in

[2]Office for National Statistics balance of payments dataset: https://www.ons.gov.uk/economy/nationalaccounts/balanceofpayments/datasets/balanceofpayments.
[3]Eurostat trade dataset: http://ec.europa.eu/eurostat/web/international-trade-in-goods/data/database.

2016 total UK trade with the EU27 (exports plus imports) constituted 12 per cent of UK GDP while total EU27 trade to the UK constituted only 3–4 per cent of EU27 GDP.

As a result, most of the economic analysis from the EU's side suggests that Brexit would not have a major effect on the EU27's economy, in aggregate. For example, Emerson *et al.* (2017) review several studies of the likely impact of Brexit on the EU27 and conclude that an EEA outcome would cost the EU27 approximately 0.1 per cent of GDP by 2030, a basic FTA deal would mean a loss of approximately 0.3–0.6 per cent of GDP, and a no deal/WTO outcome would cost the EU27 0.3–0.8 per cent of GDP. There would, however, be considerable variation between the EU member states, with Ireland suffering the most (a loss of 2.3–3.7 per cent of GDP in the event of a no deal/WTO outcome) as opposed to Germany taking only a minor hit (0.2–0.5 per cent of GDP in the event of a no deal/WTO outcome) (*cf.* Chen *et al.,* 2017; Schoof *et al.,* 2015).

In addition, there are other asymmetric economic interests that will shape negotiations. In particular, the balance of trade between the two sides means that the UK and EU27 have different interests in terms of the content of a free trade agreement. Figure 2 shows the UK–EU27 balance of trade in goods and services in 2016, when there was an overall deficit in trade between the UK and the EU27 of just over £80 billion. The relative balance of trade in goods and services would suggest that the EU has a significant incentive to sign a generous trade agreement with the UK. Nevertheless, whereas there was a large trade *deficit* between the UK and EU27 in goods (of £96 billion), there was a trade *surplus* in services (of £14 billion). In short, the EU27 sell more goods to the UK than they buy, whereas the UK sells more services to the EU27 than it buys.

The asymmetric balance of trade has strategic implications for the negotiations. Both sides have an economic interest in securing a trade agreement, and it is incorrect to see exports as positive and imports as negative, as any reduction in either imports or exports will have negative implications for consumers and/or employees and/or businesses in both the UK and the EU27. Nevertheless, at the aggregate level, which is what politicians tend to focus on, the sectoral balance of trade suggests that the EU27 are likely to be more

Figure 2: UK–EU27 Balance of Trade.

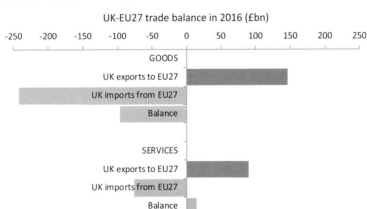

Source: Author's own calculations using data from the Office for National Statistics (2017). [Colour figure can be viewed at wileyonlinelibrary.com]

eager to sign a deal that secures zero tariffs and quotas, and as frictionless trade as possible, for goods, yet will be less eager than the UK for a deal that includes free trade in services. Services trade from the EU27 to the UK is important, worth £76 billion in 2016, but the value of EU27 services trade to the UK is swamped by the value of goods exports from the EU27 to the UK of £241 billion.

The asymmetric balance of trade presents a challenge for the UK, as one of the key elements of the 'plus' in the FTA+ model would be an agreement in services, and financial services in particular. One challenge to an agreement on financial services is that this sector is not included in any current FTA the EU has signed with any third country, even with Switzerland. The reason for the absence of financial services in EU–third country trade agreements is because the EU has not been willing to allow the access of financial services providers to the EU single market without the service provider being subject to EU regulation and oversight by EU financial services regulators and the ECJ, or the application of regulatory equivalence and the possibility that access to the EU market could be unilaterally withdrawn by the EU at any time. The UK, on the other hand, seems to want mutual recognition of financial services regulatory standards, yet such a concession would be largely incompatible with the way the EU single market works in this sector (Weatherill, 2017). In addition, the EU27 suspect that as soon as the UK is outside the EU it will be tempted to reduce the regulatory burdens in this sector in particular, and so compete 'unfairly' with the EU27.

Both sides would suffer an economic shock if there is a significant drop in trade in financial services between the UK and the EU27. Financial services make up 7 per cent of UK GDP, while Continental European firms rely heavily on the 'deep pockets' of the City of London, as well as London's connections to experienced ancillary services, such as accountancy and law firms. Nevertheless, Sapir *et al.* (2017) estimate that Brexit could mean 30 per cent of the wholesale financial services market leaving the UK for Frankfurt, Paris, Dublin, Amsterdam or Luxembourg. This would hit both sides in the short term, but in the medium term, Frankfurt, in particular, could replace many of the services London-based banks supply to Continental European clients.

In sum, from a purely economic-interest perspective, the UK and EU27 share a similar rank-ordering over the Brexit options: an EEA outcome would minimize potential economic consequences, while a no deal/WTO outcome would be the worst outcome for both sides, and the various bespoke arrangements would be somewhere between these extremes. Nevertheless, the asymmetric economic costs suggest that the UK is more eager to avoid a no deal outcome than the EU side, which gives the EU an upper-hand in bargaining. In addition, whereas for the UK an FTA+ deal covering financial services is strongly preferred to a basic FTA agreement, the EU27 are indifferent between these two options.

III. The Politics of Brexit

Economic calculations are only one side of the story. The other side is politics. The vote on 23 June 2016 was driven less by economic interests and more by cultural and ideological values. For example, looking at the NatCen survey data from immediately after the vote, Curtice (2017, p. 34) concludes that:

'Only a minority felt that leaving the EU would be bad for Britain's economy. Meanwhile around a half expressed concern about the impact of EU membership on the country's distinctive sense of identity while over half reckoned that immigration would fall if Britain left'.

The key 'project fear' message of the Remain campaign, which emphasized the likely economic consequences of leaving the EU, was trumped by the emphasis on national sovereignty of the 'take back control' message of the official Leave campaign and the explicitly nationalist message of the unofficial UKIP-led Leave.EU campaign.

Mirroring the two Leave campaigns, there are now two competing narratives about where the UK is heading post-Brexit. The so-called 'liberal leavers' present a free market vision of the UK outside the EU: regaining sovereignty to deregulate the economy, abolishing 'Brussels red tape' (EU social and environmental standards, presumably), signing free trade agreements with partners across the world and even unilaterally cutting tariffs and quotas on imports, and pursuing a liberal immigration policy. This narrative is often characterized as a 'Singapore-on-Thames' strategy for the UK and is associated with libertarian think-tanks like the Adam Smith Institute (Smith, 2016), the Economists for Free Trade (Minford, 2017), the Legatum Institute (Singham *et al.*, 2017), the Institute of Economic Affairs (Booth, 2018), and the Initiative for Free Trade.[4] Some of these groups are more liberal on immigration than others, and not all of them support the UK unilaterally removing tariffs and quotas. Nonetheless, prominent Leavers in the Cabinet, including David Davis, Boris Johnson and Liam Fox broadly support this liberal-leaver case and are closely linked to one or more of these groups.

The problem for these 'liberal leavers', though, is that the second narrative, of a Britain which is more socially conservative and economically interventionist post-Brexit is supported by a far larger number of Leave voters, as well as many Remain voters. This is illustrated in Figure 3, which shows the results of a multivariate analysis of the relationship between different social and economic values and the probability of voting Leave in the June 2016 referendum, using the Wave 9 survey of the British Election Study in July 2016 (see Appendix Table A1 for the full results).

Every 'socially liberal' value in the survey is *negatively* correlated with voting to leave the EU. Leave voters are more likely to support the death penalty, believe that children should be taught to obey, be in favour of censorship, be opposed to equality for women, ethnic minorities, and gays and lesbians, and be opposed to more immigration (*cf.* Kaufmann, 2016). Opposition to immigration most strongly correlates with voting to leave the EU. These results also hold when controlling for party identification; meaning that these views predict support for leaving the EU independently of which political party a person supports.

Perhaps more strikingly, given the debate about ending the free movement of people from the EU27, in other research with Eric Kaufmann and Thomas Leeper (Hix et al., 2017), we found that not only do Leave voters want to reduce net immigration more than Remain voters, but no matter how the British public is divided up – for example, by referendum vote, party support, age, income, education, region or gender – every sub-group wants to reduce immigration from outside the EU *more* than immigration from the EU27 (which, of course, is unrelated to the UK's membership of the EU). This underlying opposition to non-EU immigration will be a major challenge for the UK government, as

---

[4]http://www.ifreetrade.org/about.

Figure 3: Social and Economic Values of Leave Voters.

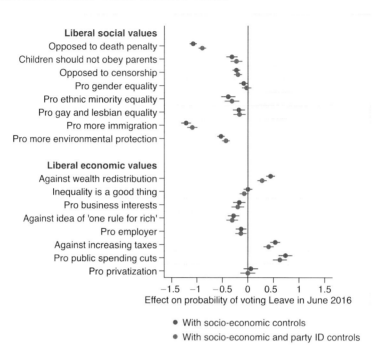

Source: Author's calculations from British Election Study 2015 Wave 9 (July 2016) data. Appendix Table A1 shows the full results of the models. The models include control variables for educational level, household income, ethnicity, age, gender and region. [Colour figure can be viewed at wileyonlinelibrary.com]

successive governments have failed to bring down non-EU immigration despite increasing restrictions on visas and family reunification. Against public attitudes, then, Brexit is likely to lead to a growing gap between falling immigration from the EU and stable, or even increasing, immigration from outside Europe.

In addition, Leave voters do not have clearly 'liberal' economic values. Leave voters tend to support public spending cuts and oppose higher taxes and wealth redistribution. But, Leave voters are also more likely to oppose the interests of businesses and employers, to believe that there is 'one rule for the rich', and to neither oppose nor support privatization. Indeed, following their own survey of public attitudes, the Legatum Institute reluctantly conceded that the British public post-Brexit generally support higher taxes, more public spending, nationalization of key industries, and more regulation of markets and labour markets in particular (Elliott & Kanagasooriam, 2018). Similarly, YouGov found that after the 2017 General Election a clear majority of the public now supports the re-nationalization of the railways and the energy and utilities companies, including over 40 per cent of Conservative voters.[5] In short, so-called 'liberal leavers' are a minority amongst the public, but are concentrated amongst the Conservative elite.

[5]Smith (2017).

Furthermore, if the UK government is to deliver a Brexit that satisfies the political preferences of Leave voters, then the final settlement should maximize the sovereignty of the UK Parliament and bring an end to the free movement of people from the EU27. Not surprisingly, these are the two main 'red lines', that hence make the EEA option politically unacceptable, despite the fact that it was favoured by many liberal leavers immediately after the referendum. An EEA– option would end the free movement of people, but would breach the sovereignty red line. Hence, from a political perspective, the UK probably prefers an FTA+ (or even a basic FTA option) to the two softer versions of Brexit, as YouGov indeed find in their own survey of public preferences of the eventual outcomes (Wells, 2016).

The EU27 also have some key political interests. The EU27 and the UK share many defence and security concerns, and so are likely to be able to reach agreement on continued defence co-operation, and security data sharing. Nevertheless, the EU27 have other political interests that conflict with the UK's interests. In particular, the EU27 does not want to undermine the integrity of the four freedoms (of goods, services, capital and persons) in the single market. One aspect of this preference relates to the current agreements the EU has with third countries. Any special arrangement for the UK, for example for financial services access, would lead Switzerland, South Korea, Canada, and others to demand similar arrangements, under the WTO Most-Favoured-Nation rules.

A second aspect of the 'no cherry picking' line is against the potential unravelling of the EU itself; driven by a fear of Brexit contagion to other member states. Support for anti-EU populist parties has grown in a large number of member states since the mid-2000s. Several of these parties, such as the Danish People's Party, have called for a 'British style in/out referendum'. Regardless of how painful the process of Brexit will be for the UK, once the UK is out the other side of the process, there will be a new exit model: a 'British model' (*cf.* Hix & Sitter, 2018). This model might be attractive to several countries who, like the UK, are not members of the Euro nor support deeper political integration, especially if the new 'British model' means considerable access to the EU single market and a special customs relationship to minimize transactions costs for supply-chains while at the same time controlling the free movement of people. Hence, the EU27 have a strategic interest to refuse a deal that would give the UK free movement of goods, services and capital but allow the UK to control the free movement of people.

Nevertheless, as Figure 4 shows, the level of trade integration in the single market of almost all the other EU27 states is considerably higher than for the UK. These different levels of trade integration suggest that while the potential economic consequences of Brexit might be large for the UK, the economic consequences would almost certainly be an order of magnitude larger for any other country. The even larger economic consequences of leaving the EU for other member states suggests that the threat of Brexit contagion to other member states is probably lower than some people claim, and also perhaps explains why several anti-EU populist parties that once supported leaving the EU or the Euro have started to tone-down their rhetoric, including the French *Front National* and the Italian *Lega*.

That said, the EU is not a united front in its interests *vis-à-vis* the UK. In addition to the differential economic exposure to Brexit of each member state, there are close political relations between the UK and several member states. In particular, the traditional economic allies of the UK in Northern Europe – Ireland, the Netherlands, Denmark, Sweden and Finland – fear being marginalized in an EU27 without the UK, which could

Figure 4: Goods and Services Trade Integration in the EU Single Market. a. Trade in goods. b. Trade in services.

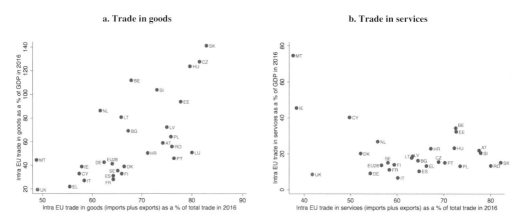

Source: Author's own calculations from Eurostat trade dataset. [Colour figure can be viewed at wileyonlinelibrary.com]

be dominated by a renewed Franco-German axis (see Huhe *et al.,* 2017). Also, without the UK, the Eurozone will dominate the EU: constituting 87 per cent of the EU27's GDP, as opposed to 73 per cent of the EU-28's GDP. Of the UK's traditional strategic allies, the dominance of the Eurozone in the EU27 could put Sweden and Denmark, as non-Eurozone member states, in a particularly difficult position going forward. As a result of these different political interests it might be difficult for the EU27 to maintain a united front when dealing with the UK as an external actor (*cf.* Durrant *et al.,* 2018; Springford *et al.,* 2018).

IV. The Bargaining Game and Likely Outcome

On the basis of this analysis we can estimate how the two sides rank the five Brexit outcomes. If the UK and EU27 have 'single-peaked preferences' along a common dimension, then the bargaining solution would be straightforward. For example, the two sides would have single-peaked preferences if, on the continuum in Figure 1, the UK's most-preferred outcome was a basic FTA and the EU's most-preferred outcome was the EEA, and the two sides ranked the other outcomes in decreasing order of preference the further they were from these 'ideal points'. In such a situation, the bargaining agreement would be somewhere between the EEA and a basic FTA, such as either an FTA+ or EEA–; although the outcome would probably be closer to the EU27's ideal point because of its larger bargaining power.

However, the Brexit bargaining game is not so simple, because the two sides do not have single-peaked preferences on a common single dimension. From the UK's side, on the assumption that political interests – and particularly the red-lines on sovereignty and ending the free movement of people – over-ride economic interests, the UK rank-order of the five outcomes is probably as follows:

1. FTA+/Canada Plus
2. FTA/Canada
3. EEA–/Norway Minus
4. EEA/Norway
5. No Deal/WTO.

Meanwhile, from the EU27's side, the two most preferred outcomes from a political point of view – in terms of maintaining the integrity of the single market – are the EEA and a basic FTA. Of these two, the EEA would have a lower negative economic impact for the EU27. Then, amongst the other two outcomes, the EU27 are probably indifferent. On the one hand, an FTA+ would undermine the four freedoms less than an EEA–, since allowing the UK a derogation on the free movement of people in the EEA would effectively end the EEA as it currently works. On the other hand, an EEA– deal would have a smaller economic impact for the EU, as the effect on trade in goods and services would be smaller than from an FTA+. So, this gives an EU27 ranking of:

1. EEA/Norway
2. FTA/Canada
3= FTA+/Canada Plus
3= EEA–/Norway Minus
5. No Deal/WTO.

As both the UK and the EU27 prefer any outcome to No Deal, this takes No Deal off the table. Some radical Brexiters, such as Jacob Rees-Mogg, claim that they prefer no agreement and a chaotic Brexit to any compromise, but these views are not held by a majority of Conservative MPs, let alone a majority of MPs in the House of Commons.

This reasoning, hence, leaves us with four outcomes, and a bargaining game as shown in Figure 5. There is only one equilibrium in this game: a basic FTA. In this set-up, the EU27 would play 'hardball' because they prefer an EEA or a basic FTA to any other outcome. The UK's 'best response' to this strategy would be to also play hardball, as they prefer a basic FTA to an EEA. Furthermore, neither the EU27 nor the UK have an incentive to deviate from this equilibrium. As a result, neither side has an incentive to 'compromise'.

This analysis does not mean that other outcomes are not possible. In fact, the analysis helps us think about what would have to change for a different outcome to emerge. For example, for the final outcome to be an FTA+ rather than a basic FTA, the EU27 would need to be willing to compromise rather than play hardball, while the UK's preferences over the outcomes would not need to change. This would require either EU politics to shift, to allow UK 'cherry picking', or the UK to make significant 'side payments' to the EU27, so that the EU27's interests shift – such as further payments into the EU budget (which is unlikely), or a major defence and security agreement. On the last of these issues, the weakness for the UK is that the two sides have mutual security and defence interests, so threatening not to reach a security and defence agreement is not a credible threat for the UK.

Alternatively, for the final outcome to be the UK remaining in the EEA rather than a basic FTA, the UK would need to see compromising as the best response to the EU27 playing hardball. This would require domestic politics in the UK to shift, so that the 'red lines' on ECJ jurisdiction, adhering to EU regulatory rules, and the continued free

Figure 5: Bargaining Game Between the UK and the EU27.

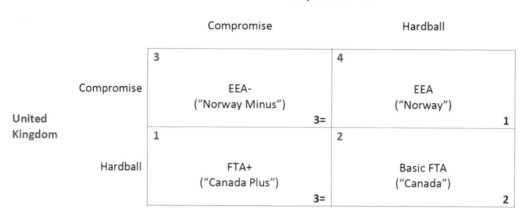

Note: EEA = European Economic Area,
EEA– = EEA minus free movement of people,
FTA+ = free trade agreement plus financial services,
FTA = basic free trade agreement, mainly covering goods.
The values represent the rank-order preferences of the two sides. [Colour figure can be viewed at wileyonlinelibrary.com]

movement of people are removed. This is unlikely given the preferences of Theresa May, the composition of the UK Cabinet, or the views of the majority in the House of Commons. Nevertheless, these preferences could change, for example if there is a surprise defeat in the House of Commons, if public attitudes on the free movement of people start to change, or if there is a sudden and significant economic shock that shifts Conservative MPs' views about staying in the single market.

Then, for the final outcome to be an EEA– rather than a basic FTA, both the EU27 and the UK would need to see compromising as securing a better outcome than playing hardball. This would mean both the EU27 preferences shifting on UK 'cherry picking' *and* domestic politics in the UK shifting, to remove the key red lines on ECJ jurisdiction, EU regulatory rules and the free movement of people. This, then, is perhaps the least likely outcome of all.

Finally, even if the preferences of the UK or the EU27 change, a further limitation on any movement away from a basic FTA is the ratification hurdle for the final agreement – unanimity in the Council and ratification in more than 30 national and regional parliaments – will make it very difficult for the EU27 to shift from their most preferred position. Every 'veto player' would need to prefer the same alternative to a basic FTA for a different deal to emerge. And, there is not much time to complete and ratify an agreement between March 2019 and the end of the transition period at the end of December 2020.

V. Longer-term Implications

I am not suggesting that a basic FTA between the UK and the EU27 would be the end of the story. Rather, this outcome would only be the end of the initial Brexit process, and the beginning of an ongoing set of negotiations that could lead to future 'bolt-ons' to the initial agreement. And, in time, one of these bolt-ons could cover trade in financial services, particularly if the EU is persuaded that the UK outside the single market can be trusted to maintain high regulatory standards in this sector (as well as other sectors), which could help secure agreement on a regulatory equivalence framework. Other deals could cover the free movement of people, at least for highly-skilled workers, or UK universities participating in European research funding programmes, and so on.

One problem for the UK, though, is that these deals may turn out to be more difficult after the UK has left the EU, from a domestic point of view. The reason for this is that public opinion in the UK may become increasingly anti-European, not increasingly pro-European. This is what happened in Norway and Switzerland after they decided not to join in the EU in the mid 1990s, as Figure 6 shows.[6]

In the mid-1990s, public attitudes towards the EU in Norway and Switzerland were only slightly lower than in their neighbours who had decided to join the EU: Sweden and Austria, respectively. However, from the early 2000s onwards, whereas support for the EU rose in Sweden and Austria, support for the EU declined in Norway and Switzerland (cf. Christin & Trechsel, 2002). This is probably explained by the fact that these two states had to accept deals from the EU that were more favourable to the EU side than to Norway or Switzerland; such as access to the single market in return for applying EU rules which they have no say over. Even if the UK signs only a basic FTA with the EU, UK goods and services exporters will have to apply EU product as well as process standards to gain access to the single market. Process standards are likely to be more intrusive than produce standards, as they cover things like phytosanitary standards, the use and disposal of chemicals and other health and safety rules. Applying these rules will not feel like 'taking back control', and like the Swiss and Norwegian publics, the British public might gradually turn even more against the EU. There have already been headlines in some English tabloids that the EU is a 'bully'.[7] The EU will feel even more like a bully once the UK is outside the EU; just ask Switzerland and Norway.

Conclusion

Much has been written and claimed about the potential economic costs of Brexit. What I have tried to focus on today is how political bargaining over the final Brexit deal might play out, based on underlying economic and political interests – although I have not addressed the unresolved Irish border question. This analysis leads me to believe that we are probably heading towards a basic free trade agreement between the EU27 and the UK, which mainly covers zero tariffs and quotas on goods and some special customs arrangements, but with not much more on services than is in the EU's existing trade agreements with Canada, South Korea and Japan. Zero tariffs and quotas on goods would be relatively easy for both sides to agree, as this is the current status quo, and the EU27 has a significant net trade surplus in goods with the UK.

[6]For the EU member states, the figure shows responses to the 'membership' question and the 'EU image' question in the Eurobarometer surveys because the membership question was not included in the surveys after 2011.
[7]For example: 'STOP BREXIT BULLYING: EU told they'll LOSE if they take on UK as Leavers issue OWN threats', *The Express*, 18 March 2018, 'QUIT THE BULLYING: EU told to 'stop pushing us around' or UK will not hand over a penny', *The Sun*, 18 March 2018.

Figure 6: Attitudes Towards the EU in Austria, Sweden, the UK, Norway and Switzerland.

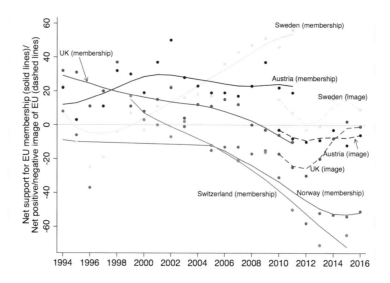

Source: Author's calculations from Eurobarometer data (for UK, Sweden, Austria, and Norway before 2003), from Sentio, Norstaft and Response surveys in Norway after 2003, and from ISSP and Mosaich surveys in Switzerland.

The questions were as follows:

Membership question (UK, Sweden, Austria): 'Generally speaking, do you think that (your country's) membership of the EU is: A good thing, A bad thing, Neither good nor bad, or Don't know?' The figure shows the percentage who responded 'A good thing' minus the percentage that responded 'A bad thing', excluding 'Neither good nor bad' and 'Don't Know'.

Image question (UK, Sweden, Austria): 'In general, does the European Union conjure up for you a very positive, fairly positive, neutral, fairly negative or very negative image?' The figure shows the total percentage of positive responses ('very positive' plus 'fairly positive') minus the total percentage of negative responses ('very negative' plus 'fairly negative').

Membership question (Norway): 'Generally speaking, do you think that (your country's) membership of the EU would be: A good thing, A bad thing, Neither good nor bad, or Don't know?' The figure shows the percentage who responded 'A good thing' minus the percentage that responded 'A bad thing', excluding 'Neither good nor bad' and 'Don't Know'.

Membership question (Switzerland): 'If a vote on Switzerland's accession to the European Union took place next Sunday, how would you vote? Don't know, Certainly for, Rather for, Rather against, Certainly against'. The figure shows the total percentage of responses 'for' ('Certainly for' plus 'Rather for') minus the total percentage of responses against ('Certainly against' plus 'Rather against'). [Colour figure can be viewed at wileyonlinelibrary.com]

What will be more difficult to agree will be the 'plus' part of a free trade agreement that the UK wants, in the area of financial services. The EU27 would suffer an economic hit if there are limitations on the access of financial service providers in the City of London to the single market. However, the economic impact for the EU27 would be much smaller than for the UK. In the medium term, large parts of the UK financial services industry could move to Frankfurt, Paris, Dublin, Amsterdam and Luxembourg. And, the political cost for the EU27 of compromising in this area could damage the integrity of the internal regulatory and mutual recognition frameworks of the single market, which the EU seems determined to avoid. On top of all that, the negotiating time will be short and the ratification hurdles will be high (unanimity in the EU Council, majorities in over 30 national and regional parliaments throughout the EU, and even possibly a referendum in Ireland and several other member states). Put another way: now is not the time to try to pass a trade agreement through the Wallonia regional parliament or the French National Assembly that gives City of London bankers easy access to the single market, and without having to apply EU rules or be subject to ECJ jurisdiction.

But, a basic free trade agreement would not be the end of the process. Instead, such an agreement could be the start of a new chapter in the UK's relationship with the EU. As Switzerland has learned, renegotiating the terms of the UK's agreements with the EU will probably become a permanent and highly-salient feature of domestic politics (a scary thought!). But, if this does become the case, and if the EU is seen to be repeatedly 'winning' in the various bargaining rounds, as it has done with Norway and Switzerland, then public opinion in the UK might become even more opposed to closer co-operation with the EU, which could then mean that the UK becomes stuck with a rather basic free trade deal for quite a long time to come.

Appendix

Table A1: Figure 3 results

Independent variable	(1)		(2)	
	coef.	std. error	coef.	std. error
Opposed to death penalty	−1.078***	0.039	−0.899***	0.033
Children should not obey parents	−0.316***	0.053	−0.227***	0.055
Opposed to censorship	−0.227***	0.035	−0.197***	0.036
Pro gender equality	−0.0831**	0.041	−0.0270	0.042
Pro ethnic minority equality	−0.389***	0.067	−0.315***	0.069
Pro gay and lesbian equality	−0.178***	0.056	−0.166***	0.058
Pro more immigration	−1.217***	0.046	−1.093***	0.047
Pro more environmental protection	−0.531***	0.033	−0.434***	0.034
Against wealth redistribution	0.441***	0.040	0.277***	0.042
Inequality is a good thing	0.002	0.039	−0.073*	0.041
Pro business interests	−0.169***	0.058	−0.198***	0.059
Against idea of 'one rule for the rich'	−0.281***	0.054	−0.308***	0.055
Pro employer	−0.133***	0.050	−0.137***	0.051
Against increasing taxes	0.534***	0.045	0.405***	0.046
Pro public spending cuts	0.736***	0.065	0.627***	0.066
Pro privatisation	0.059	0.068	0.001	0.070
Education level: less than A-level	0.397***	0.036	0.377***	0.037
Education level: degree or above	−0.438***	0.034	−0.399***	0.035
Household income: less than £20,000	0.316***	0.038	0.329***	0.039
Household income: more than £70,000	−0.479***	0.070	−0.453***	0.071
White British	0.108***	0.041	0.111***	0.043
Black, Asian or minority ethnic	−0.542***	0.098	−0.481***	0.101

Table A1: (Continued)

Independent variable	(1)		(2)	
	coef.	std. error	coef.	std. error
Age: 18 to 25 years	−0.791***	0.058	−0.840***	0.061
Age: 66 years or above	0.154***	0.036	0.153***	0.038
Male	0.010	0.029	−0.002	0.031
Region: London	0.204***	0.054	0.171***	0.056
Region: North or Midlands	0.244***	0.033	0.242***	0.035
Party ID: Conservative			0.017	0.042
Party ID: Labour			−0.751***	0.040
Party ID: LibDem			−1.091***	0.067
Party ID: SNP			−0.771***	0.083
Party ID: UKIP			3.553***	0.205
Party ID: Green			−1.218***	0.121
Constant	0.594***	0.042	0.756***	0.050
Observations	28,069		28,069	
Pseudo R-squared	0.220		0.275	

Note: Dependent variable: Vote 'Leave' vote (1,0) in June 2016 referendum.*** $p<0.01$, ** $p<0.05$, * $p<0.10$.
Source: British Election Study 2015 Wave 9, July 2016.

References

BBC News (2017) *'Brexit: David Davis wants 'Canada Plus Plus Plus' Trade Deal'*, 10 December. Available online at: http://www.bbc.co.uk/news/uk-politics-42298971.

Booth, P. (2018) *'Free Trade Should Empower Consumers – Not the Lawyers Who Write Trade Agreements'*, Institute of Economic Affairs, blog, 1 March. Available online at: https://iea.org.uk/free-trade-should-empower-consumers-not-the-lawyers-who-write-trade-agreements.

Chen, W., Los, B., McCann, P., Ortega-Argilés, R., Thissen, M. and van Oort, F. (2017) 'The Continental Divide? Economic Exposure to Brexit in Regions and Countries on Both Sides of The Channel'. *Papers in Regional Science*, Vol. 97, No. 1, pp. 25–54.

Christin, T. and Trechsel, A.H. (2002) 'Joining the EU? Explaining Public Opinion in Switzerland'. *European Union Politics*, Vol. 3, No. 4, pp. 415–43.

Curtice, J. (2017) 'Why Leave Won the UK's EU Referendum'. *JCMS*, Vol. 55, No. Annual Review, pp. 19–37.

Dhingra, S., Huang, H., Ottaviano, G., Pessoa, J. P., Sampson, T. and Van Reenen, J. (2017) The Costs and Benefits of Leaving the EU: Trade Effects, CEP Discussion Paper No 1478, London: LSE Centre for Economic Performance.

Durrant, T., Stojanovic, A. and Lloyd, L. (2018) *Negotiating Brexit: The Views of the EU27* (London: Institute for Government).

Elliott, M. and Kanagasooriam, J. (2018) *Publica Opinion in the Post-Brexit Era: Economic Attitudes in Modern Britain* (London: Legatum Institute).

Emerson, M., Busse, M., Di Salvo, M., Gros, D. and Pelkmans, J. (2017) *An Assessment of the Economic Impact of Brexit on the EU27, Study for the IMCO Committee (PE595.374)* (Brussels: European Parliament).

Hix, S., Kaufmann, E. and Leeper, T. (2017) *'UK Voters, Including Leavers, Care More About Reducing Non-EU Than EU Migration'*, LSE blog, 30 May. Available online at: http://blogs.lse.ac.uk/politicsandpolicy/non-eu-migration-is-what-uk-voters-care-most-about.

Hix, S. and Sitter, N. (2018) *'Svexit or Huxit? How Another Country Could Follow the UK out of the EU'*, LSE blog, 30 January. Available online at: http://blogs.lse.ac.uk/brexit/2018/01/30/svexit-or-huxit-how-another-country-could-follow-the-uk-out-of-the-eu.

House of Commons Exiting the European Union Committee (2018) *EU Exit Analysis: Cross Whitehall Briefing* (London: House of Commons Exiting the European Union Committee).

Huhe, N., Naurin, D. and Thomson, R. (2017) 'With or Without You? Policy Impact and Networks in the Council of the EU After Brexit', *European Policy Analysis*, August 2017 Issue, (Stockholm: Stockholm Institute for European Policy Studies).

Kaufmann, E. (2016) *'It's NOT the Economy, Stupid: Brexit as a Story of Personal Values'*, LSE blog, 7 July. Available online at: http://blogs.lse.ac.uk/politicsandpolicy/personal-values-brexit-vote.

Kern, A., Barnard, C., Ferran, E., Lang, A. and Moloney, N. (2018) *Brexit and Financial Services: Law and Policy* (Oxford: Hart Publishing).

Minford, P. (2017) *From Project Fear to Project Prosperity* (London: Economists for Free Trade).

Office for National Statistics (2017) 'UK Balance of Payments'. In *The Pink Book: 2017* (London: Office for National Statistics).

Pisani-Ferry, J., Röttgen, N., Sapir, A., Tucker, P. and Wolff, G.B. (2016) *Europe after Brexit: A Proposal for a Continental Partnership* (Brussels: Bruegel).

Portes, J. (2017) *Free Movement After Brexit: Policy Options*, London: ESRC UK in a Changing Europe Programme.

Portes, J. and Forte, G. (2016) *The Economic Impact of Brexit-induced Reductions in Migration* (London: National Institute of Economic and Social Research).

Sapir, A., Schoenmaker, D. and Véron, N. (2017) *Making the Best of Brexit for the EU27 Financial System, Policy Brief*, Issue 1, Brussels: Bruegel.

Schoof, U., Peteren, T., Aichele, R. and Felbermayr, G. (2015) *Brexit: Potential Economic Consequences if the UK Exits the EU*, Policy Brief 2015/05 (Gütersloh: Bertelsmann Stiftung).

Singham, S., Tylecote, R. and Hewson, V. (2017) *The Brexit Inflection Point: The Pathway to Prosperity* (London: Legatum Institute).

Smith, M. (2017) *'Nationalisation vs Privatisation: The Public View'*, YouGov, 19 May. Available online at: https://yougov.co.uk/news/2017/05/19/nationalisation-vs-privatisation-public-view.

Smith, R. (2016) *The Liberal Case for 'Leave'* (London: Adam Smith Institute).

Springford, J., Lowe, S. and Oppenheim, B. (2018) *Will the Unity of the 27 Crack?* (London: Centre for European Reform).

Taylor, G. (2017) *Financial Services: Contribution to the UK Economy*, Briefing Paper 6193, 31 March 2017 (London: House of Commons Library).

Weatherill, S. (2017) *'What 'MAppendutual Recognition' Really Entails: Analysis of the Prime Minister's Mansion House Brexit Policy Speech'*, EU Law Analysis blog, 4 March. Available online at: http://eulawanalysis.blogspot.co.uk/2018/03/what-mutual-recognition-really-entails.html.

Wells, A. (2016) *'Canada Option' is Most Popular Type of Brexit Deal'*, YouGov, 18 August. Available online at: https://yougov.co.uk/news/2016/08/18/majority-people-think-freedom-movement-fair-price.

JCMS 2018 Volume 56. Annual Review pp. 28–38   DOI: 10.1111/jcms.12771

A Different Europe is Possible: The Professionalization of EU Studies and the Dilemmas of Integration in the 21st Century

IAN MANNERS and BEN ROSAMOND
University of Copenhagen

Introduction: Addressing the Deeper Implications of Current Crises

Rather than celebrating 60 years of the Treaty of Rome, 2017 looks like going down as the year in which the European Union (EU) faced a seemingly 'perfect storm' of crises (associated with the eurozone, the management of refugee flows, the politics of Brexit, the rise to prominence of explicitly 'illiberal' governments within the EU and the general rise of populist far-right politics across Europe) that together constituted a truly 'existential' moment for European integration (Dinan *et al.*, 2017). It is, of course, normal for academic fields to respond to 'crises'. Real world events are bound to stimulate a scholarly reflex within established fields whose purpose must – by definition – incorporate the analysis of challenges to and change within their objects of study. This is a pattern that seems to have held throughout the six decades of scholarly work on the politics of European integration.

But it is also well established by sociologists of science that the nature of a field's response to 'external' events is driven and determined by path-dependent norms, standards and practices from *within* the field itself. Put crudely, this means that prevailing standards of 'normal science' within a field tend to mediate between real world events and the field's (internal) capture of those events (Abbott, 2001; Jasanoff, 2005). We know that different theoretical approaches within EU studies work with distinct understandings of what 'crisis' means (Schimmelfennig, 2017), which should remind us that 'crises' are never phenomena that are exogenously given. Rather crises are constituted discursively by both policy actors and academics. The former seek narrative clarity and appropriate problem and solution sets in the face of uncertainty, and the resultant crisis constructions may foreground particular political claims over others (Hay, 1996, 2016). The latter, sampling from the empirical past and established theory, develop claims about crises as punctuations that serve the goals of explanation and understanding (Blyth, 2006). But equally, the successful establishment of a scholarly narrative about what the object of study is and what is happening has the potential to privilege some approaches over others. Moreover, the policy and academic domains are not necessarily separated, and there is a growing body of work to suggest that the relationship between the two fields – in the co-production of knowledge – should be of particular interest to scholars of the EU (Adler-Nissen and Kropp, 2015; Mudge and Vauchez, 2012; Ryner, 2012; White, 2003).

Focussing on political science as the dominant scholarly mode within EU studies, our suggestion here is that the particular constitution of the field is important. We argue that scholarship in EU studies has been structured in ways that have taken the field away from exploring the kinds of deep questions that would have aided not only explanation of the crisis *ex post*, but also understanding of various long-standing pathologies of the integration process that themselves stimulate and amplify the effects of crises dynamics within Europe. In part this is an issue of the extent to which the political science of the EU, practised within normal parameters, was ever able to anticipate the possibly disintegrative tendencies now at play on the continent (Joerges and Kreuder-Sonnen, 2017; Manners, 2003, 2007). It also presents us with a paradox: that the very real successes of EU studies in recent decades may have prevented the field from fully addressing the deeper implications of current crises.

How might this be so? We offer a potentially provocative answer that centres on the dynamic of 'professionalization' within the field (Schmitter, 2002). Professionalization in this sense is associated with the appeal to particular forms of scientific rigour, methodological tightening, the eschewal of normativity, the narrowing of empirical foci and the proliferation of specialized subfields. Therefore, properly understood, professionalization within the academy inevitably involves various types of boundary drawing that in turn (and by implication) ensure the exclusion of perspectives and voices from the field as well as its internal fragmentation, albeit into sub-fields and sub-sub-fields that accord with standard disciplinary norms. While it is important to recognize that such dynamics are integral to (and inescapable in) just about every scholarly field, we maintain that they have, since the late 1980s in particular, operated in a quite distinctive way in EU studies. This period is important because it represents the moment in which 'EU studies' came to be fully constituted as a self-aware field of knowledge production in which crucial boundary work was accomplished. The version of the field that became 'EU studies' (at least in its political science variant) relied, we suggest, on the normalization of the EU as a polity whose character could be most fruitfully discerned through the application of the tenets of mainstream political science. This move also set aside and marginalized 'integration' as a central guiding *problematique* for the field, and this in turn relied upon a particular narrative of the pre-history of EU studies as – in effect – 'unprofessional'. These developments in EU studies were a subset of broader trends in political science, but they produced local field-specific effects. Our argument is that the professionalization of the field has also hidden from view a series of key analytical and political dilemmas. This contribution sketches out some of the mechanisms through which the professionalization of the field has informed the way in which the field has encountered recent and ongoing crises.

I. Twists, Turns and the Professionalization of EU Studies

In recent decades, the various 'twists' in the evolution of the EU (such as treaty reform, institutional change, enlargement, redefinitions of policy competence, the growth of the single market, the emergence of monetary union, the rise of euroscepticism and a more differentiated approach to integration) have been accompanied by various 'turns' in EU studies (for example the comparative politics, governance, normative, constructivist and Europeanization turns). There is, of course, some merit in identifying the sources of 'turns' in the various 'twists'.

As already suggested, this is a simplistic picture that treats 'turns' as largely benign intellectual reactions to events that take place within the object of study. For one thing, one key facet of 'turns' (understood here as identifiable scholarly movements within a sub-field) is their capacity to define the very nature and scope of their object of study. In other words, what is understood as 'going on' within the EU is endogenous to scholarly dis-courses that – as a matter of necessity – are defining the EU in ways that are congruent with the terms of those scholarly discourses. To be clear, this is a precondition of ordered inquiry. But it does mean that other ways of reading an object like the EU are marginalized or indeed excluded in the process (Abels and MacRae, 2016; Manners and Whitman, 2016). For example, as comparativists sought to redefine and 'normalize' (Kreppel, 2012) the European Communities/EU as a political system with state-like features, so they actively displaced 'integration' as the central *problematique* of the field. That move was justified, we would argue, via a very partial reading of the literature on regional integration (Rosamond, 2016), a point to which we return below.

Also 'turns' in a field often reflect prevailing norms of inquiry in parent disciplines and/or the broader social sciences. There is no space to argue the point in detail here, but it should not be controversial to suggest that the types of work that have prevailed in EU studies over the past 25 years have almost always been rooted in broader trends within political science and its constituent subfields (Aspinwall and Schneider, 2000; Dowding, 2000; Rosamond, 2007). This is one aspect of what has often been thought of as the 'professionalization' of EU studies – its integration into the disciplinary main-stream of political science. Disciplinary mainstreaming is not simply about the adoption of widely used theoretical approaches and the treatment of the EU as a potential case of certain general phenomena. It is also about the adoption of wider disciplinary norms re-garding what types of work count as valid and admissible science (Luke, 1999). Mainstreaming has done more than anything to deal with EU studies' 'n = 1 problem' and has helped to ensure that the study of the EU has not become ghettoized as a self-contained and insular sub-field. But it also risks the reproduction of the hard boundaries and exclusions for which (mainstream US) political science has often been criticized (Monroe, 2005).

Aside from determining both the substance and the conduct of inquiry, professionali-zation also provokes a degree of fragmentation as new sub-fields develop and consolidate themselves within the broader field. Again, this variation is often noted as a distinguishing feature of EU studies, particularly since the 'boom' in the field that is typically dated from the early 1990s (Jensen and Kristensen, 2013; Keeler, 2005; Paterson *et al.*, 2010). Fragmentation is, as we have noted, a standard feature of academic subfields, and its recent history cannot be separated from broader trends within the academy and higher ed-ucation, which are in turn nested within and constitutive of a broader political economy of knowledge production (Becher and Trowler, 2001). The consolidation and progress of subfields within disciplines and of subfields within subfields brings with it the risk of non-communication amongst the resultant scholarly silos (Almond, 1990). There is some evidence that the general journals (especially the *Journal of Common Market Studies* and the *Journal of European Public Policy*) perform something of an integrating function within EU studies (Jensen and Kristensen, 2013). But even if the coverage in general journals is representative of the field as a whole, it is doubtful that many scholars read each issue cover-to-cover. And with key research material on the EU being published in discipline (political science) and field (public administration, comparative politics, International Relations) journals, it becomes harder for EU scholars to follow all of (even

Anglophone) EU scholarship – as was certainly possible in the 1960s. The sociology of the discipline matters here, especially in contexts where self-identification as a 'Europeanist' or as an 'EU scholar' is at variance with the standard sub-field configuration of political science (Andrews, 2012; Kaufman-Osborn, 2006). In other words, fragmentation brings with it an incentive to mainstream.

So far we have thought about professionalization in EU studies in terms of two key features: conformity to the norms of the parent discipline and increasing specialization/fragmentation within the field. Both features can be thought of as carrying advantages and risks for the field. There is also a third feature of professionalization that has been rather neglected to date, namely the very constitution of 'EU studies' as a field in its own right. The concept of 'EU studies' was itself a product of changes taking place in the field in the late 1980s/early 1990s – the period typically associated with the rise of 'professionalization' and the displacement of older scholarly frames (Manners and Whitman, 2016, pp. 5–6). Google Scholar data[1] suggest that 'EU studies' was unused before 1994 and it was not until 1995 that the term gained any sort of traction – and even then sparingly. Yet by the late 1990s 'EU studies' had become a very common marker for work being done on European integration and its institutional expressions. It might be assumed that the shift is a direct field reflex to the changed language of the EU itself following the ratification of the Maastricht Treaty, but the same data show that obvious antecedents such as 'EC studies', 'European integration studies' or 'regional integration studies' were hardly used prior to the early 1990s. For example, Google Scholar finds just one recorded mention of either 'regional integration studies' or 'European integration studies' during the whole of the 1960s.

This implies that the early 1990s marked not just a key juncture in the field's history, but also the advent of the discursive construction of the field itself. This matters because the emergence of 'EU studies' was also the moment where 'professionalization', in terms of both practice and discourse really began. It follows that the various 'turns' in the field are perhaps better read in terms of the solidification of professionalizing practices and thereby the re-definition and de-limitation of EU studies' object of study, rather than as evidence of the field simply responding to developments within its object of study. Moreover, this constitutive moment was also made possible through the development of narratives about the field's past, some of which are virtually impossible to sustain empirically (Rosamond, 2016). The resultant stories about the (pre-)history of EU studies, aside from deploying simplified narratives of both the contours of past debate and the substance of previous scholarship, also had the effect of actively 'forgetting' or at least downgrading certain lines of scholarship that were no longer seen as relevant to explaining or understanding the 'new Europe'.

II. Integration as the Central *Problematique* of EU Studies

One of the key features of the 'professionalization' of EU studies and the associated scholarly 'turns' was the displacement of 'integration' as the central *problematique* of the field. The upshot is that most of the subsequent 'turns' in EU studies have tended to treat the EU as a polity of some kind (Hix, 2007; Jachtenfuchs, 2007; Kreppel,

[1]Searches at scholar.google.com undertaken on 21 June 2017.

2012). Our argument is not that the comparative politics and governance 'turns' represent some kind of historic mistake – far from it. Rather, we suggest deeper exploration of the idea that losing sight of 'integration' in EU studies has had some negative consequences, particularly in relation to how the field deals with the current constellation of crises.

It is worth noting two misrepresentations that are typically built into the claim that the field in the 1960s and 1970s was shaped by an increasingly unproductive conversation about 'integration'. The first is that the past of the field was dominated by work from scholars of International Relations, that there was little input from the cutting edge political science of the time and (thus) that there was little treatment of the communities as a nascent political system. A glance at the work of Lindberg (1963), Etzioni (1965), Lindberg and Scheingold (1970) and the papers gathered by Lindberg and Scheingold (1971) should be enough to, at the very least, qualify this claim (see also Rosamond, 2007). The second point is more central to our argument. It is to note that the conception of 'integration' built into the standard narrative of the field's past relies upon a bifurcation between simplified renditions of neofunctionalist and intergovernmentalist uses of the concept (roughly spillover plus supranational activism versus the primacy of power politics and governmental interests). This bifurcation certainly captures something important, but it strips much of this scholarship of its granulation and nuance. Ernst Haas described the project of integration theory as the observation of 'the peaceful creation of possible new types of human communities at a very high level of organisation and of the processes which may lead to such conditions' (1971, p. 4). Indeed, much of the neofunctionalist work of the 1960s and early 1970s focused on the necessary and sufficient background conditions that would enable post-national integration projects to become sustainable.

We suggest that a renewed focus on integration (broadly conceived) would enable the field to contemplate the ways in which crisis dynamics interconnect with and amplify three founding and (and unresolved) dilemmas of the European project (see also Rosamond, 2017). These can be summarized as (a) the constant tension between the goal of delivering an EU-wide market order versus the desire to ensure social solidarity, (b) the tension between the development of a legal-constitutional order versus the need to secure appropriate channels for democratic authorization of policy decisions, and (c) the tension between a developing cosmopolitan social order characterized by free movement on the one hand and ongoing national communitarian impulses on the other. These tensions open space for different theoretical perspectives on the dilemmas of the European project, in particular an agonistic cosmopolitical approach from within critical social theory (Manners, 2013). Put bluntly, we wonder whether the downgrading of the *problematique* of 'integration' and the 'normalization' of EU studies has taken scholarship away from problems that have undoubtedly been exacerbated by the current crises, but which were always hiding in plain sight. These three dilemmas cannot be captured or explored through a simplified dichotomy, but they are undoubtedly puzzles of 'integration', that might – in turn – put us in a better position to understand the spectre of 'disintegration' and the extent to which the cluster of current crises are associated with the onset of disintegrative dynamics in the EU. Put another way, did forgetting about integration make it harder to think about disintegration?

III. Researching Integration in EU Studies

It should be understood that the problem of 'forgetting' integration is not simply about a shift in the core subject matter of EU studies, which in turn provokes an inability to ask appropriate and salient questions. Our point is rather that this has tended to be accompanied by a 'professional' approach to social inquiry that rests solely on the achievement of internal disciplinary criteria to deliver scholarly progress. Once again, this is an entirely valid and necessary pursuit. We simply suggest that it comes at a cost and that this cost could and should be offset by the field constituting itself in ways that treat as valid and admissible concerns about normativity and the input of hitherto marginalized scholarly voices included through more agonistic cosmopolitics. This amounts to advocacy of a version of EU studies that balances the quest for systematic knowledge about its object with intellectual openness, an aversion to unnecessary boundary-drawing and a willingness to re-integrate normative concerns as a central feature of academic practice.

Addressing the three dilemmas of integration is paramount to opening spaces that make a different Europe possible through research agendas that actively connect questions of public interest, democratic sovereignty and transnational solidarity (Scholl and Freyberg-Inan, 2018). We suggest that this move is especially important in light of questions and crises that sit at the heart of the pieces assembled for this issue of the *Annual Review*. Addressing the first dilemma (a) of the tension between EU-wide market order and social solidarity requires both the deep *interrogation of austerity policies* that have, for several years now, been the default economic policy instruments of eurozone governance and the acknowledgement of the public interest stated in Article 3 of the Treaty on European Union: the sustainable development of Europe. The shocking socio-economic evidence of the failure of austerity in Greece and the UK reinforces the intellectual and institutional rejection of austerity measures by the OECD and IMF (Blyth, 2013; OECD, 2016; Ostry *et al.*, 2016). The importance of research into this economic integration dilemma demands work that explores the EU public interest found in achieving sustainable development through balanced economic growth and price stability, full employment and social progress, and environmental protection (Art. 3.3 TEU). In particular, post-crisis research into the public interest in maintaining sustainable public services of general interest is crucial (Art. 14 and Prot. 26 TFEU). Approaches that analyze and critique the ideological 'common sense' of economic orthodoxy (such as constructivist political economy, historical materialism and neo-Gramscianism) develop quite distinct understandings of economic sustainability and social justice. They also self-consciously seek to break with the integration codes that have been characteristic of both scholarly and policy practice in the EU (Bieling *et al.*, 2016; Ryner, 2012).

Addressing the second dilemma (b) of the tension between EU legal-constitutional order and democratic authorization requires scholarship that works from the premise of *defending democracy* and the acknowledgement of democratic sovereignty found in Article 10 of the Treaty on European Union: 'the functioning of the Union shall be founded on representative democracy'. The defence of democracy involves striking a democratic balance between political forces driving where the 'Union acts to better achieve together what cannot be achieved apart' (Manners, 2013, p. 487) and democratic needs where 'decisions are taken as openly as possible and as closely as possible to the citizen' (Art. 1 TEU). The importance of the democratic integration dilemma suggests that research should be directed towards core questions of EU democratic sovereignty: the achievement of representative democracy throughout all EU policy competences, particularly socio-economic policy, in order to ensure that shared competence, the ordinary legislative procedure, and publicly-open democratic debate and decision-making is found throughout the EU Parliament and Council, as well as member state, regional and local legislatures. Focal points for post-crisis research and debate into democratic sovereignty should include economic and monetary union generally, the role of an EU economic and finance Commissioner/minister responsible for the eurozone, EP Parliamentary and public scrutiny of the eurozone council/group meetings, and public oversight of a common eurozone budget, bonds, or monetary fund. In terms of theoretical voices, the likes of Habermasian critical theories of the public sphere and feminist theories of the power of masculinities within EU and member states' public spheres provide different understandings of democratic sovereignty (Kronsell, 2016; Manners, 2007).

Addressing the third dilemma (c) of the tension between EU cosmopolitan social order and 'national' communitarianism requires exploration of the prospects for *co-ordinated transnational solidarity* and the acknowledgement of transnational solidarity as stated in Article 3 of the Treaty on European Union: 'the promotion of economic, social and territorial cohesion, and solidarity among Member States'. The necessity of research into EU and member state support for co-ordinated transnational solidarity to help vocalize and institutionalize opposition and counter-proposals to orthodox policies within the EU can be found in an engagement with the critical social theory of agonistic cosmopolitics – work that links local politics to global ethics (Manners, 2013, pp. 482–485; Scholl and Freyberg-Inan, 2018, pp. 115–117). The agonistic actors that require support for transnational solidarity are those that act across member state spaces in support of economic and social cohesion and solidarity, including representative associations, parties representative of socioeconomic and civic civil society, trade unions and representatives of employers' organizations (Art. 11 TEU; Arts. 15, 163, 300 TFEU). Research should thus focus on how critical and agonistic actors can be supported through institutionalized transnational civil society, trade unions, youth and educational programmes, without compromising the integrity and critique of their heterodox, anti-austerity, non-national democratic grass-roots. The theoretical perspectives of critical social theory of agonistic cosmopolitics, postcolonial theories of ethno-cultural belonging, poststructural theories of violent state-bound practices, and sociological theories of cognitive framing in times of turmoil provide different understandings of transnational solidarity beyond nationalism (Borg and Diez, 2016; Kinnvall, 2016; Manners, 2013; Saurugger, 2016).

Conclusion: A Different Europe is Possible

In light of the foregoing, we conclude by sketching out a series of five suggestions for how EU studies, and thus the EU itself, can move beyond crises. Implicit throughout is our working premise that scholarly fields and their objects are mutually constitutive.

First, there must be recognition that European integration requires **historical context** – that the EU does not begin with a 'year zero' moment on 9 May 1950. This historicization must include the origins of European integration in the processes of imperialism and colonialization; nationalism and xenophobia; international trade and interwar depression; and the wars of empire. It is certainly true – as Frantz Fanon stated in the 1960s – that since its development has required the spoilation of the non-European world, 'Europe is literally the creation of the Third World' (Fanon in Manners, 2000, p. 200). As our discussion of professionalization makes clear, EU studies has increasingly lost sight of the historical context of integration as the central *problematique*. Similarly, the teaching of integration in EU studies has tended to over-look the global conflictual and political economy origins of European integration prior to 1950, while at the same time ignoring the postcolonial context of EU relations with the rest of the world (Kinnvall, 2016).

Second, there needs to be acknowledgement that the empirical agenda of EU studies has hidden in plain sight the **neoliberal preferences** for market economics over the ev-eryday socio-economic concerns of ordinary EU and non-EU citizens. In the 1980s Jacques Delors argued that a 'social Europe' was a necessary balance to the Europe of the Single Market. The need for the development of European social models to counter neoliberal globalization is widely discussed outside EU studies (European Commission, 2017), but the relative absence of mainstream EU discussions of social Europe after 1992 has had negative effects on the field of EU studies (Manners and Murray, 2016).

Third, in this context, different research agendas and theories that are underused are vital to the health and future of EU studies beyond the crises. The study of EU **public interest** in sustainable development and social progress in the opposition to intellectually-bankrupt austerity measures; of **democratic sovereignty** in representative democracy and economic and monetary union in defence of democracy; and of **transnational solidarity** in economic and social cohesion and solidarity of progressive activist groups and civil society as an agonistic heterodoxy are all vital research agendas. In parallel different theoretical approaches to European integration must be utilized to enrich the field, including historical materialist and neo-Gramscian theories of economic orthodoxy; critical theory and feminist theories of democratic sovereignty; and critical social, postcolonial, poststructural, and sociological theories of transnational solidarity beyond nationalism.

Fourth, teaching and researching the field needs to be done in a much more open way. Rather than reifying and petrifying the field, EU studies and its students need to be aware of the rich **diversity** of disciplinary and theoretical perspectives on European integration. Our discussion of professionalization shows the problems that arise as the disciplinary mainstream of political science becomes dominant within EU studies, with single-discipline textbook approaches leaving EU studies blindsided by crises (Parker, 2016). In contrast, opening EU studies to disciplinary diversity (including other humanities and social science perspectives) and cross-paradigm theoretical viewpoints (including Marxist, postcolonial, poststructural, feminist and critical social theories) enriches both research and teaching, rendering both field and subject more robust (Manners and Whitman, 2016).

Fifth, achieving such diversity involves recognizing genuine **methodological pluralism**. Different methodologies – distinct understandings of the logics, structures and procedures of inquiry – should be acknowledged and their coexistence should be encouraged in order to reap two distinct benefits (Rosamond, 2015, pp. 32–33). The first recognizes that different methodologies offer different conceptions of scientific rigour, and hence less vulnerability to the kind of paradigmatic implosion seen in communist studies and neoliberal economics. The second acknowledges that dialogue and interdisciplinarity yields far richer discussions about the research strategies beyond dichotomies, including the purpose, design and methods of different types of research (Manners *et al.*, 2015). To better reveal and address the challenges discussed here, a pluralistic field is one in which all the humanities and social sciences have something to contribute to the ontological, epistemological, and crucially methodological questions of European integration, EU studies, and understanding the EU itself in order to make a different Europe possible.

References

Abels, G. and MacRae, H. (2016) 'Why and How to Gender European Integration Theory?' In Abels, G. and MacRae, H. (eds) *Gendering European Integration Theory* (Opladen: Barbara Budrich Publishers), pp. 9–37.

Abbott, A. (2001) *Chaos of Disciplines* (Chicago, IL: University of Chicago Press).

Adler-Nissen, R. and Kropp, K. (2015) 'A Sociology of Knowledge Approach to European Integration: Four Analytical Principles'. *Journal of European Integration*, Vol. 37, No. 2, pp. 155–73.

Almond, G.A. (1990) *A Discipline Divided: Schools and Sects in Political Science* (London: Sage).

Andrews, D.M. (2012) 'The Rise and Fall of EU Studies in the USA'. *Journal of European Public Policy*, Vol. 19, No. 5, pp. 755–75.

Aspinwall, M. and Schneider, G. (2000) 'Same Menu, Separate Tables: The Institutionalist Turn in Political Science and the Study of European Integration'. *European Journal of Political Research*, Vol. 38, No. 1, pp. 1–36.

Becher, T. and Trowler, P.R. (2001) *Academic Tribes and Tendencies. Intellectual Enquiry and the Culture of Disciplines* (Buckingham: Open University Press).

Bieling, H.J., Jäger, J. and Ryner, M. (2016) 'Regulation Theory and the Political Economy of the European Union'. *JCMS*, Vol. 54, No. 1, pp. 53–69.

Blyth, M. (2006) 'Great Punctuations: Prediction, Randomness and the Evolution of Comparative Political Science'. *American Political Science Review*, Vol. 100, No. 4, pp. 493–8.

Blyth, M. (2013) *Austerity: the History of a Dangerous Idea* (Oxford: Oxford University Press).

Borg, S. and Diez, T. (2016) 'Postmodern EU? Integration between Alternative Horizons and Territorial Angst'. *JCMS*, Vol. 54, No. 1, pp. 131–51.

Dinan, D., Nugent, N. and Paterson, W.E. (eds) (2017) *The European Union in Crisis* (London: Palgrave).

Dowding, K. (2000) 'Institutionalist Research on the European Union: A Critical Review'. *European Union Politics*, Vol. 1, No. 1, pp. 125–44.

Etzioni, A. (1965) *Political Unification: A Comparative Study of Leaders and Forces* (New York: Holt, Rinehart and Winston).

European Commission (2017) 'Reflection Paper on the Social Dimension of Europe', COM (2017) 206, 26 April.

Haas, E.B. (1971) 'The Study of Regional Integration: Reflections on the Joys and Anguish of Pretheorizing'. In Lindberg, L.N. and Scheingold, S.A. (eds) *Regional Integration: Theory and Research* (Cambridge, MA: Harvard University Press), pp. 3–42.

Hay, C. (1996) 'Narrating Crisis: The Discursive Construction of the "Winter of Discontent"'. *Sociology*, Vol. 30, No. 2, pp. 253–77.

Hay, C. (2016) 'Good in a Crisis: The Ontological Institutionalism of Social Constructivism'. *New Political Economy*, Vol. 21, No. 6, pp. 520–35.

Hix, S. (2007) 'The EU as a Polity (I)'. In Jørgensen, K.-E., Pollack, M.A. and Rosamond, B. (eds) *Handbook of European Union Politics* (London: Sage), pp. 141–58.

Jachtenfuchs, M. (2007) 'The EU as a Polity (II)'. In Jørgensen, K.-E., Pollack, M.A. and Rosamond, B. (eds) *Handbook of European Union Politics* (London: Sage), pp. 159–74.

Jasanoff, S. (2005) *Designs on Nature, Science And Democracy in Europe and the United States* (Princeton, NJ: Princeton University Press).

Jensen, M.D. and Kristensen, P.M. (2013) 'The Elephant in the Room: Mapping the Latent Communication Pattern in European Union Studies'. *Journal of European Public Policy*, Vol. 20, No. 1, pp. 1–20.

Joerges, C. and Kreuder-Sonnen, C. (2017) 'European Studies and the European Crisis: Legal and Political Science between Critique and Complacency'. *European Law Journal*, Vol. 23, No. 1-2, pp. 118–39.

Kaufman-Osborn, T.V. (2006) 'Dividing the Domain of Political Science: On the Fetishization of Subfields'. *Polity*, Vol. 38, No. 1, pp. 41–71.

Keeler, J.T.S. (2005) 'Mapping EU Studies: Tthe Evolution from Boutique to Boom Field 1960–2001'. *JCMS*, Vol. 43, No. 3, pp. 551–82.

Kinnvall, C. (2016) 'The Postcolonial Has Moved into Europe: Bordering, Security and Ethno-cultural Belonging'. *JCMS*, Vol. 54, No. 1, pp. 152–68.

Kreppel, A. (2012) 'The normalization of the European Union'. *Journal of European Public Policy*, Vol. 19, No. 5, pp. 635–45.

Kronsell, A. (2016) 'The Power of EU Masculinities: A Feminist Contribution to European Integration Theory'. *JCMS*, Vol. 54, No. 1, pp. 104–20.

Lindberg, L.N. (1963) *The Political Dynamics of European Economic Integration* (Stanford, CA: Stanford University Press).

Lindberg, L.N. and Scheingold, S.A. (1970) *Europe's Would-Be Polity: Patterns of Change in the European Community* (Englewood Cliffs, NJ: Prentice Hall).

Lindberg, L.N. and Scheingold, S.A. (eds) (1971) *Regional Integration: Theory and Research* (Cambridge, MA: Harvard University Press).

Luke, T. (1999) 'The Discipline as Disciplinary Normalization: Networks of Research'. *New Political Science*, Vol. 21, No. 3, pp. 345–63.

Manners, I. (2000) 'Europe and the World: the Impact of Globalisation'. In Stevens, A. and Sakwa, R. (eds) *Contemporary Europe* (Basingstoke: Macmillan), pp. 182–201.

Manners, I. (2003) 'Europaian Studies'. *Journal of Contemporary European Studies*, Vol. 11, No. 1, pp. 67–83.

Manners, I. (2007) 'Another Europe is Possible: Critical Perspectives on European Union Politics'. In Jørgensen, K.-E., Pollack, M.A. and Rosamond, B. (eds) *Handbook of European Union Politics* (London: Sage), pp. 77–96.

Manners, I. (2013) 'European Communion: Political Theory of European Union'. *Journal of European Public Policy*, Vol. 20, No. 4, pp. 473–94.

Manners, I., Lynggaard, K. and Löfgren, K. (2015) 'Research Strategies in European Union Studies: Beyond Dichotomies'. In Lynggaard, K., Manners, I. and Löfgren, K. (eds) *Research Methods in European Union Studies* (London: Palgrave), pp. 309–21.

Manners, I. and Murray, P. (2016) 'The End of a Noble Narrative? European Integration Narratives after the Nobel Peace Prize'. *JCMS*, Vol. 54, No. 1, pp. 185–202.

Manners, I. and Whitman, R. (2016) 'Another Theory is Possible: Dissident Voices in Theorising Europe'. *JCMS*, Vol. 54, No. 1, pp. 3–18.

Monroe, K.R. (ed.) (2005) *Perestroika! The Raucous Rebellion in Political Science* (New Haven, CT: Yale University Press).

Mudge, S.L. and Vauchez, A. (2012) 'Building Europe on a Weak Field: Law, Economics and Scholarly Avatars in Transnational Politics'. *American Journal of Sociology*, Vol. 118, No. 2, pp. 449–92.

OECD (2016) *Interim Economic Outlook* (Paris: OECD).

Ostry, J., Loungani, P. and Furceri, D. (2016) 'Neoliberalism: Oversold?' *Finance & Development*, Vol. 53, No. 2, pp. 38–41.

Parker, O. (2016) 'Teaching (Dissident) Theory in Crisis European Union'. *JCMS*, Vol. 54, No. 1, pp. 37–52.

Paterson, W.E., Nugent, N. and Egan, M. (eds.) (2010) 'Hastening Slowly: European Union Studies – Between Reinvention and Continuing Fragmentation'. In Egan, M, Nugent, N. and Paterson, W.E. (eds.) *Research Agendas in EU Studies: Stalking the Elephant* (Basingstoke: Palgrave), pp. 398–419.

Rosamond, B. (2007) 'The Political Sciences of European Integration: Disciplinary History and EU Studies'. In Jørgensen, K.-E., Pollack, M.A. and Rosamond, B. (eds) *Handbook of European Union Politics* (London: Sage), pp. 7–30.

Rosamond, B. (2015) 'Methodology in European Union Studies'. In Lynggaard, K., Manners, I. and Löfgren, K. (eds) *Research Methods in European Union Studies* (London: Palgrave), pp. 18–36.

Rosamond, B. (2016) 'Field of Dreams: the Discursive Construction of EU Studies, Intellectual Dissidence and the Practice of "Normal Science"'. *JCMS*, Vol. 54, No. 1, pp. 19–36.

Rosamond, B. (2017) 'The Political Economy Context of EU Crises'. In Dinan, D., Nugent, N. and Paterson, W.E. (eds) *The European Union in Crisis* (London: Palgrave), pp. 33–53.

Ryner, M. (2012) 'Financial Crisis, Orthodoxy, Heterodoxy and the Production of Knowledge about the EU'. *Millennium: Journal of International Studies*, Vol. 40, No. 3, pp. 647–73.

Saurugger, S. (2016) 'Sociological Approaches to the European Union in Times of Turmoil'. *JCMS*, Vol. 54, No. 1, pp. 70–86.

Schimmelfennig, F. (2017) 'Theorising Crisis in European Integration'. In Dinan, D., Nugent, N. and Paterson, W.E. (eds) *The European Union in Crisis* (London Palgrave), pp. 316–35.

Schmitter, P.C. (2002) 'Seven (Disputable) Theses on the Future of "Transnationalized" or "Globalized" Political Science'. *European'. Political Science*, Vol. 1, No. 2, pp. 23–40.

Scholl, C. and Freyberg-Inan, A. (2018) 'Imagining another Europe: Building a Pan-European Counter-hegemonic Bloc around an Anti-austerity Master Frame'. *Comparative European Politics*, Vol. 16, No. 1, pp. 103–25.

White, J.P.J. (2003) 'Theory Guiding Practice: The Neofunctionalists and the Hallstein EEC Commission'. *Journal of European Integration History*, Vol. 9, No. 1, pp. 111–31.

JCMS 2018 Volume 56. Annual Review pp. 39–50

DOI: 10.1111/jcms.12751

Brexit and the 2017 UK General Election*

SARA B. HOBOLT
London School of Economics and Political Science

Introduction

The 2017 UK General Election came less than a year after one of the most significant political events in recent British and European politics history: the referendum decision of British voters to exit the European Union (EU). The snap election that was meant to strengthen the Conservative government's hand in the UK–EU Brexit negotiations, and Prime Minister Theresa May's position within her party and in parliament, resulted instead in a diminished Conservative minority government. Given the major political event that preceded the election, it was foreseeable that it might result in new patterns of voting behaviour. What was surprising, however, is that the 2017 election saw the decline of multi-party politics in Britain, despite the Brexit divide cutting across party lines. The parties that were most united in offering distinct positions on Brexit – the United Kingdom Independence Party (UKIP) with its 'hard Brexit' approach and the pro-EU Liberal Democrats and Greens with their promise of a second referendum – all lost votes. In contrast, the two major parties, that promised to honour the referendum result but were deeply internally divided on the nature of post-Brexit UK–EU relations, were rewarded with the largest combined vote share in any election since 1970. How did an election in the midst of the Brexit debate lead to the strengthening of two-party politics in Britain? Was this outcome a signal that voters were uniting behind the decision to leave the European Union? And, how did the outcome of this election affect the ongoing Brexit negotiations?

These questions are examined in this contribution. I argue that despite the ostensible consensus on Brexit by the two major parties, the public – alongside parliamentarians and political parties – remained as divided as ever. An analysis of individual-level data from the British Election Study (BES) shows that while traditional economic left–right values continued to be the main driver of electoral behaviour in British politics, other key political fault lines that were apparent in the Brexit referendum were also present in this election: the younger, progressive and degree-educated voters flocked to Labour, whereas the Conservative voter base was significantly older and more socially conservative. Moreover, the Brexit vote itself had an independent effect on vote choice, as the Conservative Party attracted more Leave voters and benefited from the collapse of UKIP, whereas Remain voters were more likely to vote for the Labour Party.

The main conclusion of this contribution is therefore that while the 2017 election resulted in the resurgence of two-party politics based on contestation along the classic

*The author would like to acknowledge the generous financial support of the ESRC Brexit Priority Grant (ES/R000573/1) and the European Research Council Consolidator Grant (ERC GA 647835/ EUDEMOS). Moreover, this contribution has benefited from insightful comments by Emanuele Massetti and Toni Rodon.

economic left–right dimension, electoral behaviour in Britain – like elsewhere in Europe – is also driven by salient cultural concerns (De Vries, 2017; Kriesi *et al.*, 2008). This reflects in part the divide created by the Brexit referendum that mobilized an underlying fault line between socially liberal cosmopolitans – mostly young and well-educated - and older, less educated socially conservative voters and which continues to reverberate (Hobolt, 2016; Jennings and Stoker, 2017). The election also had implications for Britain's negotiations on its future relationship with the EU. The surprise outcome of the ballot weakened Mrs. May's position in her party and within parliament, and this made it more difficult for the government to present a united and coherent position in the UK–EU negotiations. Rather than strengthening the British government's hands in the Brexit negotiations, the 2017 election illustrated that Britain remains deeply divided over its future in the EU and in the world – in the electorate, in parliament and even within the government itself.

I. The Surprise 2017 General Election

Both the announcement and the outcome of the June 2017 UK General Election were a surprise. The snap election was called by Conservative Prime Minister, Theresa May, who had been appointed leader of the party and the government in July 2016, after former Prime Minister David Cameron resigned in response to the unexpected Brexit referendum outcome. While Mrs. May had repeatedly ruled out a snap election, she nonetheless decided in April 2017 to call one shortly after triggering Article 50 to start the exit negotiations with the EU. Ostensibly the reason for the election was to strengthen Britain's hand in the Brexit negotiation by increasing the government's parliamentary mandate. At the time, the snap election seemed like a clever tactical decision as the Conservative party had a sizeable lead in the opinion polls of up to 20 percentage points over Labour and was widely expected to win a large majority in parliament (Prosser, 2018). However, as the campaign progressed Labour recovered ground and finished close behind the Conservatives. Shifts of this magnitude in voting intention is highly unusual during campaigns and indicate are more volatile electorate than in the past (Mellon *et al.*, 2018).

One key driver of vote switching during the campaign was the public's perception of the two contenders for the premiership, Theresa May and Labour's Jeremy Corbyn. The Conservative campaign focused heavily on Mrs. May as a strong and reliable leader who would deliver the best deal for Britain in the Brexit negotiations. But she turned out to be a much weaker campaigner than expected, while the Labour leader became increasingly popular during the campaign. Mr. Corbyn had been viewed by most commentators – including many of his own MPs – as too left-wing and largely unelectable, yet his favourability ratings improved steadily during the campaign (Mellon *et al.*, 2018). Moreover, the Labour Party chose to focus their campaign on a popular anti-austerity message of increased social spending and nationalization of key public services.

Just like Cameron's failed gamble to hold a referendum on British membership in the hope of mollifying divisions within his party and the electorate (Hobolt, 2016), May's plan to strengthen her position with a snap election did not pay off. The outcome was that the Conservatives lost their majority of seats and had to form a minority government with the support of the small right-wing Northern Irish party, the Democratic Unionist Party (DUP). Theresa May emerged much weaker as a result. Table 1 shows the vote and seat shares of the 2017 general election and the change in vote share since the last general election in 2015.

The most noticeable change in patterns of aggregate-level electoral support between 2015 and 2017 is the move towards greater two-party dominance in 2017: 82.4 per cent voted for either a Conservative or a Labour candidate with a high turnout of 68.8 per cent. The dominance of the Conservatives and Labour was particularly pronounced in England where they won 87.3 per cent of the vote. As Table 1 shows, this strengthening of the major parties was largely due to the collapse of UKIP that dropped from a vote share of over 12 per cent to under 2 per cent, but the other smaller parties (outside Northern Ireland) also lost votes.

What is perhaps surprising is that voters did not reward the parties that took the most distinct positions on the Brexit question. Despite being the most unified pro-Brexit party, UKIP was abandoned by most of the 52 per cent of the British electorate who had voted to leave the European Union. UKIP's decline can be attributed to the fact that the party's major campaigning issue of leaving the EU had been accepted by both major parties. Moreover, the referendum had allowed the Conservative Party to adopt a similar a hard-line position on reducing immigration post-Brexit; a position that had formed a major part of UKIP's electoral appeal (Ford and Goodwin, 2014). According to the British Election Study, 73 per cent of 2015 UKIP defectors voted for the Conservative Party in 2017 (57 per cent of all 2015 UKIP voters) (Mellon *et al.*, 2018). Remainers also did not reward the Liberal Democrats or the Greens that had campaigned most strongly

Table 1: 2017 UK General Election Results

Party	Leader	Brexit position	Seats 2017	Vote share 2017 (%)	Change in vote share since 2015
Conservative Party	Theresa May	Hard Brexit No 2nd referendum	317	42.3	+5.5
Labour Party	Jeremy Corbyn	"Jobs first Brexit" No 2nd referendum	262	40.0	+9.5
Scottish National Party	Nicola Sturgeon	Soft Brexit Scottish Independence referendum	35	3.0	−1.7
Liberal Democrats	Tim Farron	Soft Brexit 2nd referendum on deal	12	7.4	−0.5
Democratic Unionist Party	Arlene Foster	Hard Brexit No 2nd referendum	10	0.9	+0.3
Sinn Féin	Gerry Adams	Special status for Northern Ireland within the EU	7	0.7	+0.2
Plaid Cymru	Leanne Wood	Soft Brexit	4	0.5	−0.1
Green Party	Jonathan Bartley & Caroline Lucas	Soft Brexit 2nd referendum on deal	1	1.6	−2.1
UK Independence Party	Paul Nuttall	Hard Brexit No 2nd referendum	0	1.8	−10.8

Note: This list excludes the (Conservative) Speaker of the House of Commons, John Bercow, and the Independent Sylvia Hermon. *Hard Brexit* refers to the position of leaving the EU's Single Market. *Soft Brexit* refers to staying in the EU's Single Market and Customs Union.

against a Hard Brexit and for a second referendum on the final Brexit deal, with the option of staying in the European Union (Liberal Democrats, 2017). Both parties lost voters, with 42 per cent of 2015 Green voters switching to Labour in the 2017 election (Mellon *et al.*, 2018).

In contrast, the two major parties – the Conservatives and Labour – did not make Brexit a central theme of their campaign. Both parties were committed to honouring the referendum result, but they focused little on the details of their plans for Brexit, perhaps in part due to their internal divisions over the UK's future relationship with the EU. Mrs. May had already given a major speech on Brexit that made it explicit that the government would seek to leave not only the EU itself, but also the Single Market and the Customs Union, and therefore ruled out a so-called 'Soft Brexit'. The emphasis during the campaign was therefore on the need for a 'strong and stable government to get the best Brexit deal' (Conservative Party, 2017). The Labour Party was promising a 'Jobs First Brexit', which some interpreted as a softer approach to the negotiations, but the party made no commitment to staying in the Single Market[1] or any promises of a second referendum. Instead the focus of its campaign was a Britain 'For the Many, not the Few', which signalled a commitment to more redistribution and greater spending on the welfare state.

Given the election result, it is tempting to conclude that voters had largely united behind Brexit and that the issue was unimportant in the election. However, the polling data show a very different story As shown in Figure 1, there has been very little movement in

Figure 1: Was Britain Right or Wrong to Vote to Leave the EU?

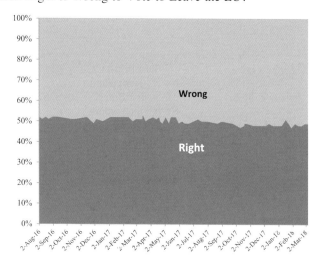

Source: YouGov/What UK Thinks (https://whatukthinks.org/eu/).

---

[1]Labour's Manifesto was ambiguous on Single Market membership (Labour Party, 2017). The party promised to 'scrap the Conservatives' Brexit White Paper and replace it with fresh negotiating priorities that have a strong emphasis on retaining the benefits of the Single Market and the Customs Union', thus emphasizing the 'benefits' of the Single Market, rather than 'membership' of the Single Market.

public opinion on Brexit since the referendum when it comes to the question of whether Britain was right or wrong to vote to leave the EU.

As Figure 1 shows, the public remains split down the middle when it comes to the question 'in hindsight, do you think Britain was right or wrong to vote to leave the EU?' Few people have changed their minds since the referendum and if anything the division between Remainers and Leavers is becoming more entrenched. Other research that I have conducted with collaborators on public attitudes and identities in the aftermath of Brexit reveals that around three-quarters of British citizens identify as either Remainers or Leavers, and these new identities cut across traditional party lines. More worryingly, our research shows that such identities go beyond political disagreement and translate into animosity towards and stereotyping of the opposite side (see Hobolt *et al.*, 2018). But to what extent were these divisions reflected in the 2017 election? This question is examined in the next section.

II. A Brexit Election?

While the two major parties, the Conservatives and Labour, adopted seemingly similar positions on the Brexit question, the Brexit question clearly continued to divide voters. Despite the reluctance of the parties to make the election about Brexit, the issue nonetheless did have an impact on their electoral support. Heath and Goodwin's (2017) analysis of constituency-level data show that Conservatives made gains from the electoral decline of UKIP in Leave-supporting areas, but lost in more Remain-supporting areas with large number of graduates and younger voters. There was also a slight tendency for Labour to perform better in Remain-supporting constituencies (Heath and Goodwin, 2017). Jennings and Stoker, in their study of aggregate-level constituency data, however, reject the description of the 2017 election as a 'Brexit election', since 'the vote is better seen as a symptom of the longer-term bifurcation of politics; less revenge of the "Remainers" and more a continuing battle of mobilisation between cosmopolitan and non-cosmopolitan areas' (Jennings and Stoker, 2017, p. 359).

These patterns in constituency-level voting thus raise important questions about the salience of Brexit to individual-level voters, as well as a broader cosmopolitan/non-cosmopolitan divide in British politics. The Brexit referendum itself had demonstrated a stark demographic and value divide between younger, better educated and more cosmopolitan voters who voted overwhelming to remain in the EU, and older, less well-educated more socially conservative voters who favoured leaving (Hobolt, 2016). Attitudes towards immigration was one of the key issues that divided Remainers and Leavers, as the latter group saw Brexit as an opportunity to restrict immigration (Clarke *et al.*, 2017; Hobolt, 2016).

This divide is not particular to British politics. Many scholars have pointed to the increasing importance of a new dimension in European politics centred not around classic economic questions about redistribution and the role of the state, but rather on a cultural divide between openness to immigration, multiculturalism and international co-operation on the one hand and traditional cultural values, nationalism and euroscepticism on the other hand (see De Vries and Hobolt, 2012; De Vries and Marks, 2012). Although the emphasis is on 'cultural' attitudes, such attitudes may well, at least in part, be rooted in the structural changes to the globalized economy that has created both winners and losers

(Kriesi *et al.*, 2006, 2008). This divide has been given various labels in the literature, such as the integration–demarcation dimension (Kriesi *et al.*, 2006, 2008), the cosmopolitan axis (Jennings and Stoker, 2017), and the transnational cleavage (Hooghe and Marks, 2018) and while there is no agreement on the exact content of this divide (De Vries, 2017), it is regarded as distinct from the traditional economic left–right dimension and focused more on identity and cultural concerns.

There is little doubt that the Brexit referendum heightened the salience of the cultural dimension of politics in ways that cut across the traditional economic and left–right dimension (Hobolt, 2016). So, the question is to what extent this cosmopolitan divide was also present in the general election, and whether the Brexit issue was salient to voters' decision-making even when accounting for these factors. To examine this, we turn to individual-level data from the British Election Study's post-election face-to-face survey (Fieldhouse *et al.*, 2018). This dataset provides a nationally representative face-to-face survey on how people voted in the election, their socio-demographic characteristics and their political attitudes as well as how they voted in the 2016 referendum, and thus provides an excellent source for examining the drivers of voting behaviour.

Our analysis focuses on the vote for the two major parties,[2] with a vote for the incumbent Conservative Party as the dependent variable (the full details of the data and results can be found in the Appendix). First, we examine the demographic predictors of the Conservative vote. To the extent that the demographic divide of the Brexit referendum is replicated, we should see that younger voters and graduates would be far less likely to vote Conservative. We also examine the impact of ethnicity and social class identity on vote choice. Figure 2 shows the marginal effects based on a logit model of Conservative vote in the 2017 general election, with Labour vote as the reference category. It clearly shows that age was a significant factor in the general election – as it was in the referendum

Figure 2: Demographic Predictors of Conservative Vote

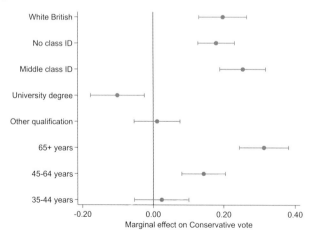

Source: BES post-election survey 2017 (http://www.britishelectionstudy.com/).

[2]The results are almost identical if we include all the minor parties in the analysis.

(Hobolt, 2016) – with voters over 65 years old 34 percentage points more likely to vote Conservative than voters below 35 years old. We also find that university graduates were 10 percentage points more likely to vote Labour than those with no qualifications. However, this educational divide is much less stark than in the referendum, perhaps is part due to the legacy of class divisions in electoral politics which meant that working class voters would traditionally vote Labour, while the better-educated middle class would vote Conservative (Evans and Tilley, 2017). We do observe that voters who self-identify as working class (reference category) were still significantly more likely to vote Labour, compared to middle class voters and those without a class identity. Voters from ethnic minority backgrounds were also more likely to vote Labour.

These individual-level demographic differences mirror the constituency-level differences between Labour-supporting urban areas with more diverse, younger and more educated voters and Conservative-voting smaller towns and rural areas, with older and less diverse populations (Jennings and Stoker, 2017). But does this mean that electoral behaviour in Britain had tilted towards the cosmopolitan axis in the 2017 election, and that economic attitudes were less relevant? And did Brexit play a role in shaping vote choices?

To examine these questions, we fit a second model that – in addition to the demographic variables above – also includes a set of attitudinal variables and an item on vote choice in the 2016 referendum. As mentioned above, there is no agreement on the main features of the 'cultural' dimension of politics or the degree to which it is correlated with, or orthogonal to, traditional left–right attitudes towards politics (De Vries, 2017). Hence, as a starting point for our analysis, we ran an exploratory factor analysis on a large set of attitudinal question items, covering both standard economic left–right items and questions on socially liberal versus socially conservative attitudes. The results show two main attitudinal dimensions that can be labelled as 'economic' and 'cultural'. The economic items capture attitudes towards state intervention in the economy and redistribution,[3] whereas the cultural items capture attitudes towards traditional values, crime, immigration and ethnic minorities.[4] On the basis of this factor analysis, I created two factor scores representing the cultural and economic attitude dimensions, as well as including a question on whether the respondent voted Leave, Remain or abstained in the Brexit referendum. The results are shown in Figure 3.

The results are striking. First, they clearly show that classic left–right economic attitudes are still the primary driver of vote choice in Britain. This should not be surprising given that post-war party competition in Britain, and in most of Western Europe, has been organized around the economic left right dimension. Moreover, given the nature of the election campaign where the two parties took very distinct positions on these economic issues – after two decades of ideological convergence – it is understandable economic left–right attitudes were also salient to voters (Evans and Tilley, 2017; Green and Hobolt,

---

[3]Economic attitudes items include: 'Private enterprise is the best way to solve Britain's economic problems'; 'It is the government's responsibility to provide a job for everyone who wants one'; 'Major public services and industries ought to be in state ownership'; and 'Make much greater efforts to make people's incomes more equal' (see Fieldhouse *et al.*, 2018).
[4]Cultural attitude items include: 'Young people today don't have enough respect for traditional British values'; 'People in Britain should be more tolerant of those who lead unconventional lives'; 'For some crimes, the death penalty is the most appropriate sentence'; 'Do you think immigration is good or bad for Britain's economy?' and 'And how do you feel about attempts to give equal opportunities to black people and Asians in Britain?' (see Fieldhouse *et al.*, 2018).

Figure 3: Attitudinal Predictors of Conservative Vote

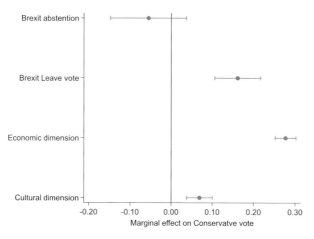

Source: BES post-election survey 2017 (http://www.britishelectionstudy.com/).

2008). But it is nonetheless an important reminder that that attitudes concerning the role of the state in the economy and redistribution are still strongly correlated with vote choice. Cultural attitudes also matter, but less than economic ones. Interestingly, we can see that the Brexit vote was a very important determinant of vote choice, even when controlling for cultural attitudes and demographics. Someone who voted to Leave the EU in 2016 was 16 percentage points more likely to vote Conservative than someone who had voted Remain, holding other attitudes constant. This suggests that despite the reluctance of the major parties to offer distinct positions on Brexit, the referendum played a role as Leavers flocked to the Conservatives and Remainers (perhaps more surprisingly) voted for Labour in larger numbers. One reason why a salient pro-EU/eurosceptic divide did not benefit smaller parties, as we have seen in the rest of Europe (see Hobolt and De Vries, 2015), is Britain's use of the first-past-the-post electoral system, which encourages voters to think more strategically about which party has a realistic chance of winning the constituency seat and of forming a government when casting a vote. Another reason is that issues other than Brexit appear to have been more important to a number of voters, notably traditional concerns about the economy and social services.

In the next section, I examine the broader consequences of this Brexit election on British politics and UK-EU negotiations.

III. Brexit Negotiations

When Mrs. May announced the snap general election in April 2017, she declared with reference to Brexit that 'the country is coming together but Westminster is not'. As shown in Figure 1, however, there is little evidence to support the claim that the country is coming together, and the election result did not lead to greater unity over Brexit, in Westminster or in the general population. This polarization of public opinion along Brexit lines makes it more difficult for the government to agree on a negotiation position that will satisfy a large proportion of the electorate. Following the disappointing election result for Mrs. May, only 34 per cent of voters thought her government was doing a good job handling Britain's exit from the EU, compared with 57 per cent who thought they were doing a bad job.[5] One of the reasons for the negative evaluation of the government's performance, even among many Leavers, is the continued uncertainty surrounding the Prime Minister's approach to Brexit. Her Cabinet has remained openly divided on the right balance between achieving the benefits of continued free trade with the European Union and avoiding a border between Northern Ireland and the Republic of Ireland on the one hand, and enforcing British priorities on restricting payments to the EU, ending freedom of movement and leaving the jurisdiction of the European Court of Justice on the other hand. While the EU – led by the Commission's negotiator Michel Barnier – has maintained a unified and consistent line throughout the negotiations, emphasizing the core principles that the UK cannot leave the Single Market and the Customs Union and maintain frictionless trade and the benefits of membership, the British government has been accused of an unrealistic 'have cake and eat it' approach to the Brexit negotiations (Hagemann, 2018).

It is not only the government that is in turmoil over the future shape of Britain's relationship with the EU. Both the Labour Party and the Conservatives are fundamentally divided in Parliament over key aspects of how the UK's relationship with the EU should be reshaped. A survey of MPs in late 2017 shows that within the Labour Party, the ordinary backbench MPs favour a softer approach to Brexit than their party leadership with 90 per cent of Labour MPs stating that membership of the Single Market is both possible outside the EU and compatible with honouring the referendum (Cowley and Wager, 2018). In contrast, a majority of Conservative MPs take a more hard-line approach to aspects of the Brexit negotiations than their government, with 74 per cent of Conservative MPs surveyed opposing the continued freedom of movement during a transition period, and 63 per cent saying they do not want any role for the ECJ after March 2019, both of which have been conceded to the EU by the British government in the discussion of transition arrangements.

The UK general election can thus be said to have weakened the British government's position in the negotiations, as it did little to provide more clarity on Britain's position on the future UK–EU relationship and damaged Theresa May's position both within her party and within parliament. Her weakness within the party – leading to her being described as a 'dead woman walking' in the aftermath of the election – has meant that she has little authority over the 'hard Brexiteers' within her Cabinet, and this makes it more difficult to compromise in the UK–EU Brexit negotiations. Moreover, her weakness within Parliament means that she is vulnerable to rebellions within her own ranks – also from Tory Remainers – and she needs the support of the hard-line DUP to ensure the survival of her minority government. This became abundantly clear in December 2017 when an agreement struck between Britain and the EU to solve the problem of the Irish border and move to the next phase of Brexit talks was thwarted at the very last minute by the DUP. An agreement was finally struck to move the Brexit negotiations to the second phase that involves the future relationship between the UK and the EU, but Mrs. May continued to find herself performing a delicate balancing act between hard-liners in her

[5]Poll by Ipsos MORI, 18 July 2017.

own party and in the DUP and a Parliament dominated by parliamentarians advocating a softer approach.

Conclusion

Less than a year after the historical referendum on Britain's membership of the EU, Prime Minister May called the election to secure an increased majority for her government and a strong mandate for the Brexit negotiations. The surprising outcome of the election was a hung parliament, resulting in a minority government led by a weakened prime minister. While Brexit was the apparent reason for the early election, it did not dominate the campaign, not least as the two major parties shared a very similar position on the Brexit issue, namely that the referendum outcome would be respected and that Britain would be leaving the EU without a second referendum. The fact that this Brexit election led to the strengthening of two-party politics – with the Conservatives and Labour winning the biggest combined share of the vote since the 1970s – is something of a conundrum. As a cross-cutting political issue, we might expect Brexit to lead to greater fragmentation of party politics (Hobolt and De Vries, 2015). Yet, instead the Conservative Party benefited from the fact that the Brexit vote allowed them to adopt a hard-line position on both Brexit and immigration. This resulted in the collapse of UKIP's electoral appeal, as voters – especially older, socially conservative voters – flocked to the Conservatives (Mellon et al., 2018). The analysis also shows that Remain voters – especially younger socially-liberal graduates – voted in larger numbers for Labour. Some Remain voters may have voted Labour in the hope that the party would adopt a 'softer' approach to Brexit in office, while others were attracted to the party's left-wing anti-austerity message. Our analysis reveals that the major parties' distinct socio-economic policies were decisive for many voters.

Overall, the election that was meant to unify the nation, and Parliament, after a divisive Brexit referendum did little to achieve that. The British public remained deeply divided on the issue of Brexit. The election also weakened the Prime Minister's position, both within her party and within Parliament. The difficult policy choices involved in negotiating Britain's exit from the European Union were thus compounded by an election that enfeebled the government and revealed deep and enduring divisions in the country.

Appendix

Table A1: Descriptive Statistics

Variable	N	Mean	Std. Dev.	Min	Max
Conservative vote	1,396	0.48	0.50	0	1
Age groups	2,175	2.73	1.10	1	4
Education groups	1,960	2.94	1.62	1	5
Middle class ID	2,137	1.01	0.88	0	2
White British	2,194	0.86	0.35	0	1
Cultural dimension	1,708	0.00	0.83	−2	2
Economic dimension	1,708	0.00	0.75	−2	2
Brexit vote	2,194	0.77	0.74	0	2

Table A2: Vote Choice Models

	Demographic Model		Full Model	
	Log odds	SE	Log odds	SE
Age (Reference: 18–34 years old)				
35–44 years old	0.25	0.23	0.22	0.28
45–64 years old	0.89*	0.17	0.77*	0.22
65+ years old	1.62*	0.19	1.27*	0.25
Education (Reference: No qualification)				
Other qualification	–0.01	0.18	0.01	0.23
Degree education	–0.49*	0.21	–0.23	0.29
Class identity (Reference: working class)				
Middle class identification	1.44*	0.18	1.29*	0.23
No class identification	1.10*	0.14	1.04*	0.19
White British (Reference: Non-white)	1.25*	0.21	0.89*	0.26
Cultural dimension			0.33*	0.12
Economic dimension			1.75*	0.14
Brexit vote (Reference: Remain)				
Voted leave			0.76*	0.19
Did not vote			–0.15	0.34
Constant	–2.67*	0.29	–2.54*	0.36
N	1,326		1,092	
Pseudo R2	0.15		0.35	

Source: British Election Study 2017 (Fieldhouse *et al.*, 2018). Dependent variable: Conservative vote. Logistic regression model. * $p<0.05$.

References

Clarke, H.D., Goodwin, M. and Whiteley, P. (2017) *Brexit* (Cambridge: Cambridge University Press).

Conservative Party (2017) Forward Together: Our Plan For A Stronger Britain And Prosperous Future (2017 Conservative Party manifesto. Available online at: https://www.conservatives.com/manifesto)

Cowley, P. and Wager, A. (2018) 'What MPs think about Brexit'. UK in a Changing Europe, 8 February 2018. Available online at: http://ukandeu.ac.uk/what-mps-think-about-brexit/.

De Vries, C.E. (2017) 'The Cosmopolitan-Parochial Divide: Changing Patterns of Party and Electoral Competition in the Netherlands and Beyond'. *Journal of European Public Policy*. https://doi.org/10.1080/13501763.2017.1339730.

De Vries, C.E. and Hobolt, S.B. (2012) 'When Dimensions Collide: The Electoral Success of Issue Entrepreneurs'. *European Union Politics*, Vol. 13, No. 2, pp. 246–68.

De Vries, C.E. and Marks, G. (2012) 'The Struggle Over Dimensionality: A Note on Theory and Empirics'. *European Union Politics*, Vol. 13, No. 2, pp. 185–93.

Evans, G. and Tilley, J. (2017) *The New Politics of Class: The Political Exclusion of the British Working Class* (Oxford: Oxford University Press).

Fieldhouse, E., Green, J., Evans, G., Schmitt, H., van der Eijk, C., Mellon, J. and Prosser, C. (2018) *British Election Study, 2017: Face-to-Face Post-Election Survey*. Available online at: www.britishelectionstudy.com/.

Ford, R. and Goodwin, M.J. (2014) *Revolt on the Right: Explaining Support for the Radical Right in Britain* (London: Routledge).

Green, J. and Hobolt, S.B. (2008) 'Owning the Issue Agenda: Party Strategies and Vote Choices in British Elections'. *Electoral Studies*, Vol. 27, No. 3, pp. 460–76.

Hagemann, S. (2018) 'The Brexit Context'. *Parliamentary Affairs*, Vol. 71, No. 1, pp. 155–70.

Heath, O. and Goodwin, M. (2017) 'The 2017 General Election, Brexit and the Return to Two-Party Politics: An Aggregate-level Analysis of the Result'. *The Political Quarterly*, Vol. 88, No. 3, pp. 345–58.

Hobolt, S.B. (2016) 'The Brexit Vote: A Divided Nation, A Divided Continent'. *Journal of European Public Policy*, Vol. 23, No. 9, pp. 1259–77.

Hobolt, S.B. and De Vries, C.E. (2015) 'Issue Entrepreneurship and Multiparty Competition'. *Comparative Political Studies*, Vol. 48, No. 9, pp. 1159–85.

Hobolt, S.B., Leeper, T. and Tilley, J. (2018) 'Emerging Brexit Identities'. In *The UK in A Changing Europe, Brexit and Public Opinion* (London: UK in a Changing Europe).

Hooghe, L. and Marks, G. (2018) ''Cleavage theory meets Europe's crises: Lipset, Rokkan, and the transnational cleavage'. *Journal of European Public Policy*, Vol. 25, No. 1, pp. 109–35.

Jennings, W. and Stoker, G. (2017) 'Tilting Towards the Cosmopolitan Axis? Political Change in England and the 2017 General Election'. *The Political Quarterly*, Vol. 88, No. 3, pp. 359–69.

Kriesi, H., Grande, E., Lachat, R., Dolezal, M., Bornschier, S. and Frey, T. (2008) *West European Politics in the Age of Globalization* (Cambridge: Cambridge University Press).

Kriesi, H., Grande, E., Lachat, R., Dolezal, M., Bornschier, S. and Frey, T. (2006) 'Globalization and the Transformation of the National Political Space: Six European Countries Compared'. *European Journal of Political Research*, Vol. 45, No. 6, pp. 921–56.

Labour Party (2017) For the Many Not the Few (Labour Party manifesto 2017). Available online at: https://labour.org.uk/wp-content/uploads/2017/10/labour-manifesto-2017.pdf.

Liberal Democrats (2017) Change Britain's Future (Liberal Democrat manifesto 2017). Available online at: https://www.libdems.org.uk/manifesto.

Mellon, J., Evans, G., Fieldhouse, E., Green, J. and Prosser, C. (2018) 'Brexit or Corbyn? Campaign and Inter-Election Vote Switching in the 2017 UK General Election'. *Parliamentary Affairs*, Vol. 71, No. 1. https://doi.org/10.1093/pa/gsy001.

Prosser, C. (2018) 'The Strange Death of Multi-Party Britain: the UK General Election of 2017'. *West European Politics.*. https://doi.org/10.1093/pa/gsy001.F.

JCMS 2018 Volume 56. Annual Review pp. 51–62   DOI: 10.1111/jcms.12756

The 2017 French and German Elections*

HANSPETER KRIESI
European University Institute, Florence

Introduction: Long-term Trends and Crisis-related Factors

Germany and France belong to the continental Western European countries whose party systems have been transformed by two waves of mobilization since the 1970s – a first wave that started in the early 1970s with the mobilization of the so-called new social movements and which gave rise to the Green parties and mainly transformed the left, and a second wave that took off in the early 1980s with the rise of the Front National in France and which has mainly transformed the right. These two waves have articulated societal conflicts that have not been taken up by the mainstream parties. The first wave was an expression of transformations that were endogenous to the European nation-states. Processes of deindustrialization, expansion of tertiary education, feminization of the workforce and occupational upgrading have been characteristic of this transformation and brought about a value change in Western Europe (Inglehart, 1977). The second wave refers to social conflicts arising from 'globalization', or, more specifically, from the opening up of national borders in economic, political and cultural terms (Kriesi *et al.*, 2008, 2012). The two waves of mobilization have in common that they concerned above all cultural issues – issues related to cultural liberalism, immigration and European integration. They primarily transformed the meaning of the cultural dimension of the party space, which, in the European context, had traditionally been dominated by issues related to religion. Interpreting the impact of the New Left, Kitschelt (1994, 1995) re-baptized the cultural dimension as a 'libertarian-authoritarian' dimension; focusing on the impact of the New Right, we chose to relabel it as the 'demarcation-integration' dimension (Kriesi *et al.*, 2008, 2012). Theorizing the joint impact of both waves, Bornschier (2010a, 2010b, 2015) suggested that the reshaped cultural dimension refers to a fundamental conflict between universalistic and traditionalist-communitarian values (traditionalism invokes the rejection of universalism, while communitarianism makes reference to the populist right's conception of community).

France and Germany differ with respect to these developments to the extent that the two waves left different legacies in their respective party systems. While Germany saw the rise of a strong Green party which emerged from the massive new social movements and experienced its breakthrough in the federal elections 1983, the New Right only developed belatedly in Germany, most importantly due to its national-socialist legacy. In France, by contrast, the legacy of the communist left constrained the development of the new social movements (see Kriesi et al., 1995) and of a viable Green

*Work on this contribution was supported by the ERC-grant 338875 (POLCON).

party, while France was at the forefront of the development of the New Right with the Front National experiencing its electoral breakthrough in the European elections 1984. Belatedly, Germany developed a party of the New Radical Right as well – the Alternative für Deutschland (AfD), which broke through in the context of the Great Recession. Originally, the AfD opposed the repeated bailouts of Europe's crisis-ridden debtor countries. But rather rapidly, it muted into a typical populist radical right party, focusing on immigration issues and joining the ranks of the New Right that had already been established in France for more than 30 years. Even though it had just been founded only seven months before, and even though it had not yet developed the typical profile of a radical populist right party, the AfD obtained 4.7 per cent of votes and only barely missed the 5 per cent threshold to enter the Bundestag in the 2013 federal elections. Subsequently, the party gained electoral ground in European and state-wide elections, both in West and East Germany. As argued by Bremer and Schulte-Cloos (2018), it probably benefited from the fact that it was initially not as closely associated with outright radical right positions as its predecessors from the New Right. In France, by contrast, the Greens who did experience a great success in the European elections in 2009, when they obtained 16.3 per cent of the vote, closely behind the PS, have been in full decline ever since. In the first round of the presidential elections 2012, their candidate only obtained 2.3 per cent, and in the 2017 elections they did not even field their own candidate but endorsed the lacklustre candidate of the PS.

As a result of the long-term trends, the dominant competition between the mainstream parties of the centre-left (Social democrats) and the centre-right (Conservatives, Liberals and Christian-Democrats) on the economic dimension of the political space has been supplemented by the competition between the New Left (Greens) and the New Right (radical populist challengers – AfD and FN in France and Germany) on the cultural dimension. In this two-dimensional space, the party configurations became tripolar. While the New Left and the mainstream left occupy rather similar positions, the right has become clearly divided between a moderate mainstream centre-right and a radical New Right.

The structure of the party system, however, not only depends on the legacy of the long-term trends, but also on unpredictable dynamics of contingent events such as the financial crisis, the euro crisis, the terrorist crisis, the refugee crisis and the Brexit crisis, which have successively shaken Europe since autumn 2008. As we have shown in a systematic analyses of the national elections in Europe during the Great Recession (Hutter and Kriesi, 2018a), the timing of the economic crisis and its articulation with the ongoing dynamics of national politics, the prevailing strategies of the parties, as well as the composition of the government at the time when the crisis hit proved to be crucial for the kind of transformation of the national party systems that was to become possible. For the outcome of the 2017 elections, it is important to keep in mind that neither Germany nor France belong to the countries most heavily hit by the economic crisis, even if Germany got through the Great Recession better than France. Moreover, we should keep in mind that, during the euro crisis, both countries became part of the group of 'creditor' countries which saw the accentuation of domestic conflict over rescue measures for the 'debtor' countries and institutional reforms of the eurozone. On the other hand, Germany is certainly the country most concerned by the refugee crisis, while France has been much more concerned by terrorism.

I. The Outcome of the 2017 Elections

Against this general background, let us consider the outcome of the 2017 elections in France and Germany. Table 1 puts the 2017 election results into perspective. It presents the election outcomes of the last two pre-crisis elections and all the post-crisis elections in the two countries. It also includes some indices for the characterization of the overall trends in the two party systems. Contrary to the pessimistic predictions by some observers (see for example Mair, 2013), voter turnout has not systematically declined over the last elections in France and Germany, nor has there been a systematic trend of convergence (as indicated by the polarization index). However, in line with the general trend that I have just sketched, the fragmentation (as indicated by the effective number of parties and the volatility of both systems has increased. In France, the respective indicators reached record levels in 2017, as a result of the destruction of the mainstream centre-left and centre-right parties and the rise of Emanuel Macron's 'République en marche' (REM). In fact, the 2017 French elections have been characterized by a 'disruptive vote' (Perrineau, 2017a). Thus, these elections led to an extraordinary renewal of parliament: no less than 60 per cent of the outgoing members who ran again were beaten, and roughly 75 per cent of the elected members of parliament have been elected for the first time (Perrineau, 2017b, p. 18). These elections represent a process of 'creative destruction' that is unique in the Fifth Republic. Compared to the French case, the German mainstream

Table 1: Election Results: Pre-crisis (2002–07) and Post-crisis (2009–17)[1]

France[2]	2002	2007		2012	2017
FG	21.0	10.7		13.4	19.6
PS	16.2	25.9		28.6	6.4
REM					24.0
UMP/UDF/MoDem/LR	26.7	49.8		36.3	20.0
FN	16.9	10.4		17.9	21.3
Turnout	71.6	83.8		79.5	77.8
Effective number of parties[3]	4.6	3.7		4.6	6.9
Polarization	0.23	0.08		0.20	0.18
Volatility	15.4	27.5		13.2	39.5

Germany	2002	2005	2009	2013	2017
Greens	8.6	8.1	10.7	8.4	8.9
Die Linke	4.0	8.7	11.9	8.6	9.2
SPD	38.5	34.2	23.0	25.7	20.5
FDP	7.4	9.8	14.6	4.8	10.8
CDU/CSU	38.5	35.2	33.8	41.5	32.9
AfD				4.7	12.6
Turnout	79.1	77.7	70.8	71.5	76.2
Polarization	0.09	0.18	0.18	0.11	0.12
Effective number of parties[3]	3.2	3.8	4.6	3.8	5.2
Volatility	6.0	8.0	11.9	15.4	14.4

Notes: [1] France: 1st round presidential elections, Germany: parliamentary elections; [2] FG: radical left, including, for earlier elections: PCF, LO, LCR, Greens (in 2017, they endorsed the PS candidate); [3] calculated based on vote shares, and for first round of legislative elections in the case of France.

parties proved to be more resilient, but they both lost voters to new challengers as well and the party system's fragmentation equally reached unprecedented levels.

The French elections saw the rise of a new challenger of an unexpected kind – a challenger neither from the New Left, nor from the New Right, but from the centre. The rise of this new centrist challenger benefited from a series of contingent events, among which the decision of François Hollande not to run again, the outcome of the primaries of the two mainstream parties and the scandal weighing down on François Fillon, the centre-right candidate, were arguably the most important ones. In particular, the role of the primaries was of extraordinary importance: they both ended with the victory of the more extreme candidate and left a space wide open in the centre of the party system. This provided an opportunity for a centrist candidate. As Strudel (2017, p. 208) points out, the opportunity was certainly there, but it took some skill to exploit it: Macron skillfully activated the Gaullist imagery of the man of the hour (l'homme providentiel'), he introduced elements of Third Way social-democracy (close to the former 'deuxième gauche' of Michel Rocard) into the French debate, and he took an unambiguously pro-European position.

The rise of the centrist challenger and the importance of the associated chance events focused the electoral campaign on the race. Thus, Piar's (2017) analysis of the main TV news channel (TF1 news at 20h) shows that the bulk of the electoral news (86 per cent) was dedicated to the events of the campaign ('jeu'), and only 14 per cent was covering the substance ('enjeux'). While the attention of the French news has always been largely focused on the electoral race and the degree of personalization of the French campaign has always been very high in comparison with other countries (Kriesi, 2011), the bias in favour of the race was exceptional in 2017. To the extent that substance mattered at all, economic issues dominated in the TF1 news, but European integration was also somewhat salient, mainly as a result of Marine Le Pen's proposal for France to leave the euro.

In addition to the rise of a centrist challenger, France also saw the rise of a new challenger from the left – 'La France insoumise' – one of the hidden winners ('vainqueur caché') of the elections (Cautrès, 2017). This 'movement-party' shares a lot of characteristics with other new radical forces from the Left, such as the campaign of Bernie Sanders in the US, the popularity of Jeremy Corbyn in the UK, or the Spanish Podemos, none of which is a product of the first wave of mobilization that gave rise to the Greens. Instead, these new radical left forces have emerged more recently as products of the Great Recession. Although they share many characteristics with their predecessors – they are also culturally liberal and open to integration, they clearly differ from them in other respects as they are economically more to the left (see Cautrès, 2017, p. 185). The French New Right (Front National) also benefited from the decline of the mainstream parties. At first sight, the upshot of this development is the emergence of a multipolar system with four almost equally sized camps – as indicated by the results of the first round in the Presidential elections: the New Left (19.6 per cent), the New Centre (24.0 per cent), the Centre-right (20.0 per cent) and the New Right (21.3 per cent) – and a greatly diminished centre-left (6.4 per cent). Given this multipolar configuration, the fact that it was the centrist challenger and the challenger from the New Right who went to the second round is somewhat of a chance event as well, which owes a lot to the strategies of the parties and their militants. Nevertheless, it is remarkable that it was two challengers and none of the mainstream parties opposing each other in the second round.

Before the 2017 elections, several observers (Gougou and Labouret, 2013; Martin, 2017; Tiberj 2013) suggested that the French party system had developed into a tripolar system, in line with the general trends I have sketched above. Certainly after the European elections in 2014 and the regional elections in 2015, it looked as if this tripolar configuration, composed of a centre-left, a centre-right and a conservative-nationalist right camp, was to constitute something like the 'new order' of the French party configuration (Martin, 2017).[1] However, what emerges from an analysis of the party-issue configurations in the 2017 elections is rather a return to a bipolar structure. Figure 1, which is based on an analysis of the newspaper coverage of the campaigns for the first round of the presidential elections, shows how the structure of the French party system has developed since the late 2000s.[2] The figure contains one image for the pre-crisis elections 2002 and 2007 combined, and one image each for the 2012 and the 2017 post-crisis elections. In each case, the space of party competition is two-dimensional with a horizontal economic dimension ranging from left (pro-welfare) to right (pro-economic liberalism) and a vertical cultural dimension going from cultural liberalism (on top) to opposition to immigration (anti-immigration) at the bottom. The two dimensions are always correlated: cultural liberalism and a pro-welfare position tend to some extent to go together. Within this two-dimensional space, we can distinguish the three poles that constitute the tripolar structure previous observers have identified: centre-left (PSF), centre-right (UPM-LR) and New Right (FN). The configuration of these three political camps is represented by shaded triangles. While the configuration of the French party system that emerges from the 2017 elections is actually not that different from the configuration which had characterized it previously, it includes the new centrist challenger and it turns out to be rather more bipolar than the previous ones.

Most importantly, in 2017 the PS and Macron's REM are located very closely together in the partisan space. In other words, REM takes the same centre-left position as the PS and, in spite of its rhetoric, it can be considered as the new centre-left. This positioning on the centre-left reflects the fact that REM attracted a much larger share of the voters from the old centre-left than it did from the centre-right (Strudel, 2017, p. 212). Opposing this couple is the Front National, while the old centre-right (LR-Les Républicains) is situated in between the two. More specifically, in 2017 the three camps mainly distinguish themselves along the cultural dimension, while they are hardly distinct from each other along the economic dimension, which points to a bipolar rather than a tripolar structure.

---

[1] Prudent as he was, Martin (2017, p. 150) also observed some weaknesses in this tripolar configuration.

[2] This figure as well as the one for the German elections is based on the content analysis of the electoral campaigns in two newspapers in each country. We selected all articles that were published within two months before the national election day and that reported on the electoral contest and national politics more generally. We then coded the selected articles by means of core sentence analysis (CSA)(for details Kleinnijenhuis *et al.*, 1997; Kriesi *et al.*, 2008). According to this procedure, each grammatical sentence is reduced to its most basic 'core sentence(s)', which contain(s) only the subject, the object, and the direction of the relationship between the two. The figures presented here are based on an analysis of the relationships between political actors (parties) and issues. The direction between party actors and issues is quantified using a scale ranging from −1 to +1. The position of a party on an issue in a given election campaign corresponds to the average direction of the core sentences it devoted to this issue. The salience of an issue for a party in an election campaign corresponds to the share of core sentences the party devoted to this particular issue. An MDS (Multi-Dimensional-Scaling) analysis of a combination of the salience of a large number of issues for the different parties and of the parties' positioning on these issues is used for the visualization of the party-issue configurations in the figures presented here. For the purposes of this analysis, the issues have been classified into a limited set of 13 categories: welfare, economic liberalism, cultural liberalism, anti-immigration, European integration, security, environment, education, defence, institutional reform, infrastructure, democratic renewal (general) and democratic reform (specific).

Figure 1: France: The Structure of the Political Space by Election.

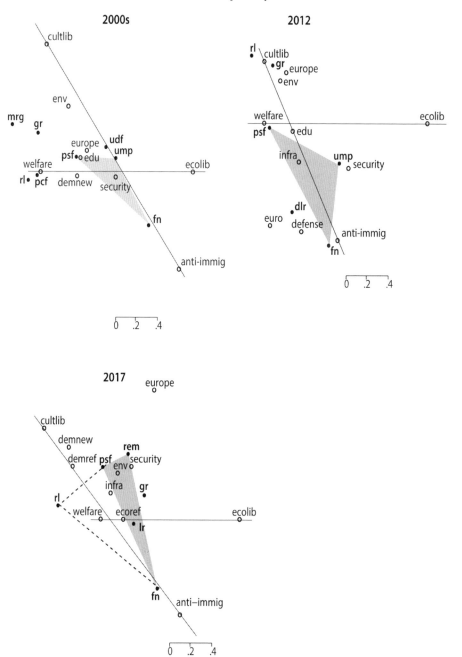

All the parties are far removed from economic liberalism, and, with the exception of the Front National, adopt a pro-welfare position. Surprisingly and contrary to its previous response to the economic crisis that included according 'top priority to the development of a comprehensive, internally consistent socio-economic, which entailed a decisive break with the dominant market ideology program' (Betz, 2015, p. 81), the Front National does not seem to have moved closer to the welfare pole in the 2017 campaign. Nevertheless, as in previous elections, the major French parties converge on economic issues and differentiate themselves above all in cultural terms.[3] This includes the new centrist challenger, the REM. At first sight, the radical left (rl-La France Insoumise), which is connected to the polar positions on the cultural dimension by dashed lines in the graph, seems to be clearly differentiated from the centre-left in 2017. Its position in the party space varies quite a bit from one election to the other. In the 2017 elections, however, contrary to the first impression one might get from Figure 1, the positioning of La France Insoumise as presented in the public debate was not clearly distinct from the PS's position, neither in cultural nor in economic terms. Thus, more detailed analyses (Hutter and Kriesi, 2018b) show that in 2017 it is not much closer to the welfare pole than the PS in economic terms, and in cultural terms it is not much more distant from cultural liberalism than the PS.[4] In 2017, what clearly differentiates it from the PS is its euroscepticism.

Turning to Germany, both incumbents lost about one fifth of their respective vote share. In absolute terms, the CDU-CSU was, however, punished more heavily, because its pervious vote share had been far larger (41.5 per cent) than that of the SPD (25.7 per cent). Arguably, the CDU-CSU was above all punished for Merkel's welcoming asylum policy, while the SPD's punishment was more a sign of general wear. The SPD had suffered most in the first crisis-election in 2009, when it lost roughly a third of its vote share, a loss from which it never recovered. Lack of a distinctive profile, a series of Chancellor's candidates (Steinmeier, Steinbrück and Schulz) lacking any charismatic appeal, and the predicament of having to serve as a minority partner in a coalition dominated by Merkel may go a long way towards explaining their decline. The Liberals and, above all, the AfD were the beneficiaries of the punishment of the incumbents in the 2017 elections. Contrary to France, the radical and the New Left (Linke and Greens) stagnated. While the return of the FDP to the Parliament did not change much in the structure of the party system, the establishment of the AfD did. As is shown in Figure 2, the emerging structure of the German party system closely resembles that of the French system. It is equally structured by an economic and a cultural dimension which are closely correlated, and it appears to be multi-polar as well.[5] However, as in the French case, this multi-polarity is more apparent than real: except for the AfD, which occupies a similar position as the Front National in France, all the parties are

---

[3]Note that Europe (European integration and the Euro) is positioned on the cultural axis opposite to the Front National. Given that economic issues dominated the substantive part of the campaign and that except for the FN neither Europe nor immigration constituted a salient issue for the major parties during the campaign, no major party is closely situated to the European pole.

[4]This assessment is based on a comparison of the relative distance of the radical left with the relative distance of the centre-left from the respective poles on each one of the two dimensions (relative economic distance=distance to welfare/distance to economic liberalism; relative cultural distance=distance to cultural liberalism/distance to anti-immigration). More precisely, the indicator corresponds to the log-odds of the relative distances of the two parties on a given dimension, that is to the natural log of the ratio of their relative distances. In the comparative analysis by Hutter and Kriesi (2018b), which includes six countries – in addition to France and Germany it also covers Austria, Britain, the Netherlands and Switzerland – the only country with a clearly differentiated left in the most recent elections is the Netherlands, where the SP is clearly distinguished from the Social-Democrats on the economic dimension and the Greens are clearly distinguished from the Social-Democrats on the cultural dimension.

[5]Note that Europe is located close to the pro-welfare pole of the German space, close to all the mainstream parties, who all support European integration, even if it was not a salient issue for them in these elections.

Figure 2: Germany: The Structure of the Political Space by Election.

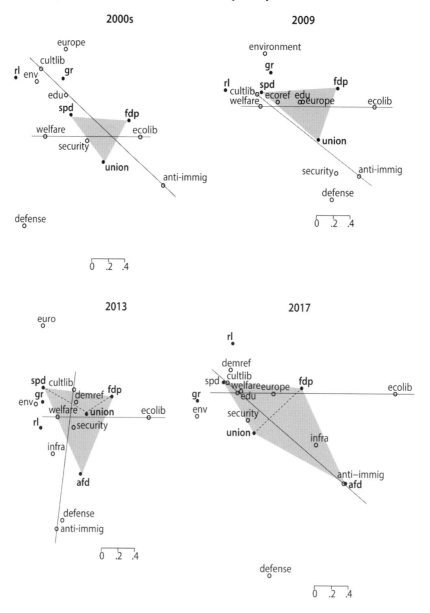

located in the upper left-hand corner of the space, relatively close to the pro-welfare pole of the economic dimension (with the exception of the FDP) and relatively close to cultural liberalism. Just as in the case of France, it is the contrast between the New Right and the rest of the parties which serves as the crucial structuring device in the party system. Even if the AfD's position in the German system is largely similar to that of the FN in France and even if it gained a lot in the 2017 elections, advancing from 4.7 to 12.6 per cent, the AfD still has a more limited electoral weight than the FN, which means that it contributes less to the polarization of the German party system than does the FN in the case of France. Compared with the position of the New Right, the differences between the remaining parties appear to be of minor importance. In particular, as in France, the divisions on the left do not appear to be justified in programmatic terms, given that all the components of the left are similarly situated in the German party space.

II. The Domestic Consequences of the Election Outcomes

As a result of these elections, we observe a strengthening of the government in France and a weakening of the government in Germany. This contrast is largely attributable to the different electoral systems of the two countries: while the French majoritarian electoral system allows for the fabrication of solid majorities in spite of the apparent fragmentation of the party system, the German proportional system has led to a fragmented composition of the German Bundestag and to protracted processes of government formation. In June, in the second round of the parliamentary elections, the presidential coalition obtained a relative majority of the cast votes (49.1 per cent), which provided it with an almost two-thirds majority (60.7 per cent) of the seats in the Assemblée Nationale and allowed it to form a cohesive government without further ado. This government immediately set out to implement the new president's reform agenda. In six months Macron has passed a series of substantial reforms, including an anti-corruption bill and a loosening of France's rigid labour laws, against the resistance of the unions which mobilized against the latter.

By contrast, the German elections resulted in a configuration in parliament which made coalition formation difficult and led to the Federal Republic's longest period without a government since World War II. A first attempt to form a so-called 'Jamaica' coalition composed of the CDU-CSU, the Liberals (FDP) and the Greens spectacularly failed in late November 2017. After this failure, a grand coalition or a CDU-CSU minority government remained as the only option. Although the leader of the SPD had originally excluded a remake of the grand coalition between the CDU-CSU and the SPD, after the intervention of the President the SPD's leadership reluctantly decided to enter coalition negotiations nevertheless. These negotiations dragged on until February and were eventually concluded with a coalition contract that still had to be approved by the two parties. In the case of the SPD, this meant consulting its 460,000 members, some of whom heavily contested the renewal of a grand coalition. After a four month stalemate, the SPD membership eventually approved the contract on 4 March by a two-thirds majority. The old and new chancellor, Angela Merkel, has paid a high price for the new coalition government. Although even more weakened in the elections than the CDU-CSU, the SPD obtained important concessions in the coalition negotiations and sees its position strengthened in the future grand coalition. After the installation of the grand coalition, there is the prospect of a sustained period of a stable albeit weak government.

III. The Implications for French–German relations and for European Integration

The election of Emanuel Macron to the French presidency greatly improved the mood in Europe. After the annus horribilis of 2016, the tides had already started to turn with the election of the Green Party candidate, Alexander van Bellen, to the Austrian presidency in December 2016, and with the Dutch elections in March 2017, when the rise of the national-populist right was checked by the voters. But it was the election of Emanuel Macron to the French presidency, which gave the greatest new impulse for the European project. In September 2017, just two days after the German elections, Macron made his great speech on a 'sovereign, unified and democratic Europe'. His big idea is captured by his slogan 'l'Europe qui protège', an idea that has many elements. Thus, among other things, Macron proposes a eurozone budget, funded by corporate-tax revenues. This budget, which would allow for launching an investment programme and for providing a cushion during economic downturns, would be overseen by a eurozone finance minister, who would answer to eurozone countries' representatives in the European Parliament. He also proposes an EU border control force, a common fund for building up European defence forces, and the integration into the national armies of members of other armies. Moreover, he envisages a social Europe that, among other things, would prevent social dumping. Last, but certainly not least, he seeks to reinforce democracy in Europe, and pleads for abandoning the well-worn method of integrating Europe without involving its people. In constructing Europe, he admonishes his fellow political leaders, they should no longer be afraid of the people. Under Macron's plan, each EU member state would hold democratic conventions to debate citizens' priorities. Their ideas would feed into a broader process involving the EU institutions and governments that want to overhaul Europe. Coalitions of the willing would then integrate faster, with a revitalized Franco-German engine driving the process forward.

As a result of the different outcome of the elections, the power relationship between the two countries is likely to be more balanced than it was previously, which holds some promise for Europe. The 'reluctant hegemon' finds a more equal partner in Macron: while Germany has been paralyzed by the protracted process of government formation, Macron has already strengthened France's role internationally. Thus, France has been chosen as *The Economist*'s country of the year,[6] for the fact that it 'confronted the drawbridge-raisers head on and beat them'. And Africa has been hit head on by the 'Macron effect' (l'effet Macron): Africans, especially the young among them, admire France for the fact that it has produced a new leader who cleaned out the old guard which had weighed down on the political scene for far too long.[7]

While it promises mostly stagnation at home, Germany's grand coalition may be the best solution for Europe: a government without the FDP could be a blessing for Europe, even if the coalition agreement uses rather vague wording in this respect. Germany, the 'sleeping beauty' may wake up once the grand coalition has got underway.[8] The enhanced status of the SPD in the grand coalition could herald a greater German openness to the proposals of the French president for reforming the EU and deepening eurozone integration. On the face of it the coalition agreement promises a more forthcoming approach of Germany towards the French president. As pointed out by a high ranking German official, 'ultimately Merkel is reactive, so not much will come from her'.[9] But she may just be the ideal partner for a young French President who is driving Europe towards new horizons. As Leonard (2017, p. 48) suggests, Brexit and Trump provide a window of opportunity for the

---

[6]*The Economist*, 19 December 2017.
[7]*Jeune Afrique,* 22 October to 4 November 2017.
[8]*The Economist*, 7 December 2017.
[9]Cited by Leonard (2017) p. 48.

French-German couple: the UK will no longer be able to block EU policies, and the US's abdication of its responsibilities as a global policeman means that the EU will have to join forces to protect itself. Even if German prudence may limit the scope of the French President's plans, the French-German couple may provide the engine for European integration once again.

Conclusion

Although very different at first sight, the outcomes of the German and French elections 2017 have much in common. The structure of the party system that emerges from these elections is largely the same, with the New Right opposing the cluster of the mainstream parties and of the various components of the radical and New Left. The striking rise of a new centrist challenger in France has actually hardly modified the structure of the French party system at all, given that it occupies virtually the same position as the old centre-left which it largely replaced. Remarkably, the centre-right has also largely come to defend similar positions both in France and in Germany. As a result, in spite of the appearance of multi-polarity, the party systems of the two countries tend to become bipolar, with the New Right opposing the rest of the competitors.

The governments that have been formed as a result of these elections are more similar than meets the eye at first sight, too. Both countries are now governed from the centre. France has a centrist government that represents, in a way, a grand coalition within one party, while Germany has a centrist grand coalition composed of the centre-left and the centre-right. Moreover, both grand coalitions are not so grand after all. The French government is based on a relative majority of 49 per cent (the result of the second round of the legislative elections), while the German grand coalition is based on a tight absolute majority of 53 per cent of the vote. In both countries, the challengers from both left and right are marginalized by the government formation, and the question is how they will react to their powerlessness. They might get their chance in the not too far future. The fact that both governments rest on a rather small popular base suggests that the electoral situation in both countries is far from stable. The major conflict between the nationalist-conservative forces defending the nation-state and its citizens and the forward-looking forces promoting cultural liberalism, European integration, and openness to immigrants is far from settled. But, as a result of the two key elections discussed here, the cosmopolitan forces have now got another chance to get their act together. Let us hope that they will seize this window of opportunity.

References

Betz, H.-G. (2015) 'The Revenge of the Ploucs: The Revival of Radical Populism under Marine Le Pen in France'. In Kriesi, H. and Pappas, T. (eds) *European Populism in the Shadow of the Great Recession* (Colchester: ECPR Press), pp. 75–90.

Bornschier, S. (2010a) *Cleavage Politics and the Populist Right. The New Cultural Conflict in Western Europe* (Philadelphia, PA: Temple University Press).

Bornschier, S. (2010b) 'The New Cultural Divide and the Two-Dimensional Political Space in Western Europe'. *West European Politics*, Vol. 33, No. 3, pp. 419–44.

Bornschier, S. (2015) 'The New Cultural Conflict, Polarization, and Representation in the Swiss Party System, 1975–2011'. *Swiss Political Science Review*, Vol. 21, No. 4, pp. 680–701.

Bremer, B. and Schulte-Cloos, J. (2018) 'No Country for the New Right? Restructuring British and German Party Politics'. In Hutter, S. and Kriesi, H. (eds.) *Restructuring European Party Politics in Times of Crises*, unpublished (Florence: European University Institute).

Cautrès, B. (2017) 'Mélenchon, 'vaniqueur caché' de la présidentielle ?' In Perrineau, P. (ed.) *Le vote disruptif. Les élections présidentielle et législatives de 2017* (Paris: SciencesPo), pp. 176–203.

Gougou, F. and Labouret, S. (2013) 'La fin de la tripartition? Les recompositions de la droite et la transformation du système partisan'. *Revue française de science politique*, Vol. 63, No. 2, pp. 279–302.

Hutter, S. and Kriesi, H. (eds) (2018a) *Restructuring European Party Politics in Times of Crises*, unpublished (Florence: European University Institute).

Hutter, S. and Kriesi, H. (2018b) 'Restructuring Party Systems in North-Western Europe. Six Countries Compared'. Paper prepared for '2017: Europe's Bumper Year of Elections' conference, RSCAS, EUI Florence, 8–9 March 2018.

Inglehart, R. (1977) *The Silent Revolution* (Princeton, NJ: Princeton University Press).

Kitschelt, H. (1994) *The Transformation of European Social Democracy* (Cambridge: Cambridge University Press).

Kitschelt, H. (1995) *The Radical Right in Western Europe: A Comparative Analysis* (Ann Arbor, MI: University of Michigan Press).

Kleinnijenhuis, J., De Ridder, J.A. and Rietberg, E.M. (1997) 'Reasoning in Economic Discourse. An Application of the Network Approach to the Dutch Press'. In Roberts, C.W. (ed.) *Text Analysis for the Social Sciences. Methods for Drawing Statistical Inferences from Texts and Transcripts* (Mahwah: Lawrence Erlbaum Associates), pp. 191–207.

Kriesi, H. (2011) 'Personalization of National Election Campaigns'. *Party Politics*, Vol. 17, No. 1, pp. 1–20.

Kriesi, H., Grande, E., Dolezal, M., Helbling, M., Höglinger, D., Hutter, S. and Wueest, B. (2012) *Political Conflict in Western Europe* (Cambridge: Cambridge University Press).

Kriesi, H., Grande, E., Lachat, R., Dolezal, M., Bornschier, S. and Frey, T. (2008) *West European Politics in the Age of Globalization* (Cambridge: Cambridge University Press).

Kriesi, H., Koopmans, R., Duyvendak, J.W. and Giugni, M.G. (1995) *New Social Movements in Western Europe. A Comparative Analysis* (Minneapolis, MN: University of Minnesota Press).

Leonard, M. (2017) 'Brave New Europe'. *The New York Review of Books*, 9 November, pp. 46–8.

Mair, P. (2013) *Ruling the Void: The Hollowing of Western Democracy* (London, New York: Verso).

Martin, P. (2017) 'V'ers un nouvel ordre électoral?' In Gougou, F. and Tiberj, V. (eds) *La déconnexion électorale. Un état des lieux de la démocratie française* (Fondation Jean Jaurès), pp. 145–51.

Perrineau, P. (ed.) (2017a) *Le vote disruptif. Les élections présidentielle et législatives de 2017* (Paris: SciencesPo).

Perrineau, P. (2017b) 'Introduction'. In Perrineau, P. (ed.) *Le vote disruptif. Les élections présidentielle et législatives de 2017* (Paris: SciencesPo), pp. 15–21.

Piar, C. (2017) 'La présidentielle vue par les JT'. In Perrineau, P. (ed.) *Le vote disruptif. Les élections présidentielle et législatives de 2017* (Paris: SciencesPo), pp. 73–99.

Strudel, S. (2017) 'Emmanuel Macron: un oxymore politique?' In Perrineau, P. (ed.) *Le vote disruptif. Les élections présidentielle et législatives de 2017* (Paris: SciencesPo), pp. 205–19.

Tiberj, V. (2013) 'Values and the Votes from Mitterand to Hollande: The Rise of Two-axis Politics'. *Parliamentary Affairs*, Vol. 66, pp. 69–86.

JCMS 2018 Volume 56. Annual Review pp. 63–73   DOI: 10.1111/jcms.12769

A Right-wing Populist Momentum? A Review of 2017 Elections Across Europe

DAPHNE HALIKIOPOULOU
University of Reading

Introduction

Right-wing populist parties competed in most electoral contests that took place in Europe in 2017, often as main contenders for power. Elections in France, the Netherlands, Austria, Germany and the Czech Republic were all characterized by an increase in the support for such parties. The French Front National (FN) progressed to the second round of the French Presidential election for the first time since 2002; the Austrian Freedom Party (FPÖ) gained access to office after forming a governing coalition with the centre-right People's Party (OVP); and the Alternative for Germany (AfD) entered parliament for the first time after substantially increasing its vote share from the previous legislative election of 2013. These results attracted extensive media attention, generating talk of a 'populist revolution' which is seen as part of a continuing trend that follows the 2014 European Parliament (EP) elections, Brexit and the election of Donald Trump; and they have coincided with increasing scholarly attention on the rise of right-wing populism in Europe and the US, with numerous accounts on both demand and supply-side dynamics driving this phenomenon (Aslanidis, 2016; Bonikowski, 2017; Gidron and Bonikowski, 2013; Inglehart and Norris, 2016; Rooduijn, 2014).

This contribution reviews the results of electoral contests that took place in 2017 in France, Norway, Bulgaria, the UK, the Netherlands, Austria, Germany and the Czech Republic, and examines them in comparative perspective. A detailed analysis, which takes into account important variations both across countries and across time, indicates that the results are not straightforward. Specifically, by focusing on these variations this contribution argues that: (1) right-wing populism is not a uniform phenomenon. What we term 'right-wing populist' parties are in fact a range of parties that differ fundamentally in terms of their rhetoric and programmatic agendas; (2) the rise of parties that we now label 'right-wing populist' is not a new phenomenon. The 2017 election results can – and should – be interpreted as part of a broader trend that commenced in the mid-1980s with the rise of parties whose electoral fortunes have been fluctuating since. Indeed, niche parties that cut across traditional partisan alignments, such as those we term right-wing populist parties, have been contesting elections in Europe for the past 30 years, often successfully, including the FPÖ, List Pim Fortuyn (LPF) and the PVV, and the FN. Support has tended to vary across time, country and election type; (3) while not new, this phenomenon does pose new challenges. These are linked to supply-side, rather than demand-side, dynamics. In most Western European countries, the parties that are increasingly enjoying the most success are those that are attempting to distance themselves from fascism, 'speak' the language of democracy, and stress 'liberal values' to justify their exclusionary agendas (Halikiopoulou et al., 2013). This makes them more able to permeate mainstream ground and influence the policy agenda; and (4) the results from Eastern Europe are more mixed. On the one hand the overall pattern there is one of 'authoritarianism, territorial revisionism and the threat from territorial minorities' (Muis and Immerzeel, 2017). However, the 2017 elections in Bulgaria and the Czech Republic again show interesting variations with steady decline in support for ATAKA in the former and the rise of the civic Freedom and Direct Democracy (SPD) in the latter.

I. Right-wing Populism: A Uniform Phenomenon?

First, it is important to place the results of 2017 within a broader theoretical framework. Since the 2014 'earthquake' EP elections (Halikiopoulou and Vasilopoulou, 2014), the electoral fortunes of parties that advocate immigration restrictions on the basis of a narrative that stresses popular sovereignty and anti-elitism have increasingly attracted academic interest. Such parties include a number of those that competed in the various 2017 elections such as the FN, the PVV, UKIP and the AfD; and others such as the Greek Golden Dawn (GD), the Danish People's Party (DF), the Swedish Democrats (SD) and the True Finns. While terminology varies, ranging from 'radical right' (Immerzeel et al., 2015), 'far right' (Halikiopoulou and Vlandas, 2016) and 'extreme right' (Arzheimer, 2009), the term 'right-wing populism' or 'populist radical right' is increasingly employed to describe these parties (see Muis and Immerzeel, 2017; Rooduijn, 2017). The focus is on two central features that the parties share: an emphasis on popular sovereignty and an emphasis on national sovereignty; or in other words, populism and nationalism. First, populism is a form of 'democratic illiberalism' (Pappas, 2016), which posits that politics should always reflect the general will of the people (Mudde, 2004). What makes these parties populist is their shared emphasis on the 'people', and more specifically their description of society as shaped by the antagonistic relationship between 'us' the pure people and 'them' the corrupt elites (Mudde, 2004). Second, nationalism is a vision of society that prioritizes the unity, autonomy and identity of the nation (Breuilly, 2005), focusing on a sharp division between in- groups and out-groups. What makes these parties nationalist is their shared focus on national homogeneity, sovereignty and the espousal of anti-immigration policies resting on the principle of the national preference – or in other words, that access to the collective goods of the state should be confined to native groups (Halikiopoulou and Vlandas, 2016).

However, the categorization of these parties as right-wing populist is to a degree problematic. The danger is that we may be lumping very different phenomena in the same category. While an anti-elite rhetoric and immigration scepticism are common among many of these parties, much more divides them, including their degree of extremism, the extent to which they adopt violence, their relationship with fascism, their position on social issues and state intervention of the economy as well as their voting base (Halikiopoulou and Vlandas, 2016). In other words, parties that we categorize as belonging to the broad umbrella of 'right-wing populism' might actually differ in kind rather than just degree. They have different ideological backgrounds, a different voting base and are often elected on very different platforms.

This is not simply a theoretical problem, but rather it affects the validity of our assessments of why these parties are increasing their electoral support. If they indeed differ in kind, then their rise cannot be traceable to a single cause (Pappas, 2016). For example, parties such as the Dutch PVV, the Bulgarian ATAKA and the Greek Golden Dawn differ fundamentally from each other and are elected on different platforms. While, therefore, it is important to identify trends and patterns, we can only do so if we can first ensure comparability. It is also important to disaggregate between the populist and nationalist attributes of these parties, that is to identify whether they are appealing because of their populism or because of their nationalism.

II. A Right-wing Populist Momentum? Variations in Electoral Support Across Country, Time and Election Type

Having identified potential theoretical and conceptual problems facing analyses on right-wing populism, this contribution proceeds to examine the 2017 election results in comparative perspective. Most right-wing populist parties that competed in the various electoral contests that took place across Europe in 2017 increased their support. These include the FN, the PVV, the AfD and the FPÖ. The Czech SPD, which ran for the first time, also achieved a good result. The FN competed in the second round of the Presidential election for the first time since 2002, receiving its highest ever percentage of 33.9 per cent in that round. The PVV received 13.1 per cent of the votes cast, increasing its representation by 5 seats. The FPÖ received 26 per cent of the votes cast and formed a coalition government with the centre-right OVP. In Germany the AfD entered parliament with 12.6 per cent of the votes cast and 94 seats. The party came third, managing to draw voters from all major parties. Finally, in the Czech Republic the newly formed SPD received 10.64 per cent of the votes cast occupying 22 seats in the Czech parliament.

On the other hand, in the UK, Bulgaria and Norway right-wing populist parties declined. In the UK, UKIP decreased its electoral support from 12.6 per cent in 2015 to 1.8 per cent in 2017. In Bulgaria, the Bulgarian Patriotic Front – a nationalist alliance between the National Front for the Salvation for Bulgaria, ATAKA and the National Movement (IMRO-BNM) – received 9.07 per cent of the votes cast in 2017. This percentage is smaller compared to the 11.83-combined percentage that three parties received in 2014.[1] In Norway, the Norwegian Progress Party also declined, but just marginally from 16.3 per cent in 2013 to 15.2 per cent in 2017 losing 2 seats. However, the loss was smaller than expected as Progress Party leaders feared that they would lose support from anti-establishment voters having entered government in 2013 (Aardal and Bergh, 2018). The results are summarized in Table 1.

The snapshot of the 2017 results offered above indeed illustrates that the majority of right-wing populist parties that competed across Europe performed well. An examination of the performance of the same parties across time, however, indicates that this phenomenon is neither linear nor new. First, a look at the wider picture illustrates that indeed the events of 2017 can be interpreted as part of a broader trend that commenced in the mid-1980s. As Figure 1 illustrates, since then the electoral performance of such parties

---

[1] This result includes ATAKA, which ran separately during the 2014 election and obtained 4.53 per cent of the votes cast and 11 seats; and the Patriotic Front consisting of the remaining two parties, which obtained 7.3 per cent of the votes cast and 19 seats.

Table 1: Right-wing Populist Party performance in 2017 Elections across Europe

Country	Party	Votes Cast % 2017	Seats 2017	Previous Election year	Votes cast % Previous Election Year	Seats Previous Election Year
Legislative elections						
Netherlands	PVV	13.1	20	2012	10.08	15
Bulgaria	Patriotic Front*	9.07	27	2014	11.83**	30
France	FN	13.20 (Round 1) 8.75 (Round 2)	8	2012	13.26 (Round 1) 3.7 (Round 2)	2
UK	UKIP	1.8	0	2015	12.6	1
Norway	Progress Party	15.2	27	2013	16.3	29
Germany	AfD	12.6	94	2013	4.7	0
Austria	FPÖ	26.0	51	2013	20.51	40
Czech Republic	SPD	10.64	22	2013	-	-
Presidential elections						
France	FN	21.3 (Round 1) 33.9 (Round 2)	N/A	2012	17.9 (Round 1) N/A (Round 2)	N/A

Notes: * A nationalist alliance between the National Front for the Salvation for Bulgaria, ATAKA and the National Movement (IMRO-BNM). ** This result includes ATAKA, which ran separately during the 2014 election and obtained 4.53 per cent of the votes cast and 11 seats; and the Patriotic Front, which obtained 7.3 per cent of the votes cast and 19 seats.

Figure 1: Average Far-right Vote 1960–2015[2]

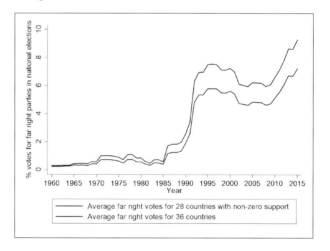

Note: Top line indicates average far right votes for 28 countries with non-zero support; bottom line indicates average far right votes for 36 countries
Source: Armingeon *et al.* (2017).

has fluctuated: there was a sharp increase from 1985 onwards, a peak in the late 1990s, a decline in the 2000s and an increase again after 2009.

A turn to specific parties reveals a similar picture. With regards to the cases where there was an increase in electoral support during 2017 elections, the longer-term analysis

[2] The use of the label far-right as opposed to right-wing populist is intentional here, as the figure includes both extreme and radical variants.

shows that these increases are not unprecedented. In France, for example, FN performance has fluctuated significantly since the 1980s and has varied across election type. With regards to parliamentary elections since 1993: the highest percentage the party has received in the first round is 15.25 per cent in 1997; the lowest is 4.9 per cent in 2007. In the second round, percentages are slightly lower in all years, the highest being 8.75 per cent the party received in 2017.

With regards to Presidential elections, since 1995 the party has progressed to the second round twice: in 2002 and in 2017. In round 1 the lowest percentage the party has received was 10.44 per cent in 2007; and the highest was 21.3 per cent in 2017. In the second round, the party received 17.79 per cent of the votes cast in 2002 and 33.9 per cent in 2017. This is the highest percentage the party has received and it is notable that it was able to retain a fairly high percentage in the second round. However, this could be explained as a protest vote, as given the winner-takes-all nature of the election, supporters did not expect the FN to win (see Figures 2 and 3).

An examination of List Pim Fortuyn (LPF) and PVV performance in the Netherlands reveals similar fluctuations. The highest vote share of a right-wing populist party in the Netherlands since the early 2000s is 17 per cent, received in 2002 by the LPF. The lowest is the same party's 5.7 per cent, received in elections held during the following year. The

Figure 2: FN Performance- French Legislative Elections 1993–2017 (% Votes Cast)

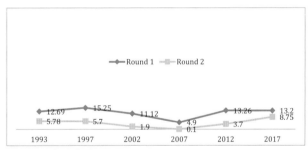

Source: Ministère de l'intérieur, 2018

Source: Ministère de l'intérieur (2018).

Figure 3: FN Performance- Presidential Elections 1995–2017 (% Votes Cast)

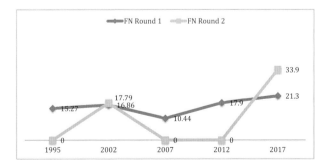

Source: Ministère de l'intérieur (2018).

Figure 4: Right-wing Populist Party Performance (LPF and PVV) in Dutch Legislative Elections 2002–2017

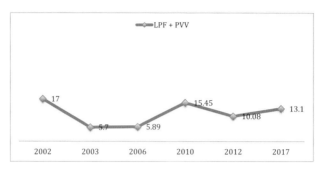

Source: European Election Database, 2018.

Figure 5: FPÖ Performance in Austrian Legislative Elections 1990–2017 (% Votes Cast)

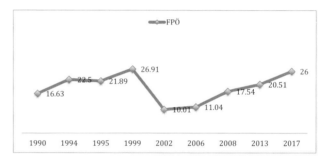

Source: European Election Database, 2018.

PVV's highest percentage is 15.45 per cent, received in 2010. The party subsequently decreased its support in 2012 with 10.08 per cent, which it increased to 13.1 per cent in 2017. While an increase from the previous election, this figure is lower than the 2002 LPF vote and its own 2010 vote (see Figure 4).

The FPÖ follows a similar pattern. Figure 5 traces the party's performance in legislative elections from 1990 to 2017. The party's electoral fortunes have fluctuated significantly across time. Its best performance was in 1999 when the party received 26.91 per cent of the votes cast. It also fared well in 2017 with 26 per cent, in 1995 with 21.89 per cent, and in 2013 with 21.51 per cent. Its worst performance was in 2002 with 10.01 per cent and in 2006 with 11.04 per cent. The party also entered a coalition government in 1999.

The German AfD and the Czech SPD are relatively new parties, not allowing for cross-time comparisons similar to those carried out above. It is important to note, however, that the AfD increased its support significantly since the previous election held in 2013.

III. Supply-side Patterns: The 'New Winning Formula'?

While this phenomenon is not necessarily new, the electoral fortunes of these parties do represent a new challenge with regards to their progressive entrenchment in their

Figure 6: Far-right Party Performance In Legislative Elections: Germany 1998–2017[3]

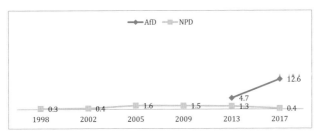

Source: Federal Returning Officer (2017).

respective political systems. Parties are in many ways themselves independent variables, determining their own electoral fortunes (Mudde, 2010). A closer look at the parties themselves, their narratives and their programmatic agendas, points to interesting supply-side patterns. Both within-country variations and variations across time reveal a similar trend: in their majority, the parties most likely to fare well electorally in Western Europe are those that have (at least seemingly) distanced themselves from fascism and racism in their programmatic agendas in favour of a narrative that stresses ideological rather than biological rationalizations of national belonging. While they are still nationalist, and offer 'nationalist solutions' to all socio-economic problems (Vasilopoulou and Halikiopoulou, 2015), they identify the out-group not on the basis of ascriptive and immutable criteria of national membership such as race and common descent, but rather on the basis of toleration, excluding those who do not share 'our' liberal values such as democracy, multiculturalism and the rule of law (Halikiopoulou *et al.*, 2013).

I will briefly focus on two examples: the AfD and the FN. First, the German case is interesting as it allows us to make this observation by looking at within-country variations. Two parties located on the far right of the political spectrum, which competed both in the 2013 and the 2017 elections include the AfD and the National Democratic Party of Germany (NPD). In both elections it was the AfD rather than the extreme right NPD that appealed to voters. Indeed, the NPD has remained marginalized in the past decades never receiving more than 1.6 per cent (in the 2005 elections). The key difference is that while the NPD is nativist – or ethnic nationalist – the AfD draws on civic nationalism excluding on the basis of ideology rather than race (see Figure 6).

While there is a debate among scholars as to whether the AfD can be classified as a populist radical right party, it is 'indeed located at the far-right end of Germany's political spectrum because of its nationalism, its stance against state support for sexual diversity and gender mainstreaming, and its market liberalism' (Arzheimer, 2015, p. 551). In its 2013 manifesto, the AfD put forward a 'soft' euroscepticism opposing the currency union and all bailouts, but showing a commitment to the European project itself. In terms of immigration, the party 'appeared to subscribe to the principles of free movement and free choice of residence for all EU citizens, although it wants to limit benefits (of which the

---

[3]The label far-right as opposed to right-wing populist is intentional here as the figure includes both the populist right (AfD) and the extreme right NPD.

party is critical in general) to long-term residents and their offspring' (Arzheimer, 2015, p. 546). The AfD, therefore, is not a straightforward case of 'nativism' (Arzheimer, 2015). The party is however, nationalist as discussed above. Its 2017 electoral campaign makes this point clear indicating that the party adopts a civic form of nationalism: an opposition to Islam and Muslims, which the party portrays as a threat to democracy, tolerance and liberalism. While the AfD is not nativist because it doesn't exclude on the basis of ascriptive criteria, it is nationalist because it defines the out-group and justifies its exclusion on the basis of ideology.

Second, the French case is interesting because it allows us to make this observation across time. The FN has increased its electoral support substantially after Marine Le Pen took over the party's leadership from her father. Marine Le Pen has reached a broader electoral base that captures 'younger' votes (see Stockemer and Amengay, 2015) and achieves a closing of the far-right gender gap in France (Mayer, 2015). What is distinctive about Marine Le Pen's leadership is her strategy of 'de-demonization' of the party and a 'softening of its rhetoric' (Ivaldi, 2015; Mayer, 2015). This process has included a shift of emphasis from *préférence* to *priorité nationale* in order to disassociate the party from the negative connotations of Jean-Marie Le Pen's rhetoric and create distance from the party's reputation for exclusionist discrimination (Alduy and Wahnich, 2015). There are similarities here with the AfD: an attempt to exclude the out-group on the basis of toleration, that is to exclude those who are 'intolerant of us' and don't like our way of life. This has resulted in a heavily anti-Muslim rhetoric also coinciding with the series of terrorist attacks in France in the past years.

We may place these two case studies within a broader European trend. Across Western Europe, right-wing populist parties are more likely to compete successfully with other actors in the system when they are better able to tailor their discourse to present themselves and their ideologies as the true authentic defenders of the nation's unique reputation for democracy, diversity and tolerance (Halikiopoulou *et al.*, 2013). This new 'winning formula' utilizes a form of civic nationalism that mobilizes around ideology rather than race (Halikiopoulou *et al.*, 2013). This also explains why these parties focus heavily on Muslims – regardless of their citizenship – by presenting them as a threat to democratic values and a terrorist risk. It is an important observation, which suggests that it is nationalism, rather than populism, that offers a successful strategy for attracting voters and justifying policies.

IV. Eastern Europe

The Eastern European pattern is somewhat different to that of Western Europe as 'the historical legacies and idiosyncrasies of the post-communist context have played a prominent role in shaping these parties' ideology' (Pirro, 2014, p. 600). Lower levels of immigration, a particular type of political culture related to the communist experience and absence of civil society have entailed the success of mostly extreme right variants, for example Jobbik in Hungary and Kotleba People's Party Our Slovakia. Specifically, such parties in Eastern Europe endorse 'clericalism and irredentism, adopt "social national" economics, and focus specifically on ethnic minorities, corruption and the EU' (Pirro, 2014, p. 604).

The electoral contests that took place in Bulgaria and the Czech Republic in 2017 should be examined within this broader context. In Bulgaria, ATAKA fits the Eastern European trajectory discussed above. The party portrays itself as a Bulgarian patriotic party. It aspires to unite the nation under the common creed of Christianity, adopts an irredentist rhetoric, appeals to economic nationalism calling for a stronger role of the state in the economy, and places extensive emphasis on the salient issue of ethnic minorities. The party also places extensive focus on corruption (Pirro, 2014). ATAKA has experienced steady decline, decreasing its support despite running as a part of a nationalist alliance with the National Front for the Salvation for Bulgaria and the National Movement (IMRO-BNM). The picture in the Czech Republic is different: the newly formed SPD mostly resembles the Western European anti-immigrant parties, focusing heavily on the anti-EU and 'Islamization' narrative.

Conclusion

The brief comparative analysis offered above has illustrated that what we term 'right-wing populism' is neither a uniform, new nor linear phenomenon. This does not mean that the electoral fortunes of parties that competed in the series of elections that took place in 2017, such as the FN, the PVV, the FPÖ and the AfD are unimportant. On the contrary: the FN's 33.9 per cent in the second round of the French presidential election is the highest percentage the party has ever received. The PVV and the FPÖ increased their support. The biggest winner of 2017 was perhaps the AfD which entered Parliament for the first time, defying theories suggesting that parties on the far-right end of the political spectrum have limited opportunities in countries such as Germany. These results do suggest that in many ways right-wing populist parties pose challenges both to their domestic political systems and Europe more broadly. However, in order to understand these challenges, it is important to focus on variations in right-wing populist support within countries, across countries and across time.

These variations point to the importance of supply-side dynamics: while social discontent is present in all societies, support for right-wing populism varies. In other words, while the multiple insecurities – including economic, cultural and personal – that drive voters open up opportunities for parties that operate in the fringes of the political system, these opportunities are not always utilized- or they are utilized by different types of party. It is supply-side factors that determine which parties will seize them and when.

Specifically, the persistence of this phenomenon, and the new challenges it poses are linked both to how these parties compete with other actors in the system and how they frame their programmatic agendas to become appealing to voters. The former is about party competition with both the centre-right and the centre-left and is addressed elsewhere in this *Annual Review*; the latter is the 'new winning formula' described above, that is the ability of these parties to justify their exclusionary policies on the basis of ideological rather than biological rationalizations of national belonging.

In other words, these parties – especially in Western Europe – have 'learned' and are better equipped to compete with other actors in the system by presenting themselves as legitimate to the electorate. The greatest challenge is these parties' ability to permeate mainstream ground. Accommodating such parties' anti-immigrant positions is not new. Anti-immigrant parties have indeed had a contagion effect on other parties' immigration policy positions since 1990 (Van Spanje, 2010). What is new – and became more apparent during the various electoral contests that took place in 2017 across Europe – is the extent to which this has intensified: the legitimation of accommodative strategies is making right-wing populist parties more effective in driving the policy agenda and setting the terms on which mainstream actors compete.

References

Aardal, B. and Bergh, J. (2018) 'The 2017 Norwegian election'. *West European Politics*. https://doi.org/10.1080/01402382.2017.1415778.

Alduy, C. and Wahnich, S. (2015) *Marine Le Pen prise aux mots: Décrytpage du nouveau discours frontiste* (Paris: Seuil).

Armingeon, K., Wenger, V., Wiedemeier, F., Isler, C., Knöpfel, L., Weisstanner, D. and Engler, S. (2017) *Comparative Political Data Set 1960–2015* (Bern: Institute of Political Science, University of Berne).

Arzheimer, K. (2009) 'Contextual Factors and the Extreme Right Vote in Western Europe, 1980–2002'. *American Journal of Political Science*, Vol. 53, No. 2, pp. 259–75.

Arzheimer, K. (2015) 'The AfD: Finally a Successful Right-Wing Populist Eurosceptic Party for Germany?' *West European Politics*, Vol. 38, No. 3, pp. 535–56.

Aslanidis, P. (2016) 'Is Populism an Ideology? A Refutation and a New Perspective'. *Political Studies*, Vol. 64, No. 1, pp. 88–104.

Bonikowski, B. (2017) 'Ethno-Nationalist Populism and the Mobilization of Collective Resentment'. *The British Journal of Sociology*, Vol. 68, No. 1, pp. 181–213.

Breuilly, J. (2005) 'Dating the Nation: How Old is an Old Nation?' In Ichijo, A. and Uzelac, G. (eds) *When is the Nation? Towards an Understanding of Theories of Nationalism* (London: Routledge), pp. 15–39.

Federal Returning Officer (2017) *Bundestag election 2017* (Wiesbaden: Germany) Available online at: https://www.bundeswahlleiter.de/en/bundestagswahlen/2017.html. Accessed 29 May 2018.

Gidron, N. and Bonikowski, B. (2013) 'Varieties of Populism: Literature Review and Research Agenda'. Weatherhead Working Paper Series, No. 13-0004

Halikiopoulou, D., Mock, S. and Vasilopoulou, S. (2013) 'The Civic Zeitgeist: Nationalism and Liberal Values in the European Radical Right'. *Nations and Nationalism*, Vol. 19, No. 1, pp. 107–27.

Halikiopoulou, D. and Vasilopoulou, S. (2014) 'Support for the Far Right in the 2014 European Parliament Elections: A Comparative Perspective'. *The Political Quarterly*, Vol. 85, No. 3, pp. 285–8.

Halikiopoulou, D. and Vlandas, T. (2016) 'Risks, Costs and Labour Markets: Explaining Cross-National Patterns of Far-Right Party Success in European Parliament Elections'. *JCMS*, Vol. 54, No. 3, pp. 636–55.

Immerzeel, T., Lubbers, M. and Coffé, H. (2015) 'Competing with the Radical Right: Distances Between the European Radical Right and other Parties on Typical Radical Right Issues'. *Party Politics*, Vol. 22, No. 6, pp. 823–34.

Inglehart, R. and Norris, P. (2016) 'Trump, Brexit, and the Rise of Populism: Economic Have-Nots and Cultural Backlash', Harvard Kennedy School Faculty Research Working Paper Series, No RWP16-026.

Ivaldi, G. (2015) 'Towards the Median Economic Crisis Voter? The New Leftist Economic Agenda of the Front National in France'. *French Politics*, Vol. 13, No. 4, pp. 346–69.

Mayer, N. (2015) 'The Closing of the Radical Right Gender Gap in France?' *French Politics*, Vol. 13, No. 4, pp. 391–414.

Ministère de l'intérieur (2018) *Les résultats* (Paris: France) Available online at: http://www.interieur.gouv.fr/Elections/Les-resultats. Accessed 29 May 2018.

Mudde, C. (2004) 'The Populist Zeitgeist'. *Government and Opposition*, Vol. 39, No. 4, pp. 542–63.

Mudde, C. (2010) 'The Populist Radical Right: A Pathological Normalcy'. *West European Politics*, Vol. 33, No. 6, pp. 1167–86.

Muis, J. and Immerzeel, T. (2017) 'Causes and Consequences of the Rise of Populist Radical Right Parties and Movements in Europe'. *Current Sociology*, Vol. 65, No. 6, pp. 909–30.

Norwegian Centre for Research Data (2018) *European Election Database* (Bergen: Norway) Available online at: http://eed.nsd.uib.no/webview/index.jsp?study=http://129.177.90.166:80/obj/fStudy/ATEP2004_Display&node=0&mode=cube&v=2&cube=http://129.177.90.166:80/obj/fCube/ATEP2004_Display_C1&top=yes. Accessed 29 May 2018.

Pappas, T.S. (2016) 'The Spectre Haunting Europe: Distinguishing Liberal Democracy's Challengers'. *Journal of Democracy*, Vol. 27, No. 4, pp. 22–36.

Pirro, A.L.P. (2014) 'Populist Radical Right Parties in Central and Eastern Europe: The Different Context and Issues of the Prophets of the Patria'. *Government and Opposition*, Vol. 49, No. 4, pp. 599–628.

Rooduijn, M. (2014) 'Vox Populismus: A Populist Radical Right Attitude among the Public?' *Nations and Nationalism*, Vol. 20, No. 1, pp. 80–92.

Rooduijn, M. (2017) 'What Unites the Voter Bases of Populist Parties? Comparing the Electorates of 15 Populist Parties'. *European Political Science Review*, pp. 1–18.

Stockemer, D. and Amengay, A. (2015) 'The Voters of the FN under Jean-Marie Le Pen and Marine Le Pen: Continuity or Change?' *French Politics*, Vol. 13, No. 4, pp. 370–90.

Van Spanje, J. (2010) 'Contagious Parties: Anti-Immigrant Parties and their Impact on Other Parties' Immigration Stances in Contemporary Western Europe'. *Party Politics*, Vol. 16, No. 5, pp. 563–86.

Vasilopoulou, S. and Halikiopoulou, D. (2015) *The Golden Dawn's Nationalist Solution: Explaining the Rise of the Far Right in Greece* (New York: Palgrave).

JCMS 2018 Volume 56. Annual Review pp. 74–84

DOI: 10.1111/jcms.12773

Institutional Architecture of the Euro Area*

AMY VERDUN
University of Victoria

Introduction

The year 2017 was characterized by an uptake in economic growth, a decline in unemployment and an increase in optimism about the state of the economy and in so doing continued the trend of the year before (European Central Bank, 2018; Hodson, 2017). Headline indicators suggested that the euro area had managed to depart convincingly from the difficulties of the crisis; even Greece showed a more solid path to economic growth.[1]

This contribution looks at the institutional architecture of the euro area. It first takes a look at the elections that took place in 2017 as they set the stage for the political will that there might be going forward. It then reviews the institutional architecture of the euro area as it stood in 2017. This is followed by a discussion of the White Paper on the Future of Europe that came out in March 2017 and a discussion of the May 2017 Reflection Paper on EMU, offering an in-depth analysis of these reports. Finally, the contribution concludes that even though the developments seem small and incremental, there are traces leading toward deeper integration. Despite the salience of Brexit on the EU agenda, the institutional architecture of the euro area remains an important item.

I. Elections: Anti-European Populism or Renewed European Integration?

In 2017, numerous important elections were scheduled to take place, many of which were awaited with some trepidation. Many observers asked themselves whether these elections would continue the somewhat 'populist' trend that had shocked the United Kingdom (UK), when the outcome of the 23 June 2016 referendum on EU membership ended in favour of 'leave', and the result of the United States (US) presidential election, which brought Donald Trump to power; or whether it would open a space for a renewed vision about the future of the euro area. It would become a year of elections that would determine what opportunities there would be for major change in Europe.

The first major elections that could signal where the winds were blowing from were the Dutch general elections that took place on 15 March 2017. In the run-up to these elections, during and in the wake of the US presidential elections of November 2016, opinion polls in the Netherlands suggested that the political party of right-wing populist

* This research was supported by the Social Sciences and Humanities Research Council of Canada. An earlier version of this article was presented at the *JCMS Annual Review Roundtable* Panel, 11th ECSA-C Biennial Conference, Toronto, 9-11 May 2018. The author thanks the editors of the Annual Review and Heather Hartung-MacRae for the opportunity and its participants for helpful feedback on the earlier version.
[1] Figure 1 and Figure 2 are reproduced from European Commission (2018) *European Economy* February, from respectively Graph 1.5 and Graph 2.8, found on p. 4 and p. 15).

Figure 1: Real GDP and its Components, Euro Area

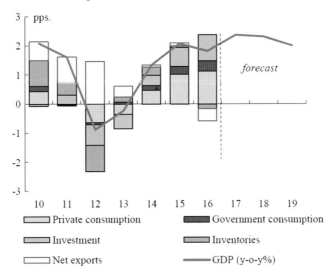

Figure 2: Real GDP Growth and Contributions in Greece.

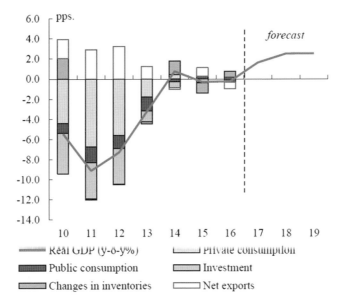

leader, Geert Wilders, who was campaigning on a eurosceptic platform, would become the largest party on Election Day. However, the day after the actual elections it transpired that the populist momentum stalled somewhat, with the party only able to attract 13 per cent of the vote, leading numerous commentators arguing that the populist wave had been halted – for now (Hazenberg, 2017).

A similar fear had taken hold of France with many wondering whether Marine Le Pen of the *Front National* could sway a sufficient number of people to defeat contenders. Though she was never considered likely to become the next president, the final run-off on 23 April and 7 May was between her and centrist Emmanuel Macron. Luckily for those who were worried about the continued right-wing populist wave, the French presidential elections led to a victory of centrist newcomer Emmanuel Macron with his '*En Marche*' movement. In June 2017 (the renamed) '*La République En Marche*' gained 350 of the 577 seats giving Macron a clear majority in the French legislative elections.

Another election also being watched with great anxiety was the German federal election that took place on 24 September 2017. It ended favourably for the incumbent Chancellor, Angela Merkel, of the Christian Democratic Union (CDU). Merkel was able to start her fourth term as Chancellor, but it took until well into 2018 before the coalition with the Social Democratic Party (SPD) was agreed to.

In this climate of anxiety about elections and what their results might mean for the future of Europe, one other election was called to the surprise of all: UK Prime Minister, Theresa May, announced on 18 April 2017 that she would hold a snap general election, which was to be held on 8 June 2017. May had expected to be able to easily win the election (given her lead in the polls). However, it proved to be a poor decision as not only did she fail to capitalize on the lead, she actually *lost* seats. Other contributions within this *Annual Review* offer extensive accounts of the outcomes of these elections across Europe.

Other than the snap UK election, the other contests had been on the election calendar for a while and policy-makers and politicians were aware that the results of these elections (especially the German and the French ones) needed to favour pro-European forces in order for the EU to pick up the momentum for deeper integration. In this sense, the winds of change in 2017 ultimately favoured the integration momentum and in their immediate aftermath, in autumn 2017, there was considerable enthusiasm about what the future might bring regarding a possible deepening of EU integration in particular in the economic and monetary domain.

II. Euro Area Architecture in 2017

In 2017, an assessment of the EU's Economic and Monetary Union (EMU) was that it was still incomplete and 'asymmetrical' (Verdun, 1996, 2000). True, 'E' 'M' 'U' was increasingly mirroring the structure of a complete institutional edifice, but there were still aspects that had not been completed or had been left incomplete. The 'E' usually refers to the four freedoms (movement of capital, labour, goods and services) and the economic governance that is needed to ensure this level of integration. The 'M' is often referred to as that part that deals with monetary policy, the management of the single currency, and thus the policies of the European Central Bank (ECB). The euro area crisis that erupted in 2010 and lasted several years, highlighted that in order for the whole institutional structure to work, centralized financial supervision would need to be strengthened. Scholars such as De Rynck (2016), Donnelly (2014), Howarth and Quaglia (2016), Leblond (2014), Mayes (2017) and Véron (2012), have researched why it took until 2012 for much of the Banking Union to be put onto the agenda, and longer still to complete it. To date the EU has managed to take steps towards a Single Supervisory Mechanism and a single resolution mechanism (SRM). Yet, it has not quite managed to finalize proposals for a European Deposit Insurance scheme (EDIS) for instance (see also Schure and Verdun, 2018). The euro area crisis also unearthed the vulnerability of having a single currency without a fully-fledged political union – or, at a minimum, not having access to collectively backed loans or access to emergency funding in case of crisis. By 2017, significant progress had been made, but particularly what some have called a 'financing union' has still not been accomplished (Claeys, 2017).

As has been the case in recent years, most of the co-ordination of macro-economic policy in 2017 was organized through the so-called European Semester (Verdun and Zeitlin, 2017). The European Commission backed up by the European Council sets out policy priorities for the year in the so-called annual growth survey. It then develops recommendations on economic policy of the euro area for the year. Based on these issues the Commission issues Country Specific Recommendations (CSR) for each member state that suggest which types of issues are out of line with priorities and guidelines. Member states have an opportunity to address these imbalances and, in this way, it is hoped that the co-ordination process will advance. Early research on whether the Commission is able to influence member states' policies suggests that the domestic setting does matter (Maatsch, 2017). Nonetheless, the ECB in its annual report points out that few of the CSRs have been met completely (ECB, 2018, p. 21) – an observation confirmed in the Commission documents that show that only 9 per cent of CSRs between 2011--16 has been fully implemented (European Commission, 2017b, p. 6; see also European Parliament, 2017).

The European Semester is an innovative form of governance (Tömmel and Verdun, 2008, 2009; see also Zeitlin and Vanhercke, 2017. Although the Commission has not gained a lot of formal competence, according to various accounts, the Commission managed to gain considerable sway over the policy-making process (Bauer and Becker, 2014; Dehousse, 2016; Savage and Verdun, 2016). Yet, looking at the EMU architecture, there are still numerous issues that need careful attention and need some form of deeper integration. In anticipation of the elections that were to follow in the year, two important documents were issued in the Spring of 2017 addressing these issues: (a) the White Paper on the Future of Europe, and (b) the Reflection Paper on EMU. Let us discuss each of them in turn.

III. White Paper on the Future of Europe

The institutional architecture of the euro area had been conceptualized in a number of earlier reports that were issued in response to the sovereign debt crisis and the difficulties that various EU member states faced following the onset of the financial crisis (Ioannou *et al.*, 2015). Whether articulated by scholars (De Grauwe, 2013; Featherstone, 2011; Tsoukalis, 2011) or in EU reports on the matter (Juncker *et al.*, 2015; Van Rompuy, 2012), EMU was incomplete. The EU needed to develop paths for deepening EMU. The White Paper on the Future of Europe (European Commission, 2017a) was conceived as a document to celebrate 60 years of European integration with the signing of the Rome Treaties on 25 March 1957. It also offered an opportunity to say something about the likely architecture of EMU, should the political will be there. It was awaited with great eagerness and excitement within the circles of Brussels.

Conscious of the concerns of the day however, the eventual version of the White Paper that was published on 1 March, was sufficiently more cautious than some europhiles may have expected. The concerns that the authors had considered included the Brexit vote, and the aforementioned national elections that had not yet taken place by the publication date of the White Paper. It also included the ongoing sense of crisis produced by the backlash that had been taking place against the increasing numbers of migrants in the EU – itself a result of the EU migrant crisis – which on the whole gave the impression of an continuous multifaceted crisis (D'Erman and Verdun, 2018). This environment, together with the enduring economic difficulties related to the incompleteness of EMU, meant that Commission officials wrote up a White Paper that offered five possible scenarios which included not only the widely anticipated proposals for further deepening, but also more pragmatic – even gloomy ones. The five scenarios were in order:

(1). carrying on;
(2). nothing but the single market;
(3). those who want more do more;
(4). doing less more efficiently; and
(5). doing much more together (European Commission, 2017a, pp. 16–25).

It is clear from reading these scenarios that they are in part written to imagine what a Europe *à la carte* might look like. Or, put differently, what the EU might look like post-Brexit, possibly if others are not as enthusiastic about deepened integration. The first scenario 'Carrying on' (1) already envisages 'incremental progress on improving the functioning of the euro area'. The second scenario (2) stresses that the Single Market is the bottom line. But even in scenario (3), in which some member states might want to deepen their co-operation, it is spelled out in which areas deepening might occur. Of course, in the domain of EMU there already is a 'Europe of different speeds'. Thus, in scenario (3) the group of countries that is already part of EMU might deepen co-operation in areas such as taxation or social policy. If scenario (4) materializes ('doing less more efficiently'), insofar as EMU is concerned, the EU would be envisaged to do less in areas such as employment and social policy but would take steps to 'consolidate the euro area'. The most ambitious scenario (5) 'Doing much more together' includes achieving the goals set out in the Five Presidents' Reports of June 2015 which envisions deepening in fiscal and financial integration (Juncker *et al.*, 2015).

IV. Reflection Paper on EMU

The Reflection Paper on EMU (European Commission, 2017c), the third in a series following the White Paper, discussed the progress that EMU had made to date with the political component now needing the next bit of attention. Citing a number of successes, such as the current support for the common currency among the citizens of the euro area (72 per cent in April 2017 – the highest support since 2004), the report highlights the real costs of EMU in recent years, in particular the effects of the Great Recession that was triggered by the financial crisis that started in 2007–08. Economic activity dropped and with it, growth and employment. Still in 2017 unemployment is higher in the euro area than before 2009 and the divergences among euro area member states are even starker with

Figure 3: Unemployment Rates in Percentage across Europe (March 2017).

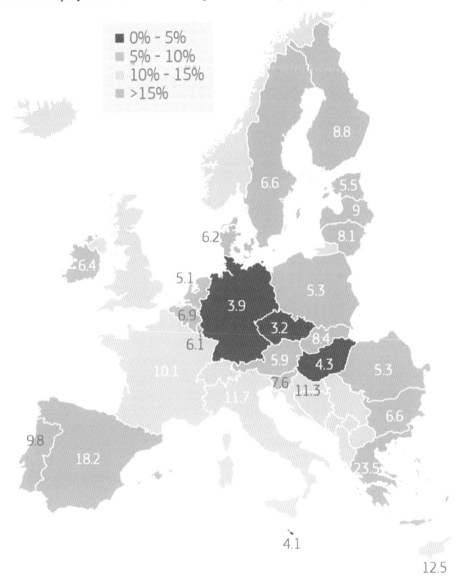

Source: Reflection Paper (European Commission, 2017c, p. 13). [Colour figure can be viewed at wileyonlinelibrary.com]

Southern Europe carrying the brunt of unemployment, particularly amongst youth and young adults (see Figure 3).

   Public funds were diverted to paying for failing banks, and to refinance public debt. Investment fell and, although the euro area in 2017 is in the fifth year of its recovery, the level of investment into the euro area as a whole has not yet returned to pre-crisis levels. Furthermore, the overall levels of public debt are still considerably higher in

2017 than they were in the ten years prior. Moreover, although banks have been recapitalized, there are still a large number of non-performing loans in the system. In 2017, there was a real concern that the Italian financial system would fail as the fourth largest bank of Italy was failing and two Italian banks in the north of the country collapsed. Many observers pointed to weak regulatory oversight of bad loans. Eventually, the Italian state rescued the two banks in Northern Italy (Banca Popolare di Vicenza SpA and Veneto Banca SpA) in addition to a bailout of Monte dei Paschi di Siena, spending in total 20 billion euros for the bailout, but not after many observed that the new banking regulation rules had been flouted (*Financial Times,* 2017; *Reuters,* 2017).

In terms of next steps towards deeper integration, the Reflection Paper proceeds to advance a few suggestions on how to strengthen the euro area's architecture. One such proposal rests on the notion of deepening the euro area's so-called 'fiscal union' (European Commission, 2017c, p. 15). Such a union would call for (1) sound public finances; (2) complementing stabilization tools at the level of the euro area as a whole; and (3) a shared rulebook. Another major point of concern, raised by the Reflection Paper, is that the role of the ECB in EMU is what is called 'overdetermined' because monetary policy is centralized, whereas budgetary policy is left to a complex decentralized system, much of which is without clear carrots and sticks (or even if clear, these mechanisms are politically sensitive to use). Thus, a further reform is needed to the governance system (European Commission, 2017c, p. 17). A third area is to find a so-called 'fiscal backstop' for the banking union (a Single Resolution Fund (SRF) that serves as a backup – a lender of last resort). A fourth major area would be to develop what the Reflection Paper calls a 'European Safe Asset' (a European version of the US Treasury Bill). Besides a number of other proposals, the Reflection Paper also hones in on the need to improve euro area governance, in particular legitimacy and transparency.

A major aspect of a strengthened EMU architecture concentrates on the political and legal framework – in particular anchoring EMU within a more solid democratic mechanism of checks and balances. Rather than going for a big-bang approach, the Reflection Paper advocates an incremental, step-by-step, approach towards deeper political integration. This could be done either by treaty change, an intergovernmental approach (outside the Treaties) or a mix of both (European Commission, 2017c, p. 27).

In order to improve the governance framework of the euro area changes to the legal provisions are necessary. What is required is incrementally increasing euro area competence in this area using the existing legal framework. Given the challenges of EU treaty change, the Reflection Paper suggests possibly first setting up rules through international treaties and perhaps at a later stage integrating those rules into the EU treaty. This path for legal change has been tried and tested in a number of cases (such as with the Schengen agreement). Some of the necessary provisions are already in the so-called Fiscal Compact[2] (itself an international treaty). Member states had agreed earlier that eventually the goal would be to have those provisions included in the EU treaties. The Reflection Paper furthermore suggests that depending on the model chosen, the European Stability Mechanism (ESM) Treaty could also be included into the EU treaties (even though member states had not explicitly agreed to do so in the first place).

[2]The formal name of the Fiscal Compact is the Treaty on the Stability, Coordination and Governance in the Economic and Monetary Union (TSCG).

To enhance democratic accountability the Reflection Paper advocates for greater powers of oversight to both national member state parliaments and the European Parliament (EP). Although there is currently considerable good practice in reporting to the EP, these practices are not yet spelled out in the treaties. The Reflection Paper advocates that these practices should be formalized. Another thought would be to advance further the democratic accountability of the euro area *per se*. This might first take the form of an *ad hoc* arrangement. If successful then it could be incorporated into the EU treaties at a later stage.

Finally, another major institutional innovation could be the creation of a euro area Treasury and possibly the issuing of what the Reflection Paper refers to as a 'European Safe Asset' (European Commission, 2017c, p. 28). An earlier document referred to something similar as a Eurobond or blue asset (see Claessens *et al.*, 2012; Favero and Missale, 2010; Jones, 2012). A euro area Treasury could bring together competences and services that are currently spread out across different institutions (such as economic and fiscal surveillance, macroeconomic stabilization and liquidity assistance to member states) alongside the possibility of co-ordinating a 'safe asset' and last resort backstop to the Banking Union (European Commission, 2017c, p. 28). In terms of the timing, the Reflection Paper reinforces what had been incorporated into the Five Presidents' Report, by stating that the 'second phase' should take place within the timeframe 2020–25.

V. Analysis

The White Paper has been commented on mostly in the press immediately following its publication. Some of the commentators regretted the strong leadership taken by the European Commission to point to possibly deepening European integration, arguing that the President of the Commission lacks the full democratic support of EU citizens along the lines of a usual representative democracy (Bartholomeusz, 2017). Others point out that change is going to come, simply because of the advent of Brexit (Ackrill, 2017). The commentators of the Reflection Paper have pointed to a number of weaknesses in the approach proposed by the Commission. Begg (2018) questions whether a 'rules-based' approach would be the best choice. He argues that although such a 'rules-based' approach has led to keeping budgetary deficits under control, public debts have not kept the same pace. Furthermore, he argues that there still is considerable non-compliance by various member states in terms of keeping national budgets under control. He also questions whether the early-warning stage of the Macroeconomic Imbalances Procedure (MIP) can adequately take into consideration the divergence in circumstances in each of the member states. He points out that the MIP has only had a limited impact. Begg's main concern is that the EU first needs to better define the essence of the EU's fiscal constitution. In order to do that, he recommends that the fiscal rules be rationalized and that greater emphasis be placed on sustainability of debt and on national rules. He also recommends that fiscal councils be better integrated into the EU governance framework and to enhance their legitimacy and that of the EU governance framework more generally. These views are repeated by Määttänen and Alcidi (2018) who come to similar conclusions.

As the year 2017 unfolded many were wondering whether with the renewed enthusiasm for European integration with a pro-European leader in France and a seasoned German Chancellor who played an important role in dealing with the euro area crisis

(Mushaben, 2017, pp. 161–212) one would expect the EU to advance to deeper integration. By the close of 2017 it was however still unclear what the path ahead would be for 2018 and the immediate years to come. Considerable push is made on concluding the Banking Union and other technocratic aspects of completing the EU economic, monetary and fiscal architecture. However, any larger changes, involving transferring competence (requiring Treaty changes) were not being proposed.

Conclusion

The year 2017 was important for the institutional architecture of the euro area. It continued a process that began in 2016 with the gradual end to the euro area crisis and continued positive economic conditions. Coming on the heels of a multifaceted crisis, and against the backdrop of discussions around the impending departure of the UK from the EU, the main question in 2017 was whether the EU would move towards more fragmentation or further deepening. With various elections in 2017 having settled in favour of more moderate forces (as opposed to more dramatic populist tendencies) the stage was set for a process where there might be more room for gradual changes in the institutional architecture of the euro area to potentially deal with the many asymmetries of EMU. This contribution looked more closely at the plans put forward by the Commission (the White Paper on the Future of Europe of March and the May Reflection Paper on EMU). Although the action taken is small and incremental, the path seems to be leading toward deeper integration. Currently, the challenges of the Brexit negotiations are taking up considerable time but, in the margins, the institutional architecture of the euro area remains an important item on the EU agenda.

References

Ackrill, R. (2017) 'Reflections on the Reflection Paper on the Future of EU Finances'. *Political Quarterly*, Vol. 88, No. 4, pp. 716–20.

Bartholomeusz, J. (2017) ''Juncker's White Paper Has the Answers – and That is the Great Tragedy'. Heinrich Böll Stiftung'. *European Union*, 23 March.

Bauer, M.W. and Becker, S. (2014) 'The Unexpected Winner of the Crisis: The European Commission's Strengthened Role in Economic Governance'. *Journal of European Integration*, Vol. 36, No. 3, pp. 213–29.

Begg, I. (2018) 'Should Rules Continue to Rule? Policy Report from the FIRSTRUN project', FIRSTRUN Deliverable 6.6.

Claeys, G. (2017) 'The Missing Pieces of the Euro Architecture', *Bruegel Policy Contribution* Issue No. 28, October.

Claessens, S., Mody, A. and Vallee, S. (2012) 'Paths to Eurobonds', Bruegel Working Paper, 2012/10.

De Grauwe, P. (2013) 'Design Failures in the Eurozone: Can They Be Fixed?' LSE Europe in Question Discussion Paper Series (LEQS) Paper No. 57/2013.

D'Erman, V. and Verdun, A. (2018) 'Introduction: Integration Through Crises'. *Review of European and Russian Affairs* (RERA) Vol. 12 No. 1 Special Issue on the theme 'Crises of the EU and their Impact on European Integration', pp. 1–16.

De Rynck, S. (2016) 'Banking on a Union: The Politics of Changing Eurozone Banking Supervision'. *Journal of European Public Policy*, Vol. 23, No. 1, pp. 119–35.

Dehousse, R. (2016) 'Why has EU Macroeconomic Governance Become More Supranational?' *Journal of European Integration*, Vol. 38, No. 5, pp. 617–31.

Donnelly, S. (2014) 'Banking Union in Europe and Implications for Financial Stability'. *Studia Diplomatica*, Vol. 67, No. 2, pp. 21–34.

European Central Bank (2018) *Annual Report 2017* (Frankfurt: ECB).

European Commission (2017a) 'White Paper on the Future of Europe and the Way Forward. Reflections and Scenarios for the EU27 by 2025', COM(2017)2025, Brussels, 1 March.

European Commission (2017b) '2017 European Semester: Country-Specific Recommendations', COM(2007) 500 final, Brussels, 22 May.

European Commission (2017c) 'Reflection Paper on the Deepening of the Economic and Monetary Union', Brussels, 31 May.

European Commission Directorate General Economic and Financial Affairs (2018) 'European Economic Forecast'. *European Economy Institutional Papers,* No. 073 (February) (Luxembourg: Publications Office of the European Union).

European Parliament (2017) 'Country Specific Recommendations for 2016 and 2017: A Comparison and an Overview of Implementation', Directorate-General for Internal Policies, Economic Governance Support Unit, PE 602.081, 23 May.

Favero, C.A. and Missale A. (2010) *EU Public Debt and Public Management Eurobonds* (Brussels: European Parliament, Committee Economic and Monetary Affairs, September).

Featherstone, K. (2011) 'The JCMS Annual Lecture: The Greek Sovereign Debt Crisis and EMU: A Failing State in a Skewed Regime'. *JCMS*, Vol. 49, No. 2, pp. 193–217.

Financial Times (2017) 'Why Italy's €17bn Bank Rescue Deal Is Making Waves Across Europe', 26 June.

Hazenberg, J. (2017) 'The Dutch Election: Populism Loses a Round, but Democracy Is Still in Trouble', Heinrich Boll Stiftung, 20 March. Available online at: https://eu.boell.org/en/2017/03/20/dutch-election-populism-loses-round-democracy-still-trouble.

Hodson, D. (2017) 'Eurozone Governance in 2016: The Italian Banking Crisis, Fiscal Flexibility and Brexit (Plus Plus Plus)'. *JCMS*, Vol. 55, No. S1, pp. 118–32.

Howarth, D. and Quaglia, L. (2016) *The Political Economy of European Banking Union* (Oxford: Oxford University Press).

Ioannou, D., Leblond, P. and Niemann, A. (2015) 'European Integration and the Crisis: Practice and Theory'. *Journal of European Public Policy*, Vol. 22, No. 2, pp. 155–76.

Jones, E. (2012) 'Eurobonds, Flight to Quality, and TARGET2 Imbalances'. *Swedish Institute for European Policy Studies (SIEPS)*, April, Issue 4, pp. 1–10.

Juncker, J.-C., Tusk, D., Dijsselbloem, J., Dragi, M. and Schulz, M. (2015) *Completing Europe's Economic and Monetary Union* (Brussels: European Commission).

Leblond, P. (2014) 'The Logic of a Banking Union for Europe'. *Journal of Banking Regulation*, Vol. 15, No. 3–4, pp. 288–98.

Määttänen, N. and Alcidi, C. (2018) 'Policy Report from the FIRSTRUN Project', FIRSTRUN Deliverable 1.7, 28 February.

Maatsch, A. (2017) 'Effectiveness of the European Semester: Explaining Domestic Consent and Contestation'. *Parliamentary Affairs*, Vol. 70, No. 4, pp. 691–709.

Mayes, D.G. (2017) 'Banking Union: The Problem of Untried Systems'. *Journal of Economic Policy Reform*, Published Online 4 November. Available online at: https://doi.org/10.1080/17487870.2017.1396901.

Mushaben, J.M. (2017) *Becoming Madam Chancellor. Angela Merkel and the Berlin Republic* (Cambridge: Cambridge University Press).

Reuters (2017) 'EU Clears Italy's $6 Billion State Bailout for Monte dei Paschi', 4 July. Available online at: https://www.reuters.com/article/us-eu-montepaschi-stateaid/eu-clears-italys-6-billion-state-bailout-for-monte-dei-paschi-idUSKBN19P1PQ.

Savage, J.D. and Verdun, A. (2016) 'Strengthening the European Commission's Budgetary and Economic Surveillance Capacity since Greece and the Euro Area Crisis: A Study of Five Directorates-General'. *Journal of European Public Policy*, Vol. 23, No. 1, pp. 101–18.

Schure, P. and Verdun, A. (2018) 'The Single Market and Economic and Monetary Integration'. In Brunet-Jailly, E., Hurrelmann, A. and Verdun, A. (eds) *European Union Governance and Policy Making: A Canadian Perspective* (Toronto: University of Toronto Press), pp. 127–54.

Tsoukalis, L. (2011) 'The JCMS Annual Review Lecture. The Shattering of Illusions – And What Next?' *JCMS*, Vol. 49, No. S1, pp. 19–44.

Tömmel, I. and Verdun, A. (eds) (2008) *Innovative Governance in the European Union: The Politics of Multilevel Policy-Making* (Boulder, CO: Lynne Rienner).

Van Rompuy, H. (2012) 'Towards a Genuine Economic and Monetary Union'. Report by President of the European Council Herman Van Rompuy', EUCO 120/12; Presse 296; PR PCE 102; Brussels, 26 June.

Verdun, A. (1996) 'An "Asymmetrical" Economic and Monetary Union in the EU: Perceptions of Monetary Authorities and Social Partners'. *Journal of European Integration*, Vol. 20, No. 1, pp. 59–81.

Verdun, A. (2000) *European Responses to Globalization and Financial Market Integration: Perceptions of Economic and Monetary Union in Britain, France and Germany* (Basingstoke: Palgrave Macmillan) DOI https://doi.org/10.1057/9780230535824

Verdun, A. (2009) 'Regulation and Cooperation in European Monetary and Economic Policy'. In Tömmel, I. and Verdun, A. (eds) *Innovative Governance in the European Union: The Politics of Multilevel Policy-Making* (Boulder, CO: Lynne Rienner), pp. 75–86.

Verdun, A. and Zeitlin, J. (2017) 'Introduction: the European Semester as a New Architecture of EU Socioeconomic Governance in Theory and Practice'. *Journal of European Public Policy*, Vol. 25, No. 2, pp. 137–48.

Véron, N. (2012) 'Europe's Single Supervisory Mechanism and the Long Journey Towards Banking Union'. Bruegel Policy Contribution, 2012/16.

Zeitlin, J. and Vanhercke, B. (2017) 'Socializing the European Semester: EU Social and Economy Policy Co-Ordination in Crisis and Beyond'. *Journal of European Public Policy*, Vol. 25, No. 2, pp. 149–74.

JCMS 2018 Volume 56. Annual Review pp. 85–95

DOI: 10.1111/jcms.12768

Halfway Through the Better Regulation Strategy of the Juncker Commission: What Does the Evidence Say?*

CLAUDIO M. RADAELLI
University of Exeter

Setting the scene

Better regulation – as identified in the discourse of the European Union (EU) – is a set of activities and evidence-based policy instruments. Its aims are to appraise new policies (regulatory or not), to carry out systematic consultation, to undertake evaluations of regulations and domains of the *acquis*, and to provide regulatory management.

Better regulation has its own distinctive processes, actors, problems, inter-institutional agreements and instruments, for example, impact assessment, legislative evaluation and consultation. Consequently, we can call it a public policy. The difference with other policies like health and safety or environmental protection policy is that better regulation is supposed to be systematic in its goals and activities, no matter what policy sector is considered. It is horizontal so to speak – international organizations call this the 'whole of government approach' to regulatory quality (OECD, 2015).

Of course, the fact that this policy is called by the EU institutions and others 'better regulation' does not necessarily mean that it delivers on high quality regulation, or that the very notion of regulatory quality is accepted by every player. Objectively, the EU better regulation policy is one possible incarnation of some ideas about regulatory reform and the governance of EU legislation. With this caveat, we can carry on with the terminology adopted in the official documents of the EU, which, after some oscillations in the past between 'smart' and 'better' regulation (European Commission, 2010, 2015a), seems now to have settled on 'better'.

I. Better Regulation: Policy and Politics

To grasp the fundamentals of the year in review, it is useful to go back to 2015 when the First Vice-President of the Commission Frans Timmermans defined his strategy for this policy domain (European Commission, 2015a). There are other prominent actors, including the European Parliament, the Council of the European Union, the member states, the business community and non-governmental organizations – we will consider some of them in due course. But at the very least the Commission has the advantage of moving first when it comes to defining the agenda.

*Research for this contribution was funded by the European Research Council, advanced grant Protego / Procedural Tools for Effective Governance 694632. I wish to thank Thibaud Deruelle for research assistance and Claire Dunlop for having read the first draft. Lorna Schrefler kindly provided detailed comments on an early draft. Many thanks to Theofanis Exadaktylos for his substantial and editorial suggestions.

   The early attempts in this field dated back to the 1990s, with a more consistent effort to align objectives and instruments since 2002. In May 2015, the Commission defined the scope of better regulation for the Juncker Commission. The highlights of the Communication by Timmermans (European Commission, 2015a) and accompanying documents were: the objective of closing the policy cycle by putting *ex-post* evaluation at the beginning of any work on new proposals (the so-called 'evaluate first' principle, European Commission, 2010); an enhanced flow of consultations involving stakeholders at different stages of the policy cycle; a re-defined body for the scrutiny of better regulation activities (the Regulatory Scrutiny Board); and a single set of methodological templates for better regulation activities (a toolbox running above 400 pages, re-adjusted in summer 2017 to take into account the experience of the first two years). In a sense, this is the technical/instrumental level, enshrined in, or accompanied by, a political setting – if you wish, you can call the former policy and the latter politics.

   On the policy dimension, three observations are necessary. First, *ex-post* regulatory and legislative evaluation is a complex activity where most of the OECD countries have just raised awareness (OECD, 2014). By taking the decision to embark on both systematic *ex-post* evaluation and making evaluation the first step in the planning of new legislation, the Commission set a very high bar. Second, massive doses of consultation across the board, new platforms for stakeholders, fitness checks where consultation is the main method to appraise regulatory burdens and compliance costs mean that the Commission, in the period considered, has been seeking legitimacy from the input given by stakeholders. Whether this is for the Commission more important than legitimacy provided by accurate economic analysis and reputation for independence we cannot tell.

   Third, the Regulatory Scrutiny Board (RSB) emerged since 2015 as more than just a watchdog. Although the Commission had the experience of the Impact Assessment Board since 2007 (a body staffed part-time by Commission's high level officials from selected Directorates General), the RSB is chaired by a Commission's director general and consists of three independent experts recruited from outside the EU institutions and three high-level Commission officials. All RSB members work full-time, are bound to the principle of collective responsibility – this has generated a common intent and *esprit de corps* – and have a mandate that is wider than that of the old Impact Assessment Board. The RSB in fact evaluates the quality of impact assessments of new legislation, major *ex-post* regulatory evaluations and fitness checks of existing legislation. It can intervene on implementing and delegated acts, as well as being able to offer advice on methods and issues that cut across different types of assessment. Behind the emergence of the RSB lies a tension between some member states (led by Germany, the Netherlands and the UK in this case) who wanted a totally independent regulatory oversight body, and the Commission, close to the idea of keeping oversight within the perimeter of its treaty-defined right to initiate legislation.

   With this observation, we have already entered the politics dimension. Scratch beneath decisions on the scope, mission and membership of the RSB and you will discover fundamental questions about who is and should be in control of the life-cycle of policy. Arguably, member states would have more trust in a regulatory oversight body with no Commission officials. For the Commission, instead, opinions on the quality of impact assessments of proposed initiatives should remain a component of the internal process of monitoring and learning – that is, the policy conversation among the Secretariat General, the Directorates General, and the Commissioners.

The second feature of the politics dimension is the bold statement made by the Commission that all the activities of the annual work programme are informed, appraised and supported by better regulation. Take the work programme for 2016, for example: here we read that all initiatives for the Digital Single Market, the Energy Union, Security, Migration, the Capital Markets Union, the Action Plan for Fair and Efficient Corporate Taxation, the Single Market Strategy for goods and services 'are underpinned by the Commission's new Better Regulation Agenda' (European Commission, 2015b, p. 2). Similarly, in the work programme for 2018 we learn that: 'Today, more than ever, there is a need for sound preparations, evaluations and evidence-based policy-making. Any decision, any proposal must take into account all available facts and evidence in a structured and comprehensive way. The stakes are too high, the challenges too complex, to take any other approach. This is why Better Regulation underpins all the Commission's work and continues to ensure that our proposals are based on the best available information' (European Commission, 2017c, p. 13). This implies that the Commission is prepared to be judged on the quality and usage of the evidence-based instruments deployed in all these areas.

At the same time (this is the third politics-relevant annotation), the Commission since 2015 has made it clear that it is no longer prepared to take the blame for the inefficiency and poor quality of regulatory outcomes. On the one hand, it accepts the high bar of evidence-based standards for its own activities. On the other, responsibilities should be separate. It should be clear to the public if and when the European Parliament and the Council impose amendments that generate new administrative obligations and higher compliance costs, or when member states customise legislation by introducing new regulatory costs.

For this reason, the Commission put on the table a new inter-governmental agreement on better regulation – to bind the Council and the Parliament to evidence-based appraisals of their major amendments. It has also insisted that member states should report on their additional regulatory obligations, beyond EU regulatory floors. A 2003 inter-institutional agreement on these matters was never properly implemented. The new agreement was negotiated and eventually agreed in 2016 with the name Inter-Institutional Agreement on Better Law-Making.[1] The reference to *law-making* instead of *regulation* is a good sign, because it goes beyond better regulation to capture in principle all law-making activities where the three main institutions of the EU need to co-operate on evidence-based policy. The change of label hopefully means more involvement of the EU legislator – up until now *better regulation* has been perceived as a policy of the Commission, whilst there is no doubt that *law-making* points towards all institutions involved in making legislation.

The fourth politics element is tricky. It is about the relationship between better regulation and subsidiarity. In the period 2015–17, the Commission has taken a number of decisions grounded in Juncker and Timmermans's beliefs about the legitimate scope of subsidiarity and the notion that the Commission should be, as they often put it, big on big things and small on small things (see for example, Juncker, 2014). To illustrate, in

[1]OJ L 123 vol. 59, 12 May 2016.

2015 the Commission withdrew 73 proposals – not because they did not pass an impact assessment or there was no sufficient evaluation of the existing legislation, but because they were not considered acceptable given the approach of the Juncker Commission to subsidiarity or, in other cases, did not have realistic changes to go through the legislative procedure. Although this has created political controversy and a Court's decision on the scope of the power to withdraw (Case C-409/13), the withdrawal of proposals, in general, is not underpinned by the usage of evidence-based instruments. Rather, it is an indicator of a regulatory philosophy of a political Commission like the present one.

II. The Main Achievements of the Commission

Two years after the 2015 Communication, we can appraise some preliminary results of the better regulation strategy. The Commission published a mid-term review of the better regulation agenda (European Commission, 2017a). The European Court of Auditors (2018) published its performance audit on the EU system of *ex-post* review of legislation. Thus, it is an appropriate time for social scientists too to review the evidence available.

The main achievements of the Commission are the strong emphasis on consultation, the attempts made to include *ex-post* legislative evaluation into the policy cycle, the *de facto* independence of the RSB and its capacity to handle different types of scrutiny. On the minus side of the equation, there are questions about domains where impact assessment is not carried out or not done properly (for example, the governance architecture of the eurozone); whether impact assessment really informs the development of the proposals of the Commission (note that the final impact assessment and the proposal are published simultaneously); the methodological robustness and timing of the *ex-post* evaluations; and the fact that, considering the amount of work done, the RSB members are not adequately supported by a team of economists and social scientists.

Let us start with the core of regulatory oversight, the RSB, whose independence is also crucial for the legitimacy of the overall better regulation agenda. On impact assessment, the RSB provides an opinion. It can approve or ask the relevant Directorate General to review and re-submit the report. By late 2016, the RSB started to publish a third type of opinion: 'positive with reservations'.

In 2017, the RSB scrutinized 53 impact assessments. Seven evaluations were examined by the RSB in 2016, with a jump to 17 in 2017. The RSB focuses on the staff working document (SWD) in which the Commission reflects on the evaluation. This SWD is the document where the service of the Commission signals its ownership of the evaluation carried out by the consultants and other activities (such as a stakeholders conferences) that inform the learning-from-the-results process.

How does the RSB go about its scrutiny function? In 2017 the first opinion on impact assessment was negative in 23 cases, positive in another 12 and positive with reservations in the remaining 18 cases. As for second opinions on impact assessments that were found below standard at the first stage of review, 1 was negative, 12 positive with reservations and 4 were never resubmitted after the first negative opinion (RSB, 2018, p. 12). There was much discussion as to whether the Commission should still carry on with proposals with two negative RSB opinions. The answer is that the RSB does not say YES or NO to a proposal: a double-negative means that the proposal does not meet the RSB *standards for evidence-based policy*. But there may be political reasons that make the

Commission carry on. The presence of a published motivated double negative opinion adds transparency and flags up issues that should be taken into account in the legislative procedure.

The revision of the 2015 Toolbox in summer 2017 clarifies and provides guidance on the approach to evaluation of the Commission, for instance, the notion of evaluate first and back-to-back evaluations and impact assessments (European Commission, 2017d). As mentioned, the idea is that impact assessment work should draw on *ex-post* evaluations. A couple of studies deal with the results achieved in closing the policy cycle (Mastenbroek *et al.*, 2016; van Golen and van Voorst, 2016). Van Golen and van Voorst gathered 309 *ex-post* legislative evaluations and 225 impact assessments. They found that only 9 *ex-post* evaluations use impact assessment and 33 impact assessments draw in some ways on *ex-post* evaluations. Their data do not cover the last two years, though. In 2016/2017 some evaluations were published at the same time as the impact assessment and legislative proposal.

One problem is what kind of report or study meets the threshold to be called an evaluation and how close to the impact assessment is its publication date? It is very difficult to plan evaluations so that they are temporally aligned with the impact assessment and the work on new proposals. In some cases, the Commission's impact assessment reports on the presence of 'studies'. Does a study or report equal an evaluation? The RSB report for 2017 observes that in that year 30 out of 40 impact assessments aiming to revise legislation were supported by an evaluation (this is a 75 per cent rate). Interestingly, for the RSB 10 of these evaluations were inadequate, 6 not properly used, and the other 14 are cases of 'good use of evaluation' (RSB, 2018, p. 23). Mastenbroek *et al.* (2016) have designed a scorecard to appraise the quality of legislative evaluations carried out by the Commission. The evaluations in their sample do not fare well on 'justification of methods' (only 15 per cent of the sample) and 'reliability' (29 per cent).

If evaluation ought to connect back-to-back with impact assessment, the classic evaluations of cohesion policies offer little assistance to design policy (see Dunlop and Radaelli, 2017 for details). This explains why the Commission needs to draw on *legislative* evaluations and new evidence-based instruments like REFIT, fitness checks and Cumulative Cost Assessments. A fitness check is conceptually the same as the evaluation of an individual intervention but it covers a range of rules that have common regulatory goals or share some objectives and for this reason have to be examined together (European Commission, 2017d).

REFIT (Regulatory Fitness and Performance) belongs to the attempt to review the entire *acquis* with a strong emphasis on the involvement of stakeholders. At its core, it is a simplification and burden-reduction initiative – the official slogan is 'identify opportunities for simplification and reducing unnecessary costs every time the Commission proposes to revise existing law' (European Commission, 2017e, p. 4). It is now incorporated in the annual Commission work programme as a quality review of existing EU legislation. Indeed, REFIT is designed as a rolling programme and as such identifies where to withdraw proposals – here we see a connection between better regulation and the approach to subsidiarity.

The 2018 work programme includes 17 legislative initiatives under REFIT, 15 withdrawals and 3 repeals. The programme adds 12 new REFIT simplification initiatives in the priority areas of the Juncker Commission, for example, looking at reporting requirements in the sectors of environment, the fisheries control system, consumer law, trans-European transport networks, ID cards and emergency travel documents.

The methodological foundations of REFIT remain shaky. Exactly because of its conceptual ambiguity on the policy dimension (not a proper evaluation tool since some REFIT exercises are just appraisals of some regulatory costs) REFIT has been a political springboard for a variety of actions: consulting stakeholders, preparing hit lists of regulations to be targeted, reducing administrative burdens and compliance costs for business, slowing down regulatory action in some sectors, and withdrawal of proposals.

Since 2015 the Commission has experimented with platforms to collect comments on irritating or burdensome regulations, following the example of similar platforms in the UK and Belgium. REFIT indeed has a two-tier platform for dialogue with stakeholders and member states. Essentially the platform consists of two standing groups, one for governments and one for stakeholders. Since its creation, the REFIT platform has adopted 58 opinions based on more than 280 public suggestions to make EU laws more efficient (European Commission, 2017e). Oddly enough, the REFIT platforms are chaired by Anne Bucher, the head of the Regulatory Scrutiny Board, who deputises Timmermans on this exercise. There is no conceptual connection between the RSB scrutiny activity and the REFIT platforms.

Since 2013, a tool called 'cumulative cost assessment' appeared under the REFIT umbrella. The cumulative cost assessment is not an evaluation. It performs a different function. It considers a single sector and attempts to measure the effects of different EU rules on a sample of representative facilities. The early applications of the cumulative cost tool were in the automotive, steel and aluminium sectors (Schrefler *et al.*, 2015).

III. The European Parliament and the Council

Let us turn to the other EU institutions. The European Parliament has invested in capacity building by increasing the number of members of staff with the skills necessary to exercise oversight of the Commission's impact assessments and evaluations and to brief the parliamentary committees. Looking at the detailed, meticulous work of the European Parliament Research Service (EPRS, especially directorate C, Impact assessment and European Added Value) at various stages, from inception appraisals to the final impact assessments of the Commission, one has the impression that there is some duplication of work done by the RSB. But, here is the counter-argument: the EPRS is an internal EP voice, as opposed to the external voice of the Commission – this internal voice is heard by the committees, thus raising attention and amplifying some of the RSB messages. Further, the MEPs may be interested in impacts and dimensions that for the RSB are not priorities – hence EPRS complements what the RSB does.

Be that as it may, the European Parliament scrutiny of better regulation also covers the *ex-post* dimension. In December 2015, two EPRS researchers (Schrefler and Huber, 2015) provided the Members of the European Parliament with a rolling check-list of all evaluations underway at the Commission (this includes both expenditure programmes and *ex-post* legislative evaluations). They found that at that time there were 525 planned and on-going evaluations, of which 3 per cent were originated by the Commission's work programme, specifically the commitment to 'evaluate first'.

The variety of information on these evaluations is indeed puzzling, making it difficult for the European Parliament to even just keep track of it. In November 2017, Schrefler found 507 planned and on-going evaluations. She concluded that 'Until recently, the overall picture of Commission evaluations remained complex and difficult to reconstruct for external actors. Progress towards the full implementation of the 2015 Better Regulation Guidelines has now clarified the status of on-going and planned Commission evaluations considerably. Conversely, accessing completed evaluations, namely Commission evaluation staff working documents and the underlying external studies, remains more challenging' (Schrefler, 2017, p. 5; Timmermans was challenged by a Parliamentary question on this issue[2]).

Do Members of the European Parliament (MEPs) use evaluations? In the 220 *ex-post* legislative evaluations examined by Zwaan *et al.* (2016), no question (on evaluation) has been asked by an MEP to reflect on policy performance or how legislation has achieved its goals. Most of the variance in the MEPs' questions is explained by the political muscle-flexing exercises pitching the Parliament versus the Commission. Our analysis of the questions for January 2017–March 2018 shows 39 questions that either mention an evaluation published by the Commission, call for an evaluation or discuss ongoing evaluations. When it comes to reflecting on policy performance, seven questions clearly reflect on policies that have been evaluated as underperforming, whether by not meeting clear numerical standards, (question E-006722-17 on the tap water directive), imperfectly achieving the aim of said policy (question E-001017-18 on the legal instrument to achieve goals set in the 'EU blood directive'), or in ways that do not warrant the conclusions drawn by the Commission (question O-000034/2017 on the implementation of the Nature directives). Five questions on on-going evaluations demand that the evaluation be geared towards dimensions of policy performance or ask the Commission to be more explicit on the evaluation strategy. In the recent period we examined (Table 1), MEPs cast a critical eye on the evaluation process, for example, by questioning the method of evaluation (17 questions), asking for actions to be taken once the evaluation is done (10 questions) or pointing towards lack of evaluation (17 questions). Sometimes the reference to policy performance is subtle or absent, as conclusions from an evaluation (e.g., in the form of a quote) will be taken as the rationale and/or introduction to the question, without clearly discussing policy performance (10 questions).

In principle, the inter-institutional agreement of 2016 binds together the Commission, the European Parliament and the Council. In particular, the agreement makes the statement that the impact assessments of the Commission should be presented in ways that facilitate the consideration by the Council and the European Parliament. The secretariat of the Council has elaborated a procedure so that the different formations should start their discussion with an examination of the underlying impact assessment, prior to getting into the details of proposed legislation.

The Council formations have responded with different degrees of commitment – arguably reflecting the silos mentality still prevalent. Definitively, there is motivation to take the better regulation agenda seriously in the Council formations that are closer to economic problems, such as the Competitiveness Council. The inter-institutional agreement

[2]See the European Parliament webpage: http://www.europarl.europa.eu/sides/getDoc.do?pubRef=-//EP//TEXT+WQ+E-2017-007614+0+DOC+XML+V0//EN&language=en).

Table 1: Parliamentary questions on evaluation (January 2017–March 2018)

Types of Parliamentary Question on Evaluation January 2017–March 2018	Number of questions
Reflecting on policy performance: questions on policy performance following an evaluation, or on the gap between performance and the MEP expectations about performance.	7
Discussing ongoing evaluations (at the time of the question): questions on MEPs' demand for a preview of the evaluation, or first-hand information on either performance or impact.	5
Questioning/suggesting methods of evaluation: Rationale, dimensions, issues the MEP wants to see in an evaluation.	17
What is the follow-up once the evaluation is published? MEPs showing interest in knowing what the effect of an evaluation will be on the Commission's agenda or work programme.	10
Lack of evaluation pointed out/asking for an evaluation (explicitly or implicitly): More evaluation is sometimes demanded explicitly, other times the request is phrased implicitly e.g. 'Will the Commission conduct an evaluation of ....'	17
An existing evaluation can be identified as the rationale to ask the question, without clear reference to performance: Questions that are based on the conclusions of a specific evaluation or that refer to a programme of evaluations.	10

Source: Author's own compilation.

also states that the Council and the European Parliament will carry out impact assessments of their substantial amendments to the Commission's proposals 'when they consider this to be appropriate and necessary for the legislative process' (Art. 14). The secretariat of the Council, which is endemically under-staffed to produce impact assessments, launched a tender in autumn 2017 for a framework contract to support this analytical work.

In these inter-institutional relationships, there are also political issues – like we said, policy and politics intersect. One is that the Council is notoriously hostile to raising awareness of how member states add regulatory burdens at the stage of transposition and implementation of EU regulation (so-called gold-plating) and more generally the regulatory responsibility of member states in implementing and delivering EU legislation. The Council wants to keep the Commission accountable, not the member states. Another is that the inter-institutional agreement does not define the exact moment or threshold when the impact assessment of amendments should be carried out. It is up to the European Parliament and the Council to identify case-by-case the conditions under which this is appropriate and necessary – thus, there are no monetary thresholds above which an amendment generating additional regulatory costs should be looked at analytically.

Third, both for the European Parliament and the Council, evidence-based activities stand in the way of more political discussions. They are so to speak grains of sand that can slow down or make it more difficult to talk 'politically', especially in trilogues – although in principle robust evidence should open the eyes of the negotiators and facilitate political work.

Fourth, during the last two years the Competitive Council and the Commission have competed over the definition of what better regulation should be about. We have already seen the coordinates of the Commission's interpretation of problems and solutions. The Council agrees with the general coordinates, but on specific details it wants to see more emphasis on the reduction of administrative burdens. The political bone of contention is whether the EU should have regulatory targets similar to the UK's Business Impact Target (Department for Business, Energy & Industrial Strategy, 2016; National Audit Office, 2016). On several occasions, for example in May 2016, the Competitiveness Council urged the Commission 'to rapidly proceed on this to enable the introduction of regulatory targets in 2017' (Council of the European Union, 2016, p. 5). For the Commission, a business impact target is unfeasible and would skew the usage of evidence-based tools towards meeting the target rather than delivering net policy benefits. Noting the reluctance of the Commission, seven national regulatory bodies grouped under the RegWatchEurope banner commissioned a feasibility study on introducing EU-wide regulatory targets (Renda, 2017) – to push the Commission in this direction. The final episode (for now) in this tug-of-war was in October 2017, when the Commission stated that targets are neither feasible nor appropriate for the EU. The target 'may lead to undue deregulation because "necessary costs" to achieve regulatory benefits are not distinguished from "unnecessary costs"'. A burden-reduction policy of this sort will not have the necessary legitimacy among stake-holders' (European Commission, 2017b, p. 44).

Conclusions

This Commission is committed to the better regulation agenda. The bar has been set high, thus it is not surprising to observe the difficulty with the principles of evaluating first and closing the policy cycle. We do not have the counterfactual of how EU legislation would look if impact assessments and the tools of better regulation did not exist. The causal link between better regulation and the quality of EU rules is a fascinating yet elusive object of study, especially if we extend regulatory quality to the dimension of how rules are delivered and experienced by firms and citizens in the member states (European Commission, 2017f). Even more daunting is the question about regulation and innovation – Commissioner Moedas has started the conversation (European Commission, 2016) but this important relationship will most likely mature in the next Commission.

Politically, there is tension between the de-regulatory vision of some Council formations and some member states (the UK being a classic champion) and the approach of the Commission, as shown by the controversy on the feasibility of an EU-wide business impact target. Perhaps with Brexit the Commission will find it easier to fight for its notion that the better regulation agenda should deliver net benefits rather than just reduce regulatory costs.

The connection between better regulation and subsidiarity remains a delicate issue. In launching the new industrial strategy on 13 September 2017, Juncker (2017) announced a new task force led by Timmermans on subsidiarity and proportionality. The task force was set up in November 2017 with members from national parliaments and the Committee of the Regions. It should clarify the principles of subsidiarity and proportionality and identify policy sectors that should be given back to EU countries or re-delegated to the EU.

Thinking of the next Commission, the key questions are more likely to be around subsidiarity and better regulation, regulation and innovation, the evolution of the RSB (whether totally independent or half-and-half), the added value of the inter-institutional agreement, and whether Juncker and Timmermans will deliver a set of robust evaluations that will provide the baseline for the planning of future policies.

References

Council of the European Union (2016) 'Council Conclusions on 'Better Regulation to Strengthen Competitiveness', COMPET 21 RECH 135, 8849/16, Brussels, 18 May.

Department for Business, Energy & Industrial Strategy (2016) *Business Impact Target: Statutory Guidance*, London, November 2016.

Dunlop, C.A. and Radaelli, C.M. (2017) 'If Evaluation is the Solution, What is the Problem?' In Zahariadis, N. and Buonanno, L. (eds) *The Routledge Handbook of European Public Policy* (London: Routledge), pp. 331–43.

European Commission (2010) 'Smart Regulation in the European Union', COM (2010) 543 Final, Brussels, 8 October.

European Commission (2015a) 'Better Regulation for Better Results: An EU Agenda', COM (2015) 215 final, Brussels, 19 May.

European Commission (2015b) 'No Time for Business as Usual,' Commission work programme 2016, COM (2015) 610 final, Strasbourg, 27 October.

European Commission (2016) 'Better Regulations for Innovation-Driven Investment at EU Level' Commission staff working document, Brussels, 2 October. Available online at: https://ec.europa.eu/research/innovation-union/pdf/innovrefit_staff_working_document.pdf. Accessed March 2018.

European Commission (2017a) 'Completing the Better Regulation Agenda: Better Solutions for Better Results', COM (2017) 651 final, Brussels, 24 October.

European Commission (2017b) 'Overview of the Union's Efforts to Simplify and Reduce Regulatory Burdens', Staff working paper, SWD (2017) 675 final, Strasbourg, 24 October.

European Commission (2017c) 'An Agenda for a More United, Stronger and More Democratic Europe', Commission work programme 2018, COM (2017) 650 final, Brussels, 24 October.

European Commission (2017d) 'Better Regulation Toolbox'. Available online at: https://ec.europa.eu/info/better-regulation-toolbox_en . Accessed March 2018.

European Commission (2017e) 'REFIT Scoreboard', Brussels, 24 October. Accessed March 2018. Available online at: http://publications.europa.eu/webpub/com/refit-scoreboard/en/images/REFIT_Scoreboard.pdf. Accessed March 2018.

European Commission (2017f) 'Business Perceptions of Regulation; Flash Eurobarometer', 451. Brussels. Available online at: ec.europa.eu/commfrontoffice/publicopinion/index.cfm/ResultDoc/download/.../80138. Accessed June 2018.

European Court of Auditors (2018) 'Ex-post Review of EU Legislation: A Well-established System, But Incomplete'. Special Report No.16/2018, Luxembourg, European Court of Auditors.

Juncker, J.C. (2014) *The Juncker Commission: The Right Team to Deliver Change*, Brussels, 10 September. Available online at: http://europa.eu/rapid/press-release_SPEECH-14-585_en.htm.

Juncker, J.C. (2017) 'State of the Union Address', Brussels, 13 September 2017. Available online at: http://europa.eu/rapid/press-release_SPEECH-17-3165_en.htm'. Accessed March 2018.

Mastenbroek, E., van Voorst, S. and Meuwesc, A.C.M. (2016) 'Closing the Regulatory Cycle? A Meta Evaluation of Ex-post Legislative Evaluations by the European Commission'. *Journal of European Public Policy*, Vol. 23, No. 9, pp. 1329–48.

National Audit Office (2016) 'The Business Impact Target: Cutting the Cost of Regulation'. Report by the Comptroller and Auditor General, HC 236 session 2016–2017, 29 June.

OECD (2014) *Oecd framework for regulatory evaluation* (Paris: OECD Publications).

OECD (2015) *Regulatory Policy Outlook* (Paris: OECD Publications).

Regulatory Scrutiny Board (2018) *Annual Report 2017* (Brussels: European Commission). Available online at: https://ec.europa.eu/info/sites/info/files/rsb-report-2017_en.pdf. Accessed March 2018.

Renda, A. (2017) *Introducing EU Reduction Targets on Regulatory Costs: A Feasibility Study* (Brussels: CEPS Publications). Available online at: https://www.ceps.eu/publications/introducing-eu-reduction-targets-regulatory-costs-feasibility-study. Accessed March 2018.

Schrefler, L. (2017) *Evaluation in the European Commission: Rolling Check List and State of Play* (Brussels: EPRS). Available online at: http://www.europarl.europa.eu/RegData/etudes/STUD/2017/611020/EPRS_STU(2017)611020_EN.pdf) Accessed March 2018.

Schrefler, L., Luchetta, G. and Simonelli, F. (2015) 'A New Tool in the Box? The Cumulated Cost Assessment'. *European Journal of Risk Regulation*, Vol. 6, No. 1, pp. 68–78.

Schrefler, L. and Huber, S. (2015) *Evaluation in the European Commission: Rolling Check List and State of Play* (Brussels: EPRS). Available online at: http://www.europarl.europa.eu/thinktank/en/document.html?reference=EPRS_STU(2015)558789) Accessed March 2018.

van Golen, T. and van Voorst, S. (2016) 'Towards a Regulatory Cycle? The Use of Evaluative Information in Impact Assessments and Ex-Post Evaluations in the European Union'. *European Journal of Risk and Regulation*, Vol. 7, No. 2, pp. 388–403.

Zwaan, P., van Voorst, S. and Mastenbroek, E. (2016) 'Ex-post Legislative Evaluation in the European Union: Questioning the Usage of Evaluations as Instruments for Accountability'. *International Review of Administrative Sciences*, Vol. 82, No. 4, pp. 674–93.

JCMS 2018 Volume 56. Annual Review pp. 96–108   DOI: 10.1111/jcms.12770

European Economic Governance in 2017: A Recovery for Whom?

ROSALIND CAVAGHAN[1] and MUIREANN O'DWYER[2]
[1] Glasgow Caledonian University [2] University of Warwick

Introduction

In 2016, *JCMS*'s special issue 'Another Theory is Possible' argued that both EU Studies and the EU find themselves in need of a re-invigorated, poly-phonic debate which questions the socio-economic power structures and narratives of exclusion potentially embedded in all politics (Manners and Whitman, 2016). In this contribution focusing on the EU's economic policy, we take up this challenge applying an intersectional lens to review the positive narrative of growth and recovery that the European Commission, amongst others, deployed in 2017. Our analysis shows how EU economic policy plays a key role in establishing gendered and racialized hierarchies in the EU. Additionally, this reveals the gendered and racialized dynamics at the heart of European integration itself. We demonstrate the urgent need for EU studies to take such dynamics seriously in seeking to understand the European Union of 2017 and beyond.

Taking an intersectional, perspective, we problematize who the audience for this positive narrative is and whose economic well-being is understood to 'count'. As such, we examine the *gender constitutive effects* of the EU as an economic actor. We explore how European integration is progressing through the establishment of a common economic space (Hoskyns, 2008, p. 108) built through the pursuit of gender-blind and gender-biased economic goals promoted by the EU. This is an EU which ignores women as economic citizens and economic actors. In building this critique of the narratives of the EU's economic 'success' or of 'the end of the crisis', we draw on two existing bodies of work: existing critical political economic approaches to EU integration which have sought to understand the full implications of the shifts in the EU's economic governance structures, the flexibility and political opportunism of the EU's economic narrative (Rosamond, 2002; Ryner, 2015; Schmidt, 2016), and Feminist Political Economy critiques which have uncovered 'strategic silences' in 'mainstream' approaches to macro-economic policy (Picchio, 2015; Schuberth and Young, 2011). These perspectives are united by the way that they shed light on how the EU is (re-) shaping the contours and limits of political arena. As the EU's institutions seek to portray a break with the crisis and a return to normality, we interrogate this narrative of exiting crisis, arguing that it serves to entrench and continue economic priorities and assumptions established in the heat of the crisis. The narrow economic interests of finance and global markets that were prioritized during the crisis remain dominant in this 'post-crisis' moment, presented as universal. The pursuit of these interests does not serve those most impacted by the crisis itself: women and other marginalized groups.

It is possible to tell the story of the European economy in 2017 as one of recovery. Several prominent indicators show a growing economy, with unemployment continuing its downward trajectory, debt low and confidence among the business community high (European Commission, 2017e). The overwhelming anxiety of crisis management has dissipated and several developments suggest a return to a more 'normal' policy-making regime – albeit one that is committed to the reforms implemented in the heat of the crisis. In his, now annual, State of the Union address to the European Parliament, Commission President Jean-Claude Juncker celebrated the recovery and growth, delighting in the fact that growth in the EU has outstripped that of the United States for the past two years (European Commission, 2017e). These signals of success cannot hide many of the continuing weaknesses in the architecture of the European economy – the problems of divergent economic models remain, and there are still several banks and financial institutions that give reason for caution (Hodson, 2017), and of course, the gender blind nature of the policies, something which we critique in depth below. Nonetheless the dominant narrative of recovery has motivated discussions of future reforms. Where the review of the European economy in last year's *Annual Review* posed the question of how long the recovery could last (Benczes and Szent-Iványi, 2017) this year's contribution asks a different question: a recovery for whom?

Juncker and other key actors in European economic policy have pointed to several indicators to justify their claim that the 'sun is shining'. For example, in the Autumn forecast of 2017, the Commission begins by noting, 'The EU economy as a whole is also set to beat expectations with robust growth of 2.3% this year' (up from 1.9 per cent in spring) (European Commission, 2017a). GDP figures are key to the narrative of a successful recovery. Levels of business confidence, as measured by the Commission's Business Cycle Indicators instrument, showed impressive increases throughout 2017, especially in the third and fourth quarter (European Commission, 2017b, 2017c). Other measures are somewhat less dramatic – unemployment is down across the EU as a whole, though there remains scope for a further decline. Additionally, wage growth has been slower than could be expected in a recovery marked by such significant growth figures. This indicates the role being played in this recovery by unconventional monetary policy, as well as a strong global economic upturn. However, the reliance on these indicators in the narration of the 'recovery' also points to questions about what gets included in discussions of the European economy, and crucially, who, and what, gets left out.

The Politics of Economic Governance in 2017

> *'We are now in the fifth year of an economic recovery that really reaches every single Member State'* – Jean Claude Juncker, State of the Union Address 2017.

In 2017 we observed the continued contests between the Commission and the European Council concerning control over economic policy, and for legitimacy in this policy area. This contest perpetuates the sidelining of the European Parliament. While the Parliament has attempted to develop a voice in economic governance, and has engaged with the other institutions in informal ways, it remains secondary in the major debates (Bressanelli and Chelotti, 2017). The Parliament remains a consultative actor in economic policy, which drastically limits its ability to impact on this area. This is particularly striking, given the fact that the Parliament is more likely to offer alternative accounts of both the crisis and the recovery, and has an established track record of providing a platform to feminist political concerns. The exclusion of the Parliament reflects a wider issue of democratic legitimacy in economic policy-making. Despite widespread critique of the anti-democratic nature of much of the reforms enacted in response to the crisis (Gearty, 2015), the various proposed reforms to the regime do not address this question. In fact, the various proposals for clearer external representation in economic affairs, which dominate the sections on legitimacy and democracy in the reform documents of the Commission, for example in the White Paper published in the Summer, reflect a desire for greater competence for the Commission and other EU level actors. The issue of external representation is a recognized challenge (Hodson, 2017) however, it is not the only, or even the primary, legitimacy challenge faced by the EU in economic policy (Jones, 2009; Scharpf, 2013).

The shift back to 'normal' politics is perhaps best reflected by some of the personnel changes across various economic policy institutions. The election of a new President of the Eurogroup, once seen as a key player in protecting the existence of the Euro and thus the European project, was overshadowed in the media by the on-going Brexit negotiations. The selection of a Finance Minister, Mário Centeno, from a former bail-out country to head up the meetings of eurozone Finance Ministers reflects the transformation of Portugal's own economic image from problem child to first in class. Indeed, the lack of media attention paid to the election of its president is also a sign of the Eurogroup becoming more like a normal EU institution, and though it still lacks the formal legal underpinnings of other Council formations, its authority is widely accepted (Craig, 2017). The year 2017 also saw the debate over personnel at the European Central Bank step a level, as debates over the purpose and mandate of the ECB look set to shape the contest to replace Mario Draghi, and fill other positions on the governing board. Indicatively, the focus of this contest surrounds the speed at which unconventional monetary policy is wound up, further indicating the sense of normality returning.

In the interest of setting the agenda, the European Council produced a collection of documents advocating for reforms in October. At the December Council meeting, member state leaders argued for a reform programme that focused primarily on continuing structural reforms, and aiming for economic convergence. They also tasked the Eurogroup with developing a roadmap for completing the Banking Union, a European Monetary Fund and a capital markets union. Not to be outdone, in December the Commission published its proposed reforms. These proposals presented a more supranational approach to economic governance, with greater oversight power for the Commission itself, and a continuation of the role of DG ECFIN in driving the European Semester. However, it is notable that amongst all of the reform proposals there is a particular understanding of the democratic and legitimacy challenges being faced. We would point out that the proposals for a Eurozone Finance Minister, for example, are premised on a belief in the need for more efficient management of economic policy. Whether such a position would sit in the Council or the Commission, has proven a point of contention at the EU level, but questions of accountability have thus far not. The politics of these competing visions for economic governance tabled in these debates replicate a classic divide between intergovernmental and supranational visions of EU functioning. Notably however each of the current options on the menu are similar in the way they serve to sideline alternative visions.

The shift away from crisis narratives and the retreat of the mantra that 'There Is No Alternative' have meant that there are now some debates over the substance of future reforms. This is to be welcomed, while such debates may slow down reforms and may often simply reflect the self-interested motivations of member states and the EU institutions, we argue strongly that a continuation of the practice of imposing new reforms and structures that typified the 'crisis years' would be inherently dangerous for the democratic legitimacy of the EU. Furthermore, the presence of some debate does not, by any stretch indicate that powerful practices of exclusion and strategic framing are not still at play. In the next section, we explore how the concerns of feminists continue to be sidelined from discussions of the economic policy in 2017, and how the very measures which are motivating Juncker to speak of the 'wind in Europe's sails' systematically obscure the experiences of the economically vulnerable throughout Europe.

The sense of now being in a 'post-crisis' moment can also be seen in attempts to rebalance EU policy-making through attempts to 'bring the social back in'. Responding to criticism from many quarters, the EU this year launched the European Pillar of Social Rights. Whether or not this process has successfully 'rebalanced' the European Semester remains a highly contested issue (Maricut and Puetter, 2018). We argue that the prominence of these questions both in 2017 and previous years highlights the importance of the debate concerning the purpose of economic governance, how we measure economic progress or decline, and even how we define the economy itself. Observing how these debates play out gives us an opportunity to test for whether the economic crisis did in fact feature a discursive process of excluding social and other concerns, through the 'duty to yield' (Skjeie, 2006) generated by a crisis rhetoric that drew the boundaries around the 'crisis', in such a way as to establish and justify a hierarchy of concerns. It is in the moment of recovery that we can really explore how effective such a discourse was, and continues to be. If the justification for excluding feminist and other social input into economic policy was that such inputs were unsuited for a crisis moment, then how they continue to be excluded highlights how such sidelining was strategic, rather than pragmatic.

Beyond the establishment of the Social Pillar, other concerns and issues which were sidelined during the crisis may be returning to the agenda. For example, the Commission has launched (or re-launched) plans to tackle the gender pay gap in Europe (European Commission, 2017d). However these have originated in DG Justice, and they seem to have had limited impact upon or input from DG ECFIN, perpetuating the divide that sees gender equality concerns as political rather than economic. This reflects the continuation in 2017 of the attempts by DG ECFIN to maintain control over economic matters, and to present a distinctive definition of what counts as economic (Cavaghan, 2017).

Developing an Alternative Lens for 2017

Gender equality and the economy are firmly intertwined in a mutually constitutive relationship. Gender is often misunderstood within mainstream EU studies as 'merely another *variable* of analysis *rather than an intrinsic axis of power*' (Guerrina *et al.*, 2018). The extensive literature of feminist political science however has emphasized gender as a fluid and constantly re-negotiated system of meaning which plays a pivotal, structural, role in the distribution of power and roles and opportunities (Connell, 1990). Intersectional approaches explicitly point out that experiences of gender hierarchies vary in accordance with other structural axes of inequality such as race or class (Collins and Bilge, 2016; Hancock, 2007). Thus, intersectionality is 'a way of looking at the world that takes a principled stance ... that gender ... is simultaneously operative with other [axes of difference] like race, class, sexuality and religion' (Wekker, 2016, p. 21). Feminist and intersectional approaches highlight whose interests are understood as the default.

Feminist approaches thus go far beyond any understanding of gender as simply a variable and it is these frameworks that we apply to our discussion of current EU narratives of 'recovery', 'normality' and proposed reforms. Feminist literatures have shown how economic policies create, entrench and obscure racial and gender inequalities (Gill and Roberts, 2011; Grown *et al.*, 2000). Much of this analysis was developed in assessments of structural adjustment policies implemented in the global south in the 1980s and 1990s (Griffin, 2015; Klatzer and Schlager, 2014), which bear uncanny similarities to the EU's 'Austerity' policies. So, in the following we interrogate the production of knowledge about the economy and economic interests in Europe. We develop an intersectional analysis of 2017 by asking: who is at stake and who has authority to define public policy goals within the institutional configuration of economic governance in the EU.

Feminist approaches thus go far beyond any understanding of gender as simply a variable and it is these frameworks that we apply to our discussion of current EU narratives of 'recovery', 'normality' and proposed reforms. Feminist literatures have shown how economic policies create, entrench and obscure racial and gender inequalities (Gill and Roberts, 2011; Grown *et al.*, 2000). Much of this analysis was developed in assessments of structural adjustment policies implemented in the global south in the 1980s and 1990s (Griffin, 2015; Klatzer and Schlager, 2014), which bear uncanny similarities to the EU's 'Austerity' policies. So, in the following we interrogate the production of knowledge about the economy and economic interests in Europe. We develop an intersectional analysis of 2017 by asking: who is at stake and who has authority to define public policy goals within the institutional configuration of economic governance in the EU.

Theorizing the Gendering Effects of EU Economic Policy

Feminist political economists have argued that the financial crisis writ large has been used to constitute a 'new normal' where intersectional inequalities are being entrenched through austerity policies, presented as 'the only option' during the crisis (Griffin, 2017; Hozic and True, 2016). These literatures pointed out the political dominance of neo-classical economic paradigms in policy-making circles across the board (Balakrishnan *et al.*, 2010; Picchio, 2015) and demonstrated that the economic policies they lead to are premised on significant, though implicit, sexist assumptions (Bakker 1994, Cavaghan 2017, O'Dwyer, 2017). In revealing these assumptions and their implications, feminist accounts have made the political and economic consequences of macro-economic policies like EU austerity visible.

In the wake of the economic crisis, flagship commitments to gender mainstreaming and to increasing women's employment which had been prominent in the era of the Lisbon Strategy and the European Employment Strategy, disappeared from the EU's rhetoric (Cavaghan 2017, Karamessini and Rubery, 2014) as the financial crisis was used as a pretext to entrench rule-based economic policies (Addabbo *et al.*, 2018, p. 8). These focused on deficit and debt reduction, leading to cuts in state provision of public services in areas such as child, health and care for the elderly or reducing state support for carers and welfare support (Karamessini and Rubery, 2014). These policies dump reproductive labour back into the 'private' sphere, homes and families, where in all EU member states, it is disproportionately taken up by women. Deregulations in the labour market often described in EU policy documents as 'structural reforms' which lead to a decline in working conditions have also disproportionately affected women already clustered in part-time, lower paid and more insecure work (Karamessini and Rubery, 2014). Finally, women's employment has been disproportionately affected by public sector cuts, because women are over represented working within it.

This raises questions of whose interests are being included in the pronouncements of recovery and return to normality, now being posited by EU institutions. The EU's economic governance, instituted since the crisis, is a process which has encouraged and legitimized a withdrawal of state support for the reproductive economy. There are a number of gendered outcomes to be highlighted here. Firstly, it has eroded the sharing of these burdens amongst tax-payers and employers, dumping them onto women. Secondly, long-term upward trends in women's employment throughout the EU, a flagship element of the EU's prior economic strategies, have been halted (Karamessini and Rubery, 2014). Thirdly, inequalities in men and women's time use have increased as the proportion of women's time spent on domestic labour has increased and their leisure time has decreased (European Institute for Gender Equality 2017, p. 38). It thus appears that the 'structural subsidy' extracted from women's unpaid work for the productive economy across the EU has increased since the implementation of austerity.

Feminist critiques argue that this situation is sustained by the silence maintained around women's (diverse) economic experience as producers and reproducers (Acker, 2004; Bakker 1994; O'Dwyer, 2018) and the use of technical and (wilfully) inaccessible economic jargon which obscures the unequal economic relations between men and women that these kinds of policies entrench (Cavaghan 2017). This is a classic instance of 'the strategic silence' at work. These gendered relationships of dependence and *entrenched ignorance of them* are wrapped up in common economic conceptions and measures, such as measurements of GDP (Coyle, 2015), competitiveness (Gillespie and Khan, 2016) classification of investment and infrastructure (De Henau and Perrons, 2016), and measurements of growth. If we revisit the measures of success posited in 2017's narrations of success and a return to normality, it is precisely these types of indicators which are being used to build this narrative.

If we turn our focus to the EU's pronouncements of 'recovery' and its proposals for reform, we can interrogate them as mechanisms through with EU produces knowledge about the economy. This knowledge is loaded with assumptions about what is and is not relevant, or significant. Important critiques have emphasized that women of colour's and migrants' economic marginalization is persistently portrayed as though it were acceptable, unremarkable or simply unimportant (Bassel and Emejulu, 2017; Emejulu and Bassel, 2017; Strolovitch, 2013). These authors build on black anti-capitalist and black feminist critique, which has long emphasized the political implications of suppressing the production of knowledge concerning the political and economic marginalization of people of colour (Collins, 1990; Mills, 2007). These processes produce marginalized groups and 'minority' status (Bassel and Emejulu, 2017). Kinnvall (2016) and Wekker (2016) for example have highlighted the links between white economic and political dominance; the suppression of knowledge concerning racial oppression and economic marginalization; and the construction of 'Europe'. These dynamics are at play in current narratives of economic recovery.

In addition to the broadly conceived gendered dynamics outlined above, EU responses to the financial crisis have deepened intersectional hierarchies *between women,* intensifying problematic dynamics already set in train through the EU's flagship gender sensitive labour force activation policies (The Lisbon Strategy for instance). Here, two dynamics have worked in tandem. The EU's attention to racial discrimination and to women's specific gendered experiences of it, lags far behind its rhetoric on gender equality (Agustín, 2013) and EU institutions have a long history of confusing 'working white women' with *all* women (Hoskyns, 1996). As a result, EU policies, even before the financial crisis exacerbated social and economic polarization between white middle-class professional women on the one hand and European minority/migrant women,[1] on the other. White middle-class women's movement into paid employment has increased demand for cheap domestic labour. In parallel, minority women suffering (unaddressed) discrimination in the formal economy, found employment in the causalized home working economy, meeting demands for domestic labour (Williams, 2003). These deepening inequalities between women after the financial crisis have been acknowledged by feminist scholars and women's advocates (Karamessini and Rubery, 2014; European Institute for Gender Equality, 2017). In Greece for example women's unemployment as a whole fell by 14.3 per cent over the four years 2008–12. Migrant women's employment however plunged from 50.9 per cent to 38.6 per cent *in 21 months* between the third quarter of 2010 to the second quarter of 2012 (Karamessini, 2014, p. 171). Eighty per cent of this group are employed in domestic roles in households and this dramatic shift in migrant women's employment coincided with the implementation of tax increases and wage and pension cuts in 2010 and 2011 which lead to a decline in middle-class households' incomes (Karamessini, 2014, p.172).

The So-called Recovery and the Shape of Europe in 2017

Feminist approaches thus furnish us with a set of questions about the narrative of recovery. Does recovery or return to normality, which the Commission and others have sought to portray, mean that the long-term increase in women's employment, which was halted by austerity policies, has been restored? Is women's employment now growing at the same speed as before the crisis, so that their labour market participation is increasing in line with trends and flagship targets established in the Lisbon Strategy? Does the recovery mean that the quality of women's employment has improved to pre-austerity levels? Have intersectional inequalities between women disappeared so that minority women in Europe can expect a quality of life unaffected by patterns of racial discrimination and marginalization? Do women enjoy the same level of access to public services and carers allowances as they did before austerity? In fact, these types of

[1]North American black feminist scholars often use the descriptor 'women of colour'. In the European context however categories describing racial and migrant groups differ according to national administrative and cultural context. In view of this complexity we follow Bassel and Emejulu (2017) and use the term 'minority women' to describe women who experience the effects of racialization, class and gender domination, in instances when we require an umbrella term suitable for the European context.

measures are notably absent from the Commission's pronouncements of 'recovery' and return to normality. What kind of recovery then is this and who benefits from it?

This type of silencing and exclusion has profound implications for the character of the EU as a governance regime and emerging state-like entity. The EU's policy responses to the financial crisis eroded hard-won steps towards a more equitable sharing of reproductive labour between the state, employers and families (where women disproportionately perform reproductive labour) in the European economy. Previous economic strategies such as the Lisbon Strategy indicated *some* engagement with the relationship between the productive and the reproductive economy, including commitments to childcare, for example (Galligan, 2017). These kinds of commitments lent a liberal feminist credibility to the EU's proclamations that gender equality is a flagship EU value, something Frans Timmermans effusively claimed on International Women's day in 2017 stating 'The European Union stands by women in Europe and around the globe today, as it did at the time of its foundation'.

In the last ten years though, austerity measures have caused predictable and well-known gendered and racialized economic hardships. During this time, a notion of economic governance as technocratic, incontestable and legitimately immune from progressive critiques has been fostered. This is not a position accepted by critical political-economists, including feminist economists (Balakrishnan *et al.*, 2010). Rather, a feminist lens identifies this as a European version of 'the strategic silence' which misrepresents the relationships between the productive and the reproductive economy and which wilfully obscures the deeply entrenched gendered and racialized hierarchies which EU economic policy actively maintains.

In the first years following the onset of the crisis during the atmosphere of 'fire-fighting', the absence of intersectional gender analysis was paralleled by the absence of other social or environmental concerns. However, in 2017 as the reforms enacted in response to the crisis are being normalized, this strategic silence remains. Looking at 2017, we can see how in moving to a discourse of recovery, the exclusion of concerns with gender equality, which was previously justified through reference to emergency and crisis, has been maintained. In this light, such exclusions cannot be viewed as a temporary reflection of a heightened focus on particular areas of economic policy during the crisis. Rather, they reflect a broader exclusionary practice within EU economic policy-making that situates concerns with gender and racial equality outside of economic policy. Austerity and the 2017 normalization of the governance mechanisms associated with it are thus intensifying long-standing tendencies within EU institutions. Namely the assumption, that women's interests are part of the social policy sphere only (EU member state level), or a niche gender equality silo, rather than deeply entwined with EU economic policy. Even before austerity, feminist EU integration theorists pointed out how the EU's economic/social binary places women's interests outside the political sphere delineated by the EU (Kronsell, 2005), thus locking them out of an important part of the reconfigured state within the EU. This reinvigorated exclusion of women's interests in the dawning of the EU's new normal and recovery is the first step in the generation of an entrenched imbalance in EU policy-making which has profound and negative gender constitutive effects.

In addition, however, if we turn to institutional attempts to build up a social response to the European Semester we can see that they remain limited, and lag significantly behind.

The European Pillar of Social Rights, launched in 2017 to great fanfare, lacks any binding power. The 'rights' of the pillar are in fact objectives, with no legal standing. While the recommendations of the European Semester are also not hard law, they do have the potential to influence behaviour in ways that social recommendations, so far, cannot. This is due, firstly, to the potential for hard sanctions connected with the European Semester – while member states cannot be sanctioned for ignoring individual recommendations, if they consistently miss the targets of the Stability and Growth Pact, financial penalties are an option available to the EU. There are no such sanctions connected with social policy. Prior experience has shown that non-binding social policy measures do not reliably produce results. The EU never met the childcare objectives agreed in 2002 for example.

While the scoreboards of both economic and social policy are premised on the idea of social pressure and reputational sanction, the reputational consequences of poor economic scores exert a far more pronounced impact on EU economic policy, than poor scores in social policy. External actors, such as global markets and other financial institutions, pay far greater attention to the Macro Economic Imbalance Indicator, than to the Social Scoreboard. Outrage from, for example, organized female immigrant labour (who may not need a scoreboard to identify their own economic experiences), enjoys no audience amongst economic policy-makers convinced that detrimental racial or gender equality outcomes of their policies are irrelevant to them and should be mopped up in DG EMPL or DG JUSTICE (who have very limited influence on economic policy). The recovery being pronounced by the Commission in 2017 seems therefore to consist more of a recovery of *control*. Rule-based economic policies and associated co-ordination and surveillance mechanisms are being normalized in 2017. Competency over economic policy has been enhanced at EU level and Macro Economic Imbalance Indicators are producing figures acceptable to markets. We argue that this, rather than a return to pre-austerity living standards or commitments to gender equality, is what constitutes the European recovery proclaimed in 2017.

Conclusions

The EU's use of 'the strategic silence', which portrays unequal impacts of economic policy on people as irrelevant, also serves to justify the disproportionate power of economic policy, compared to social policy and to deflect contestation of the root-causes of their economic marginalization to ineffective channels. 'Social' impacts are addressed at EU level through non-binding aspirational objectives misleadingly named 'rights', even though they have no legal standing. This reflects the shadow side of the EU project – its policies often entrench inequalities, not only through the actual policies promoted, such as austerity, but also through the policy-making and integration structure itself. The imbalances we have discussed here reflect a broader asymmetry within European integration, one that favours deregulation and market liberalization over market correction and social regulation (Ferrera, 2017; Scharpf, 2013). Our contribution here shows how intersectional inequalities entrenched by EU economic policies, constitute a key feature of this asymmetry, which since the crisis and austerity, have now become even more acceptable to EU policy-makers and even more protected from contestation and democratic accountability in 2017.

Moreover, as we have shown in this contribution, racialized and gendered dynamics are key to the processes of economic integration. Inequalities are an outcome of economic governance, but they are also constitutive of the system of governance itself. We have shown that it is through the silencing of the experiences of marginalized groups, in particular minority women, that the structures of economic policy-making are maintained. A gendered and racialized underpinning of economic discourse and policy-making is therefore a key factor in the construction of the current process of European integration. So, in order to adequately discuss and understand the changing dynamics of the European Union, and how it is shaping the contours of the state, EU studies must not perpetuate its own silence on the gendered and racialized characteristics of EU integration.

References

Acker, J. (2004) 'Gender, Capitalism and Globalization'. *Critical Sociology*, Vol. 30, No. 1, pp. 17–41.

Addabbo, T., Klatzer, E., Schlager, C., Villa, P. and de Villota, P. (2018) 'Challenges of Austerity and Retrenchment of Gender Equality'. In O'Hagan, A. and Klatzer, E. (eds) *Gender Budgeting in Europe: Developments and Challenges* (Palgrave Macmillan), pp. 57–85.

Agustín, L.R. (2013) *Gender Equality, Intersectionality, and Diversity in Europe* (New York: Palgrave Macmillan).

Bakker, I. (1994) *The Strategic Silence: Gender and Economic Policy* (London: Zed Books).

Balakrishnan, R., Elson, D. and Patel, R. (2010) 'Rethinking Macro Economic Strategies from a Human Rights Perspective'. *Development*, Vol. 53, No. 1, pp. 27–36.

Bassel, L. and Emejulu, A. (2017) *Minority Women and Austerity: Survival and Resistance in France and Britain* (Bristol: Policy Press).

Benczes, I. and Szent-Iványi, B. (2017) 'The European Economy: The Recovery Continues, but for How Long?' *JCMS Annual Review*, Vol. 55, No. 1, pp. 133–48.

Bressanelli, E. and Chelotti, N. (2017) 'Taming the European Parliament: How Member States Reformed Economic Governance in the EU', European University Institute Working Paper. Available online at: http://hdl.handle.net/1814/48924. Last accessed 20 June 2018.

Cavaghan, R. (2017) 'The Gender Politics of EU Economic Policy: Policy Shifts and Contestations Before and After the Crisis'. In Kantola, J. and Lombardo, E. (eds) *Gender and the Economic Crisis in Europe: Politics, Institutions and Intersectionality* (Palgrave Macmillan), pp. 49–71.

Collins, P.H. (1990) *Black Feminist Thought: Knowledge, Consciousness, and the Politics of Empowerment* (London: Routledge).

Collins, P.H. and Bilge, S. (2016) *Intersectionality* (Cambridge: John Wiley & Sons).

Connell, R.W. (1990) 'The State, Gender, and Sexual Politics'. *Theory and Society*, Vol. 19, No. 5, pp. 507–44.

Coyle, D. (2015) *GDP: A Brief But Affectionate History* (Princeton, NJ: Princeton University Press).

Craig, P. (2017) 'The Eurogroup, Power and Accountability'. *European Law Journal*, Vol. 23, No. 3-4, pp. 234–49.

De Henau, J. and Perrons, D. (2016) 'Investing in the Care Economy to Boost Employment and Gender Equality'. Women's Budget Group. Available online at: https://wbg.org.uk/wp-content/uploads/2016/03/De_Henau_Perrons_WBG_CareEconomy_ITUC_briefing_final.pdf. Last accessed 20 June 2018.

Emejulu, A. and Bassel, L. (2017) 'Whose Crisis Counts? Minority Women, Austerity and Activism in France and Britain'. In Kantola, J. and Lombardo, E. (eds) *Gender and the Economic Crisis in Europe: Politics, Institutions and Intersectionality* (Palgrave Macmillan), pp. 185–208.

European Commission (2017a) *Autumn Economic Forecast 2017* (Brussels: EC). Available online at: https://ec.europa.eu/info/business-economy-euro/economic-performance-and-forecasts/economic-forecasts/autumn-2017-economic-forecast_en. Last accessed: 20 June 2018.

European Commission (2017b) *European Business Cycles Indicators 3rd Quarter 2017* (Brussels: EC). Available online at https://ec.europa.eu/info/publications/economy-finance/european-business-cycle-indicators-3rd-quarter-2017_en. Last accessed 20 June 2018.

European Commission (2017c) *European Business Cycles Indicators 4th Quarter 2017* (Brussels: EC). Available online at: https://ec.europa.eu/info/publications/economy-finance/european-business-cycle-indicators-4th-quarter-2017_en. Last accessed 20 June 2018.

European Commission (2017d) 'Equal Pay Day: Statement by First Vice-President Timmermans and Commissioners Thyssen and Jourová', Press release. Available online at: http://europa.eu/rapid/press-release_STATEMENT-17-4241_en.htm. Last accessed 20 June 2018.

European Commission (2017e) *State of the Union Address 2017*. Available online at: http://europa.eu/rapid/press-release_SPEECH-17-3165_en.htm. Last accessed 20 June 2018.

European Institute for Gender Equality (2017) 'Gender Equality Index 2017: Measuring Gender Equality in the European Union 2005–2015'. Available online at: http://eige.europa.eu/rdc/eige-publications/gender-equality-index-2017-measuring-gender-equality-european-union-2005-2015-report. Last accessed 20 June 2018.

Ferrera, M. (2017) 'The Stein Rokkan Lecture 2016 Mission Impossible? Reconciling Economic and Social Europe after the Euro Crisis and Brexit'. *European Journal of Political Research*, Vol. 56, No. 1, pp. 3–22.

Galligan, Y. (2017) 'Filtering Out, Filtering In: What Place for Gender in European Economic Plans?' In MacRae, H. and Weiner, E. (eds) *Towards Gendering Institutionalism: Equality in Europe* (London: Rowman and Littlefield), pp. 25–41.

Gearty, C. (2015) 'The State of Freedom in Europe'. *European Law Journal*, Vol. 26, No. 1, pp. 21, 706–21.

Gill, S. and Roberts, A. (2011) 'Macroeconomic Governance, Gendered Inequality, and Global Crises'. In Young, B., Bakker, I. and Elson, D. (eds) *Questioning Financial Governance from a Feminist Perspective* (Abingdon Oxon: Routledge), pp. 155–73.

Gillespie, G. and Khan, U. (2016) 'Integrating Economic and Social Policy: Childcare a Transformational Policy?' In Campbell, J. and Gillespie, M. (eds) *Feminist Economics and Public Policy* (Abingdon, Oxon: Routledge), pp. 94–100.

Griffin, P. (2015) 'Crisis, Austerity and Gendered Governance: A Feminist Perspective'. *Feminist Review*, Vol. 109, No. 1, pp. 49–72.

Griffin, P. (2017) 'Financial Governance 'after' Crisis: On the Liminality of the Global Financial Crisis and its 'Afterwards', Through a Gender Lens'. *Politics*, Vol. 37, No. 4, pp. 402–17.

Grown, K., Elson, D. and Catagay, N. (2000) 'Introduction Special Issue'. *World Development*, Vol. 28, No. 7, pp. 1145–56.

Guerrina, R., Haastrup, T., A. M. Wright, K., Masselot, A., MacRae, H. and Cavaghan, R. (2018) 'Does European Union Studies Have a Gender Problem? Experiences From Researching Brexit'. *International Journal of Feminist Politics*, Vol. 20, No. 2, pp. 252–7.

Hancock, A.M. (2007) 'When Multiplication Doesn't Equal Quick Addition: Examining Intersectionality as a Research Paradigm'. *Perspectives on Politics.*, Vol. 5, No. 1, pp. 63–79.

Hodson, D. (2017) 'Eurozone Governance in 2016: The Italian Banking Crisis, Fiscal Flexibility and Brexit (Plus Plus Plus)'. *JCMS Annual Review*, Vol. 55, pp. 118–32.

Hoskyns, C. (1996) *Integrating Gender: Women, Law and Politics in the European Union* (London: Verso).

Hoskyns, C. (2008) 'Governing the EU: Gender and Macroeconomics'. In Rai, S. and Waylen, G. (eds) *Global Governance: Feminist Perspectives* (Houndmills, Basingstoke: Palgrave Macmillan), pp), pp. 107–28.

Hozic, A.A. and True, J. (2016) *Scandalous Economics: The Spectre of Gender and Global Financial Crisis* (Oxford: Oxford University Press).

Jones, E. (2009) 'Output Legitimacy and the Global Financial Crisis: Perceptions Matter'. *JCMS*, Vol. 47, No. 5, pp. 1085–105.

Karamessini, M. (2014) 'Structural Crisis and Adjustment in Greece: Social Regression and the Challenge to Gender Equality'. In Karamessini, M. and Rubery, J. (eds) *Women and Austerity: The Economic Crisis and the Future for Gender Equality* (Oxford: Routledge), pp. 165–85.

Karamessini, M. and Rubery, J. (2014) *Women and Austerity: The Economic Crisis and the Future for Gender Equality* (London: Routledge).

Kinnvall, C. (2016) 'The Postcolonial Has Moved into Europe: Bordering, Security and Ethno-Cultural Belonging'. *JCMS*, Vol. 54, No. 1, pp. 152–68.

Klatzer, E. and Schlager, C. (2014) 'Feminist Perspectives on Macroeconomics: Reconfiguration of Gendered Power Structures and Erosion of Gender Equality Through the New Economic Governance Regime of the European Union'. In Evan, M., Hammings, C., Henry, M., Johnstone, H., Madhock, S. and Plomien, A. (eds) *The Sage Handbook of Feminist Theory* (Boulder, CO: Sage), pp. 283–99.

Kronsell, A. (2005) 'Gender, Power and European Integration Theory'. *Journal of European Public Policy*, Vol. 12, No. 6, pp. 1022–40.

Manners, I. and Whitman, R. (2016) 'Another Theory is Possible: Dissident Voices in Theorising Europe: Dissident Voices in Theorising Europe'. *JCMS*, Vol. 54, No. 1, pp. 3–18.

Maricut, A. and Puetter, U. (2018) 'Deciding on the European Semester: The European Council, The Council and the Enduring Asymmetry between Economic and Social Policy Issues'. *Journal of European Public Policy*, Vol. 25, No. 2, pp. 193–211.

Mills, C.W. (2007) 'White Ignorance'. In Sullivan, S. and Tuana, N. (eds) *Race and Epistemologies of Ignorance* (New York: State University of New York Press), pp. 13–38.

O'Dwyer, M. (2017) 'Gendering Ideational Political Economy in the European Union', Paper presented at the European Conference on Politics and Gender, Lausanne, 8–10 June.

O'Dwyer, M. (2018) 'Making Sense of Austerity: The Gendered Ideas of European Economic Policy'. *Comparative European Politics*, (forthcoming).

Picchio, A. (2015) 'A Feminist Political-Economy Narrative Against Austerity'. *International Journal of Political Economy*, Vol. 44, No. 4, pp. 250–9.

Rosamond, B. (2002) 'Imagining the European Economy: "Competitiveness" and the Social Construction of "Europe" as an Economic Space'. *New Political Economy*, Vol. 7, No. 2, pp. 157–77.

Ryner, M. (2015) 'Europe's Ordoliberal Iron Cage: Critical Political Economy, the Euro Area Crisis and its Management'. *Journal of European Public Policy*, Vol. 22, No. 2, pp. 275–94.

Scharpf, F.W. (2013) 'Political Legitimacy in a Non-Optimal Currency Area. Democratic Politics in a European Union under Stress'. In Cramme, O. and Hobolt, S. (eds) *Democratic Politics in a European Union Under Stress* (Oxford: Oxford University Press), pp. 19–47.

Schmidt, V. (2016) 'The Resilience of "Bad Ideas" in Eurozone Crisis Discourse (even as Rival Ideas Inform Changing Practices)', Paper presented at The 23rd International Conference of Europeanists, Philadelphia, 14–16 April.

Schuberth, H. and Young, B. (2011) 'The Role of Gender in Governance of the Financial Sector'. In Young, B., Bakker, I. and Elson, D. (eds) *Questioning Financial Governance from a Feminist Perspective* (Abingdon Oxon: Routledge), pp. 132–54.

Skjeie, H. (2006) 'Gender Equality: On Travel Metaphors and Duties to Yield'. In Sirkku, K.H., Holli, A.M. and Daskalova, K. (eds) *Women's Citizenship and Political Rights* (London: Palgrave Macmillan), pp. 86–104.

Strolovitch, D.Z. (2013) 'Of Mancessions and Hecoveries: Race, Gender, and the Political Construction of Economic Crises and Recoveries'. *Perspectives on Politics*, Vol. 11, No. 1, pp. 167–76.

Wekker, G. (2016) *White Innocence: Paradoxes of Colonialism and Race* (Durham, NC: Duke University Press).

Williams, F. (2003) 'Contesting "Race" and Gender in the European Union: A Multi Layered Recognition Struggle for Voice and Visibility'. In Hobson, B. (ed.) *Recognition Struggles and Social Movements Contested Identities, Agency and Power* (Cambridge: Cambridge University Press), pp. 121–44.

JCMS 2018 Volume 56. Annual Review pp. 109–119   DOI: 10.1111/jcms.12774

Austerity and the Politics of Becoming

AKWUGO EMEJULU[1] and LEAH BASSEL[2]
[1]University of Warwick [2]University of Leicester

Introduction

In this short contribution, we attempt to explore the ways in which austerity measures – deficit reductions through tax increases and cuts to public spending – generate unexpected political subjectivities among women of colour activists in Britain. In particular, we examine how the dramatic cuts to public spending and the privatization of public services simultaneously subject women of colour by further destabilizing their already precarious economic position *and* create new possibilities for women becoming radical agents for social change. We argue that the dynamic for mapping this process of women of colour becoming new (or, at least, different) political agents is found in the oftentimes disrespected and devalued social relations of caring and care work (Erel, 2011). We argue that caring for and about Others is a dual process of subjectivation through the (re) privatization of care through the roll back of the social welfare state and a politics of becoming which generates new solidarities for collective action among women of colour.

Taking seriously the dynamics of women of colour's activism under austerity matters because it disrupts the binary in EU studies scholarship that privileges a focus on the macro politics of EU institutions over the lived experiences and outcomes at the microlevel. By intruding into this space to tell a different kind of story about austerity politics, it might perhaps be possible to reframe how we think about the ongoing economic crisis, whose interests are served by governing institutions and how we might think differently about resistance to the crisis – beyond the tropes of documenting a populist far-right backlash. We begin by first mapping the changing landscape of austerity and its disproportionate impact on women of colour in Britain. We then turn to explore how women of colour confront the challenge of care by investigating how care acts as both a barrier to public space and as the fulcrum for a new public politics.

I. The Material and Discursive Violence of Austerity

The 2008 economic crisis was sparked after global financial institutions gambled with subprime mortgages through complicated synthetic financial instruments such as collateralized debt obligations, and plunged global capitalism into chaos after these supposedly 'safe' investments rapidly depreciated (Bassel and Emejulu, 2017a). In order to save the global capitalist system, nation states in which the crisis was concentrated, such as Britain and the United States, bailed out these institutions through a massive transfer of wealth. It is this transfer of wealth from public to private hands that then sparked austerity measures. In Britain, since 2008, more than £1,162 billion has been allocated to saving ailing financial institutions from collapse (National Audit Office, 2017). Unlike what took place in the eurozone,

Britain chose to undertake a voluntary programme of austerity. The massive hole in the public accounts had to be reconciled and austerity was the policy proposal taken up in Britain in 2010. Indeed, the then Conservative-Liberal Democrat government led by David Cameron saw the crisis as an opportunity to dramatically reshape the British social welfare state and the conception of social citizenship (Bassel and Emejulu, 2017a). Britain is distinctive in its response to the crisis as austerity was, for a time, justified across the political left and the right as a consequence of an overweening social welfare state. However, this surprisingly durable economic consensus among elite state actors has now fractured with the Labour Party, the official opposition, breaking ranks under the leadership of Jeremy Corbyn and the Shadow Chancellor, John McDowell, to call for an end to austerity and a return to the social welfare settlements of the post-war period (The Labour Party, 2017).

Curiously in the British context and in the context of the *JCMS Annual Review*, debates about Brexit and austerity remain almost completely separate. Although the worst is yet to come in terms of austerity with more than £12 billion of cuts to public services still to be implemented, this programme of cuts and privatizations is not necessarily informing Britain's approach to economic and monetary policy after its planned exit from the EU. Instead, austerity has largely disappeared from public debate; it seems to have been crowded out by the on-going difficulties of the protracted Brexit negotiations.

What is important to note about the economic crisis and austerity measures is that they are largely represented as crises for an undifferentiated middle class and the *white* working class. In the hegemonic discursive constructions, the middle classes experience the crisis as a new phenomenon of precarity: a university graduate will have to struggle on zero-hour contracts for long periods; permanent, well-paid jobs are difficult to find; final salary pension schemes have closed; it has become increasingly difficult to get on the housing ladder. Thus, in one sense, the crisis is represented as a temporary inconvenience for the economically privileged. For groups who can draw on their wealth to secure their economic position and buy access to vital social welfare services such as healthcare and education, austerity is largely an invisible process. The crisis and austerity have also been represented as an insurmountable challenge for the white working classes. In these discursive constructions, white working class men and women have found themselves in circumstances where local services have disappeared and the eligibility requirements for certain kinds of benefit have become more stringent (Goodhart, 2017). These tough economic conditions combine with an already existing hostility to immigration, which, in turn, become the explanatory factor for a backlash against the establishment as seen in the 2016 Brexit vote, misrepresented as the will of the 'white working class' (Emejulu, 2016).

This dominant narrative is compelling but misleading in that it erases the complex dynamics of race, class, gender and legal status that have helped to determine which groups have been hardest hit by the crisis and austerity. The economic crisis has been a slow-moving disaster for women of colour which they experience largely outside the public eye. As we have documented in great detail elsewhere (Bassel and Emejulu, 2017a, 2017b; Emejulu and Bassel, 2015, 2017a, 2017b;) women of colour are impacted by the crisis and austerity measures both discursively and materially. Firstly, women of colour largely disappear in accounts of the crisis and austerity. There can be no place for women of colour in the story of the economic crisis as their experiences confound the hegemonic narrative. Both middle class and working class women of colour – but particularly Pakistani, Bangladeshi and Black African women – have seen their household incomes plummet since 2008 (see Women's Budget Group (2018) for further details). This is for two reasons. First, women of colour, on the whole, are more likely to be living in the poorest households and are more likely to be unemployed, underemployed or in low-skilled, low-paid work. Second, women of colour are also more likely to be living in larger households with more dependents – older adults and children – requiring care. Thus when public spending – particularly real terms cuts in unemployment insurance and housing benefit – is curtailed, these women lose a vital source of household income. Importantly, when controlling for class, women of colour in a more secure economic position also see greater falls in their income in comparison to their white counterparts. This is because these women are more likely to work for the state in the feminized caring professions of teaching, social work and nursing. Thus, when public spending is cut, this also destabilizes employment – and income – for women of colour.

In this tumultuous year in which we have witnessed far right and proto-fascist groups make important breakthroughs in electoral politics particularly in Germany and Italy, women of colour disrupt the taken-for-granted narrative about the relationship between austerity and the populist far-right politics. Women of colour's precarity under austerity has not seen them turn against immigration or vote for racist and xenophobic parties. In fact, we are currently seeing a revival in radical grassroots Black feminist and Afrofeminist politics in Europe (Emejulu and Sobande, forthcoming, 2019). Thus, the dynamics under austerity are more nuanced than is usually represented. However, in order to capture this complexity we need to have an appreciation of intersecting inequalities – unequal social and economic outcomes derived from the ways in which race, class, gender and legal status interact – and an understanding of how care work in both private and public spaces, creates particular kinds of political subjectivities for women of colour. It is to this point we now turn.

II. Subjectivation by Care: Muslim Women and 'Failed Care[1]'

We now explore how caring for and about Others is a *dual* process of subjectivation. In this section we explore the first face of care. Through migrant women of colour's experiences of becoming British citizens we see the (re) privatization of care and roll back of the social welfare state at work. This face of the politics of becoming (see also Khan, 2019) is one in which care is turned against some women of colour, for not caring in the 'right ways' to instil 'British values' and prevent extremism. Yet, at the same time, the increasingly neoliberal nature of the process (Turner, 2014) exacerbates the ways in which the broader withdrawal of state care and support of women can severely hamper some women of colour's participation in the naturalization process and public life more generally.

Care acts both as a barrier to public space and as the fulcrum for a new public politics (Bassel and Emejulu, 2017b; Erel, 2011; Lister, 2008). In the process of becoming British citizens, migrant women of colour face a vortex of conflicting demands (Bassel and Khan, in progress; Bassel, 2016).[2] In particular Muslim migrant women – specifically Pakistani and Bangladeshi Muslim women – are often portrayed in public discourse and social

---

[1]The findings on the naturalization process in the UK are drawn from work supported by the Economic and Social Research Council (grant number ES/K010174/1). The research material can be accessed on the UK Data Service ReShare website, persistent identifier: 10.5255/UKDA-SN-852967.
[2]This section draws on the Economic and Social Research Council project 'The UK citizenship Process: Exploring Immigrants' Experiences' (ES/K010174/1) and specifically Bassel and Khan's article in preparation.

integration policy as victims of social isolation who need English to do their job of social-izing young people better (more generally see Luibhéid, 2006; Tyler, 2013). We can un-derstand the ways in which these Muslim women are interpellated by the state as 'failed care'. Muslim women are portrayed as isolated victims for whom no one cares (except, grudgingly the state) and also passive objects who fail to care for – and sufficiently con-trol – their sons which leads to violent disorder and extremism.

These refrains of failed care have been consistently repeated by state actors – on both the left and the right – for almost 20 years. One of the earliest instances of the deployment of failed care is seen in the Labour government's response to rioting in the northern En-glish cities of Oldham, Bradford and Burnley in 2001. The multiple causes of these riots, including intimidation and violence by far right groups, were largely ignored. Instead, the disorder was attributed to the lack of English proficiency, particularly of mothers of the young men who participated in the disorder (who, it should be noted, did not participate in the rioting and for whom it was assumed they could not speak English). A 'meaningful concept of citizenship' was needed, that would foster loyalty to the nation (Turner, 2014, p. 337).[3] Understanding English was linked with social cohesion and ultimately led in 2005 to the introduction of a naturalization process that seeks to bureaucratically impose 'British values' via citizenship tests, a ceremony, and administrative procedures in order to 'become' a British citizen. The citizenship test, in particular, was posited as the solution to a lack of community cohesion and the failed care of Muslim mothers.

More recently and especially in the context of young British people travelling to Syria to join Islamic State (IS), the former Prime Minister David Cameron called for an end to the 'passive tolerance' of separate communities which, he argued, left many Muslim women facing discrimination and social isolation, and proposed the launch of a £20 mil-lion language fund (*The Guardian*, 2016). The proposals mandated that migrant women demonstrate proficiency in the English language if they were living in the United Kingdom on a five year spousal visa, and left open the possibility that these women would be detained and deported if they were unable to provide evidence of improvement in the language. Similar to the Labour government's response in 2001, young Muslims' disor-der was attributed to their mothers' failed care and lack of English.

Dame Louise Casey's *Review into Opportunity and Integration* (2016) commissioned by David Cameron evokes the same failed care figure: the Muslim woman – particularly the Pakistani and/or Bangladeshi Muslim woman – who is simultaneously a victim of domestic violence, socially isolated, facing discrimination in the job market and unemployed, failing to learn English and, as a result, struggling to manage her children. In addition to language provision for these women, Casey proposed to reinvent the pro-cess through which one becomes a British citizen 'which is of huge national, cultural and symbolic value' to include 'an Oath of Integration with British Values and Society on arrival, rather than awaiting a final citizenship test' (Casey, 2016, p. 168).

Cameron's pledge to support Muslim women to learn English and Casey's very gen-eral recommendation to support 'targeted English language provision' are silent on the state withdrawal of care through austerity. They do not acknowledge the legacy of

---

[3]Adrian Blackledge notes the significance of extending the language requirement to those applying on the basis of marriage in the Nationality Act 2002. 'Asian immigrant women should be required to learn English as soon as possible, because their failure to do so brings about community segregation and lack of social cohesion which threatens society' (Blackledge, 2005).

funding cuts to English for Speakers of Other Languages (ESOL) services which have contributed to social isolation. Instead, failed care, which is transmitted through culture and religion, are constructed as the problem, and English language training and a new and improved citizenship test process, the solution (Bassel, 2016). English language, as before, is to act as the 'panacea' (Greenwood and Robins, 2002, p. 507; Sasse, 2005, p. 678) to the ills caused by a lack of integration (Khan, 2013) and serve as an antidote to radicalization. These Muslim migrant women are the vehicle for this panacea of English language because they are biological and social 'reproducers' of the nation (Yuval-Davis and Anthias, 1989; Yuval-Davis and Anthias, 1997), who will, it is argued, raise young people with the correct values (Lonergan, 2017; Yuval-Davis et al., 2005; see also Morrice, 2016a). It is vital, according to Casey, for this existing culture of failed care to be transformed by using the English language as the vehicle to impose the correct British values – and in turn, the correct forms of care and control – on Muslim groups.

Yet, for those women of colour targeted by these discourses and policies, austerity looms large in experiences of becoming British. Government funding for ESOL has been dramatically cut back and a 2011 Equality Impact Assessment demonstrated that women and ethnic minorities would be disproportionately affected (BIS, 2011). In July 2015 the Skills Funding Agency announced that ESOL courses for students receiving Job Seeker's Allowance would be cut with immediate effect, affecting 16,000 individuals and again with a disproportionate effect on female and ethnic minority learners (Ashworth, 2016).

Finally, we can see how discourses of 'failed care' intersect with a broader 'crisis of care' that shapes women of colour's experiences of becoming British citizens. According to Nancy Fraser, this crisis of care takes a particular shape: alongside state and corporate disinvestment from social welfare (particularly but not exclusively since the 2008 economic crisis), women are recruited into the paid workforce, externalizing care work onto families and communities while diminishing their capacity to perform it. The result is a new, dualized organization of social reproduction, commodified for those who can pay for it and privatized for those who cannot, as some in the second category provide care work in return for (low) wages for those in the first category (Fraser, 2016, p. 112). As we have argued above, this is not new. What changes is how the crisis is resolved for some and made worse for others, particularly women of colour. And for some poor and working class Muslim women, their failed care, in this broader crisis of care, means they become objects of state intervention and demonization.

When experiencing the process of trying to become a British citizen both material and discursive dimensions of austerity come to light.[4] Cost is a key challenge: a minimum of £1000 per adult (£50 for the test, over £1000 for naturalization, plus any preparation courses, solicitor fees, etc.) (Bassel et al., 2017, p. 19). These findings echo studies on legalization processes in the United States which document how 'gender and class intersect to make the legalization process unaffordable – and eventual legalization unachievable – for the poorest women' (Salcido and Menjívar, 2012, p. 353).

---

[4]This withdrawal coincides with increasingly demanding test requirements through which it is no longer possible to obtain citizenship through the 'ESOL with citizenship' route where a course could be taken instead of a computer-based exam. This was a realistic route for migrant women with lower language proficiency (Morrice, 2016b). Since October 2013 both language proficiency and passing the Life in the UK computer-based test were required. These challenges are erased when visibility in public debate is tied directly to being a threat to British values and a victim of patriarchal oppression.

The lack of childcare acts as a barrier to preparation that has become more acute under austerity. Preparation strategies themselves are highly gendered in the broader context of 'time crunch' and the politics of survival that women of colour negotiate under austerity in Britain (Bassel and Emejulu, 2017a). Every minute counts between childcare responsibilities that some women of colour living the 'crisis of care' are not able to outsource so must cover themselves, while at the same time trying to meet the demanding requirements of the naturalization process. It has become increasingly difficult to access affordable preparation and English language classes that have childcare facilities, further impeding access to the ESOL classroom. Public services, particularly childcare, libraries and sports activities for children, had been the key way in which some migrant women could participate in everyday life alongside caring responsibilities (Lonergan, 2015). Cuts to these services, particularly at the local level, isolate women who are already in a precarious social and economic position.

The citizenship test process appears to be gender neutral but, in fact, interacts with gendered social structures and ideologies (Salcido and Menjívar, 2012), including the gendered division of labour and of caring responsibilities. It is part and parcel of the austere politics of becoming, literally becoming a British citizen in this case. This face of subjectivation by care is the product of border control and austerity through which migrant women of colour experience material and discursive violence and barriers to public space.

However, women of colour are not merely objects of state policy and control. In the next section, we examine how austerity spurs new resistances through which caring and care work is the spark.

III. Care as a Freedom Dream

Care creates unexpected political possibilities for women of colour. To only view care as a barrier to public space and to collective action is to misunderstand the complex ways in which care operates to simultaneously close down and open up opportunities for activism (Bassel and Emejulu, 2017b). In mapping women's of colour's activism against austerity, against the far right and for migrants' rights in London,[5] we find that care is the crucial social relationship that guides many women's activism and is an important dynamic for building solidarity for collective action.

For these activists, we can think about care as both a praxis – theory informed action – and as prefiguration – a process of becoming and creating new political subjectivities. To understand care as praxis is to recognize how *caring about Others* is a radical act. *To care about Others* requires the development of a political imagination that takes seriously the lived experiences of the most marginalized. This caring is radical particularly in the context of the commodified care as we discussed above. Caring in this sense is not mere empathy but an act of re-valuing and re-validating the views and experiences of those who are systematically dehumanized and disrespected because of their particular positioning at the intersections of race, class, gender and legal status.

[5] This section draws on the University of Warwick funded project, 'The Politics of Catastrophe', in which Akwugo Emejulu is the principal investigator. We thank Inez van der Scheer for her research assistance on this project.

For instance, this British Asian anti-deportations activist in London discusses how care and protection for Others is the foundation for how she knows and understands the social world and this care makes possible her radical activism against the British state's border regime:

> 'What is central to basically how I frame all of my politics is I know the things I do are because I have this sense of having care for the people around me ... But then how does that feed into ... sharing radical politics ... and making sure that we can continue to undo the power of ... state institutions' (Interview, MR1, London, 2018).

Here we can see how care operates as a freedom dream. Care is the organizing principle that galvanizes collective action but caring about others does not end with protecting groups from harm. To care about Others makes possible the ability to build solidarity and seek to counter state violence. We see care operate in a similar way for this British Asian prison abolitionist in London. For her, care represents a window to a new world. To care about others is to imagine a society in which everyone – but especially women of colour and migrant women – are cared for by the state and by other citizens:

> 'forty-six per cent of women in prison are also survivors of domestic violence. A lot of the women who go through the refuge system are also the women who go through the prison system ... An understanding that a world without prisons is a world where we have adequate services ... for domestic violence, for addiction, for housing, for employment, like mental health services' (Interview, PA1, London, 2017).

Note how the state functions very differently for each of these activists. For the anti-deportations activist, the state must be dismantled – there is no hope for reform. For the prison abolitionist, however, there is a possibility of reform by transforming the state from a punitive to an egalitarian and redistributive institution.

To care about Others also involves caring about the impact and consequences of one's collective action processes. For this mixed race anti-austerity activist in London, we can see how caring means recognizing Others as political subjects and struggling to build coalitions so that everyone can be free:

> 'We're completely autonomous [as a collective] ... But we have to look to where our points of reference have got the experience over many decades of how you work collectively, how you work in a way which does not undermine anybody else's struggle, but in fact does everything possible to bring ... struggles together in a principled way, and in a way that is not about personal ambition, but it's about a complete ambition for all of us, a whole movement' (Interview, AA1, London, 2018).

We can also understand care as prefiguration. By 'prefiguration' we mean politics that seek to build and live a future new world through practices in the present. For the activists we interviewed, *caring for Others* is to refuse neoliberal, racist, sexist, xenophobic, homophobic, ableist frameworks that govern their everyday lives. Thus, to care for Others is an act of refusal and an act of becoming simultaneously: care rejects hierarchical domination and attempts to create new political subjectivities.

For example, this woman of colour prison abolitionist describes her prefigurative politics like this: 'At the end of the day what I'm really interested in is creating an alternative social reality ... we've got a glimmer of what it would be like to live otherwise in a world that isn't this world and that was beautiful' (Interview, PA2, London, 2017). This activist was involved in a high profile occupation of the site of a former women's prison. In a 'place of so much pain' it was important to create 'something beautiful' (Interview, PA2, London, 2017) and live, even for a short while, the new world. The motivation for the occupation was that the prison was a place of *carelessness*: where families were broken up, where women of colour experienced institutionalized abuse and/or died under suspicious circumstances and where women, who should have been receiving support for mental health problems or as a survivors of domestic violence, were criminalized. To occupy the prison was a bold act of radical care to recognize and remember the inmates' suffering and to try to build a new politics through caring about them, their families and their struggles.

Activists also use care as a way to create radical political identities. Through self-care and by valuing themselves as activists attempting to survive everyday life, they are able to build community and take radical action – such as direct action to oppose funding cuts to anti-violence against women's services, in the case of this British Asian activist:

> 'That self-care, self-preservation Audre Lorde stuff … Like how radical is it in this world where no one wants us to have a nice time and enjoy things … It comes back down to we [women of colour activists] are more concerned about survival than like this longer term … idealised, I dunno, communist, socialist, whatever, society' (Interview, PA3, London, 2017).

Through a prefigurative politics of care, this allows the activist women we spoke with to revalue the kinds of activism that are important to them but that are too often delegitimized by ostensible social movement allies: that of everyday survival. Survival may not be prefigurative but recognizing and taking seriously the struggle to stay alive under violent and oppressive austerity measures, border enforcement and carceral regimes makes possible the ability to think expansively about what politics is, what politics looks like and who gets to be a political agent. In this way, the activist women attempt to create new political subjectivities by using care as a way to revalorise their grassroots activism and understand it as a radical politics of everyday possibility. Care also functions as a bridge to a new world in which the violent systems that devalue, disrespect and delegitimize women of colour are destroyed and a new world is built that puts caring for and about Others at its heart.

Conclusions

In this contribution we have attempted to explore the dual processes of care for women of colour in Britain. To understand what the EU is and how it functions it is important to map the ways in which those who are forcibly invisibilized and silenced speak and take action in and against governing institutions. Mapping the micropolitics of women of colour activists is crucial as a counter-narrative to the incomplete but nevertheless hegemonic story that typically gets told about European austerity politics. Exploring the dynamics of care for women of colour gives an insight to the hidden yet consequential politics of domination and resistance. On the one hand, care further subjects women to state intervention, control and violence. For Muslim migrant women in particular, a discourse of failed care is deployed against them to justify everyday state intrusions in their lives. These failed care discourses are further exacerbated by austerity measures and a tightening border regime in which women are compelled to 'become' British citizens but the means to do so are withheld from them because of dramatic cuts to local services and seemingly impossible eligibility requirements for naturalization and citizenship. Care, however, also functions as a galvanizing force for collective action. In the context of the current Conservative government's hostile environment policy and on-going austerity measures, caring for and about Others functions as a practice of freedom – a refusal to re-produce hierarchical exclusions and violence. Caring for and about others also functions as a hopeful and hoped for future. To care for others – especially the despised and disrespected – helps to build the new world in the present. To care is to make real a fragile and precarious utopia. To care for others is to become free, even for a short time.

Care is a double-edged sword of domination and resistance. Care is a politics of be-coming. For women of colour, care is a process by which one is compelled to act. Women of colour's struggle for justice and recognition cannot be separated from caring and care work. How women of colour care is the foundation of their public politics and the norma-tive case for care is crucial for understanding the micropolitics of EU studies.

References

Ashworth, J. (2016) *'If Cameron Wants Female Migrants To Learn English, Why Did He Cut ESOL Funding?' The Spectator*, 18 January. Available online at: http://blogs.spectator.co.uk/2016/01/if-cameron-wants-female-migrants-to-learn-english-why-did-he-cut-esol-funding/. Accessed 20 June 2018.

Bassel, L. (2016) 'The Casey Review on Opportunity and Integration: Re-Inventing the Wheel'. *Discover Society.*, Available online at: http://discoversociety.org/2016/12/09/the-casey-re-view-on-opportunity-and-integration-re-inventing-the-wheel/.

Bassel, L. and Emejulu, A. (2017a) *Minority Women and Austerity: Survival and Resistance in France and Britain* (Bristol: Policy Press).

Bassel, L. and Emejulu, A. (2017b) 'Caring Subjects: Migrant Women and the Third Sector in Scotland and England'. *Journal of Ethnic and Racial Studies*, Vol. 41, No. 1, pp. 36–54.

Bassel, L., Monforte, P., Bartram, D., Khan, K. and Misztal, B. (2017) *The UK Citizenship Test Process: Exploring Migrants' Experiences. Final Project Report* (Leicester: University of Leicester) Available online at: https://www2.le.ac.uk/departments/sociology/research/uk-citi-zenship-process/final-report.

Bassel, L. and Khan, K. in progress(forthcoming) 'Austere Citizens: Women's Experiences of the Citizenship Test Process in the United Kingdom'. *Sociology*.

BIS (2011) English for Speakers of Other Languages (ESOL) equality impact assessment (London: Department for Business, Innovation and Skills). Available online at: https://assets.publishing.service.gov.uk/government/uploads/system/uploads/attachment_data/file/32297/11-1045-english-for-speakers-of-other-languages-equality-impact.pdf.

Blackledge, A. (2005) *Discourse and Power in a Multilingual World* (Amsterdam: John Benjamin Publishing).

Casey, L. (2016) *The Casey Review: A Review into Opportunity and Integration* (London: Queen's Printer and Controller of Her Majesty's Stationery Office).

Emejulu, A. (2016) *On the Hideous Whiteness of Brexit* (Verso Books) https://www.versobooks.com/blogs/2733-on-the-hideous-whiteness-of-brexit-let-us-be-honest-about-our-past-and-our-present-if-we-truly-seek-to-dismantle-white-supremacy.

© 2018 The Authors. JCMS: Journal of Common Market Studies published by University Association for Contemporary European Studies and John Wiley & Sons Ltd

Emejulu, A. and Bassel, L. (2015) 'Minority Women, Activism and Austerity'. *Race & Class*, Vol. 57, No. 2, pp. 86–95.

Emejulu, A. and Bassel, L. (2017a) 'Whose Crisis Counts? Minority Women, Austerity and Activism in France and Britain'. In Kantola, J. and Lombardo, E. (eds) *Gender and the Economic Crisis in Europe* (London: Palgrave).

Emejulu, A. and Bassel, L. (2017b) 'Resisting Epistemic Violence: Women of Colour's Anti-Austerity Activism'. In Whyte, D. and Cooper, V. (eds) *The Violence of Austerity* (London: Pluto Press).

Emejulu, A. and Sobande, F. (eds) (2019) *To Exist is to Resist: Black Feminism in Europe* (London: Pluto Press), forthcoming.

Erel, U. (2011) 'Reframing Migrant Mothers as Citizens'. *Citizenship Studies*, Vol. 15, No. 6–7, pp. 695–709.

Fraser, N. (2016) 'Contradictions of Capital and Care'. *New Left Review*, Vol. 100, pp. 99–117.

Goodhart, D. (2017) 'Why Self-interest Isn't the Same as Racism''. *The Financial Times*, Available online at: https://www.ft.com/content/220090e0-efc1-11e6-ba01-119a44939bb6.

Greenwood, J. and Robins, L. (2002) 'Citizenship Tests and Education: Embedding a Concept'. *Parliamentary Affairs*, Vol. 55, pp. 505–22.

Khan, K. (2013) *'Becoming British: A Migrant's Journey'*, mimeo (University of Birmingham).

Khan, K. (2019) *Becoming a Citizen: Linguistic Trials and Negotiations* (London: Bloomsbury).

Party, L. (2017) *For the Many, Not the Few: The Labour Party Manifesto 2017* (London: The Labour Party) Available online at: https://labour.org.uk/wp-content/uploads/2017/10/labour-manifesto-2017.pdf.

Lister, R. (2008) 'Inclusive Citizenship: Realising the Potential'. In Isin, E.F., Nyers, P. and Turner, B.S. (eds) *Citizenship Between Past and Future* (London: Routledge).

Lonergan, G. (2015) 'Migrant Women and Social Reproduction under Austerity'. *Feminist Review*, Vol. 109, No. 1, pp. 124–45.

Lonergan, G. (2017) 'Reproducing the 'National Home': Gendering Domopolitics'. *Citizenship Studies*, Vol. 22, No. 1, pp. 1–18.

Luibhéid, E. (2006) 'Sexual Regimes and Migration Controls: Reproducing the Irish Nation-State in Transnational Contexts'. *Feminist Review*, Vol. 83, pp. 60–78.

Morrice, L. (2016a) 'Cultural Values, Moral Sentiments and the Fashioning of Gendered Migrant Identities'. *Journal of Ethnic and Migration Studies*, Vol. 43, No. 3, pp. 400–17.

Morrice, L. (2016b) 'British Citizenship, Gender and Migration: The Containment of Cultural Differences and the Stratification of Belonging'. *British Journal of Sociology of Education*, Vol. 38, No. 5, pp. 597–609.

National Audit Office (2017) Taxpayer Support for UK Banks: FAQs. Available online at: https://www.nao.org.uk/highlights/taxpayer-support-for-uk-banks-faqs/. Accessed 20 June 2018.

Salcido, O. and Menjívar, C. (2012) 'Gendered Paths to Legal Citizenship: The Case of Latin American Immigrants in Phoenix'. *Law and Society Review*, Vol. 46, No. 2, pp. 335–68.

Sasse, G. (2005) 'Securitization or Securing Rights? Exploring the Conceptual Foundations of Policies towards Minorities and Migrants in Europe'. *JCMS*, Vol. 43, No. 4, pp. 673–93.

Tyler, D.I. (2013) *Revolting Subjects: Social Abjection and Resistance in Neoliberal Britain* (London: Zed Books).

The Guardian (2016) *'Muslim Women to be Taught English in £20m Plan to Beat "Backward Attitudes"'*, 18 January.

Turner, J. (2014) 'Testing the Liberal Subject: (In) security, Responsibility and "Self-Improvement" in the UK Citizenship Test'. *Citizenship Studies*, Vol. 18, No. 3–4, pp. 332–48.

Women's Budget Group (2018) 'Intersecting Inequality: The Impact of Austerity on BME Women in the UK', 30 January. Available online at: https://wbg.org.uk/main-feature/intersecting-in-equalities-impact-austerity-bme-women-uk/

Yuval-Davis, N. and Anthias, F. (eds) (1989) *Woman, Nation, State* (London: Palgrave Macmillan).

Yuval-Davis, N. and Anthias, F. (1997) *Gender, Race and Nation* (London: Sage).

Yuval-Davis, N., Anthias, F. and Kofman, E. (2005) 'Secure Borders, Safe Haven and the Gendered Politics of Belonging: Beyond Social Cohesion'. *Ethnic and Racial Studies*, Vol. 28, No. 3, pp. 513–35.

Interviews

Interview participant	Location of interview	Date of interview
MR1 is a British Asian anti-deportations activist	London	January 2018
PA1 is a British Asian prison abolitionist	London	December 2017
AA1 is a mixed race anti-austerity activist	London	January 2018
PA2 is a woman of colour prison abolitionist	London	December 2017

JCMS 2018 Volume 56. Annual Review pp. 120–130   DOI: 10.1111/jcms.12763

The Politics of European Union Migration Governance*

ANDREW GEDDES
European University Institute

Introduction

Crises are often understood as an opportunity for change. In a strategic note prepared by the European Political Strategy Centre (EPSC) – the European Commission President's in-house think tank – it was noted not only that the 'age of migration is here to stay' but that 'the current crisis is an opportunity for system overhaul' (EPSC, 2015, p. 1). Others are more sceptical of the possibility for change, arguing that EU institutional and policy priorities on migration and asylum were established in the late 1990s and early 2000s and have led to significant path dependencies, which means that initial policy choices driven by security concerns are difficult to shift (Guiraudon, 2017). While crises attract attention, the EU's response draws from practices dating back more than 25 years. Perhaps of greater significance, in 2017, was further evidence of the political effects of migration governance. Efforts to relocate asylum applicants from Italy and Greece foundered in the face of strong opposition, particularly from the Visegrad Group (Czech Republic, Hungary, Poland and Slovakia). In December 2017, the Commission referred the Czech Republic, Hungary and Poland to the Court of Justice for their refusal to relocate asylum applicants from Greece and Italy. Immigration was a salient issue in national elections in 2017 in Austria, France, Germany and the Netherlands and contributed to relatively strong performances by anti-immigration political parties. These developments are indicative of the political effects of EU migration governance that go beyond the technical aspects of governance to expose the consequences of EU actions for the allocations of values and resources within and between EU states and with substantial effects on non-EU states too.

Four dimensions of potential change are identified and used to evaluate events in 2017. First, there can be change in the underlying drivers of migration (such as relative inequalities of income and wealth or the effects of conflict either within or between states) that can then affect decisions to migrate. It can be difficult to objectively measure the effects of potential drivers of migration (economic, social, political, demographic and environmental, plus their interactions) on actual migration flows, which means that perceptions and understandings by decision-makers and the wider public (whether accurate or not) of what is going on 'out there' have powerful effects. Second, change in EU policies and associated practices. EU policies have an 'internal' dimension (Schengen and common EU migration and asylum policies) plus an 'external' dimension attempting to affect

*The research leading to these results has received funding from the European Research Council under the European Union's Seventh Framework Programme (FP7/2007-2013)/ ERC grant agreement no. 340430 for the project 'Prospects for International Migration Governance'. Thanks to Leiza Brumat, Leila Hadj-Abdou and Emanuele Massetti for comments on an earlier draft.

actions or responses in non-EU countries. Policy change includes the depth and density of co-operation evidenced by the outputs of these processes as well as by the policy focus (for example, more or less open or closed to various kinds of migration). Third, change in the participants to involve a greater role for EU institutions, a diffusion of interest in migration within the EU institutions (certainly it is the case that almost all Directorate Generals within the Commission are now in the 'migration business'), a greater role for EU agencies such as the European Asylum Agency (EAS) and the European Border and Coast Guard Agency (EBCG), and, more involvement by international organizations such as the International Organization for Migration (IOM) or United Nations High Commissioner for Refugees (UNHCR). Fourth, change in the politics of migration including both political mobilizations on migration as well as in public attitudes to migration. Public attitudes can be influenced by objective data on, for example, the scale or type of flows or the economic or fiscal effects of migration, but evidence suggests that they are also powerfully shaped at individual level by values and emotions (Dempster and Hargrave, 2017).

I. Drivers and Routes

In 2017, the policy focus in the Mediterranean shifted to a 'Central Mediterranean' route for people crossing from North Africa to Italy. As is well known, the post-2015 migration and refugee crisis was primarily focused on people moving to the EU via dangerous Mediterranean Sea crossings and was compounded by images of death, chaos and disorder. Between January 2014 and the end of March 2018, 1.78 million people entered the EU via Mediterranean crossings with 16,045 people reported dead or missing (UNHCR, 2018). In 2017, 3,139 people were reported as dead or missing in the Mediterranean (UNHCR, 2018). Many people moving to Europe were seeking refuge from the conflict in Syria, although most displaced Syrians made shorter cross-border journeys to the next safe place. By the end of 2017, there were more than 5 million Syrian refugees in Jordan, Lebanon and Turkey (UNHCR, 2018).

The total number of Mediterranean crossings has declined since its peak in 2015 when just over 1 million arrived, of which around 450,000 originated from Syria. Greece, with around 830,000 people arriving in 2015, became a visual and political focus for the crisis with hundreds of thousands of migrants and asylum-seekers then moving on in seemingly haphazard ways through Central Europe towards Germany, which was for many the preferred destination.

The shift in the dynamics in 2017 towards the Central Mediterranean was linked to EU policy interventions. Following the EU–Turkey Statement of April 2016, the numbers of migrants moving along the 'Eastern Mediterranean' route from Turkey to Greece fell from 176,000 in 2016 to 35,000 in 2017. The Statement provided for: return of all irregularly arriving Syrian nationals from Greek Islands to Turkey; a mechanism for one vulnerable Syrian to move to the EU for every Syrian returned to Turkey; a €6 billion Facility for Refugees in Turkey; and, designation of Turkey as a 'safe third country' to allow the return of asylum applicants from the EU who had passed through Turkey (Council of the European Union, 2016). The 'Noori decision' of the Greek Council of State in September 2017 allowed the return to Turkey of a 21-year old Syrian man and thus upheld the provision within the EU–Turkey Statement that returns to Turkey were reasonable, albeit only by a knife-edge 13–12 majority (Alpes *et al.*, 2017). Because of its 'geographical limitation' from the terms of the 1951 Geneva Convention, Turkey offers refugee status only to those fleeing events in Europe. Syrian nationals in Turkey receive Temporary Protection. Between April 2016 and the end of February 2018, there were 1,554 people returned to Turkey, 91 per cent of whom were men, with the greatest number being from Pakistan (41 per cent). There were concerns about lack of procedural safeguards to protect the rights of asylum seekers in Turkey and concern about the risk of refoulement (return to a country where an individual would be at risk of persecution) (Alpes *et al.*, 2017).

After the EU–Turkey statement came into effect, the main point of arrival for those crossing the Mediterranean then became Italy where a total of 406,808 people arrived between 1 January 2016 and 18 March 2018, including 119,369 sea arrivals in 2017. A difference between the Eastern Mediterranean route to Greece (predominantly people from Syria, Iraq and Afghanistan) and the Central Mediterranean route to Italy is the diversity of origin of migrants with prominent origin countries being Nigeria, Eritrea, Guinea, Ivory Coast, Gambia, Senegal, Mali, Sudan and Bangladesh (Wittenberg, 2017). The scale of arrivals put significant pressure on systems for reception and processing of asylum applications. In a 5-year period between 2013 and 2017 there were 427,000 requests for international protection in Italy, which compares to a total of 317,000 in the preceding 37 years between 1985 and 2012 (Eurostat, 2018).[1] In 2017, 8 per cent of applicants were granted refugee status, 8 per cent a subsidiary protection status, 25 per cent humanitarian protection and 58 per cent were rejected (Ministero dell Interno, 2017).

II. Policies Old and New

Concern about actual or potential large-scale migration flows to the EU has become a normal component of EU migration governance, the history of which has been defined by a series of 'crises' dating back to the end of the Cold War. The Maastricht Treaty's Justice and Home Affairs (JHA) pillar was influenced by concern about post-Cold War large-scale migration from former Soviet bloc countries. The 'Dublin' system, defining the state responsible for determining an asylum application, was shaped by refugee flows from former Yugoslavia (Geddes, 2007). Efforts to control migration flows by externalizing migration policy through co-operation with non-EU countries can be traced to the late 1990s and early 2000s (Lavenex, 1999). Increased asylum flows in the early 2000s led the Spanish and UK governments to propose 'extra-territorial processing' of asylum applicants (Garlick, 2006). A 2006 surge in arrivals in the Canary Islands prompted a 'multilayered deterrence strategy' that is an antecedent of measures adopted in response to the Mediterranean crossings after 2015 (Godeneau and López-Sala, 2016).

The agenda-setting European Agenda for Migration (EAM) of 2015 was a response to the surge in Mediterranean arrivals, but was also built on 25 years of co-operation on migration and asylum and the associated policies and practices (CEC, 2015). The EAM rests on 4 pillars:

1. Reducing the incentives for irregular migration with a focus on 'root causes behind irregular migration in non-EU countries', on 'dismantling smuggling and trafficking networks' and on 'the better application of return policies'. The EU Emergency Trust

---

[1] I am grateful to Dr Matteo Villa of the Istituto per gli Studi di Politica Internazionale, Milan for sharing these data.

Fund for Africa agreed by EU governments in November 2015 provides up to €2 billion targeted at the root causes of irregular migration and displacement in Sahel/Lake Chad, the Horn of Africa and North Africa. A 2017 evaluation of the Trust Fund reported engagement with 26 partner countries and positive effects in terms of the help for displaced people and opportunities for economic development while also identifying a risk that longer-term objectives are side-tracked by the EU's short-term political interest in combating irregular migration (Oxfam, 2017). The darker side of the externalization of EU migration controls became evident in Libya in 2017 where EU governments were accused of being complicit in the abuse of hundreds of thousands of migrants and refugees at the hands of Libyan authorities, armed groups and militias. Working with the IOM, the EU's Regional Development and Protection Programme oversaw the return to their countries of origin of almost 7,500 migrants from Libya plus a further 4,000 from Niger (CEC, 2017b, p. 6). This was linked to a shifting focus in Mediterranean Sea operations away from 'search and rescue' (the Italian government's *Mare Nostrum* operation rescued around 150,000 people between October 2013 and October 2014) towards law enforcement and tackling smuggling routes via the Triton, Sophia and Themis operations. In February 2016, Europol established a European Migrant Smuggling Centre with a focus on dismantling smuggling networks. The underlying logic is that 'combatting smuggling organizations is key to reducing the influx of illegal immigrants' (Zhang *et al.*, 2018, p. 8). Research evidence suggests that smuggling is often more improvised and embedded in social relations within migration networks than the image of exploitative and ruthless criminal gangs would suggest (Zhang *et al.*, 2018). The understanding of migration pressures is evident in the many maps that have emerged to represent the migrant crisis that often show ominously big arrows pointing from Africa towards the EU. There are, of course, people moving from Africa to Europe, but the scale of intra-continental African migration is far greater than migration to Europe (FAO, 2017).

2. Better management of the external border through 'solidarity' towards member states such as Greece and Italy that are the particular focus of arrivals via Mediterranean routes. Creation of 'hotspots' (five in Greece and four in Italy) was an emergency response to the registration and processing of new arrivals, although there is now discussion about whether to make this a more long-term approach in the context of the ongoing budget negotiations for the period after 2020 (Beirens, 2018). The Commission identified solidarity as an element of future migration and asylum policy. In September 2015, EU member states agreed a 2-year plan to move 160,000 asylum seekers from Greece and Italy to other member states, according to a distribution key based on population, national income, numbers of asylum applicants and unemployment rates. The scheme formally ended on 26 September 2017, by which time just over 30,000 people had been relocated (CEC, 2018). In June 2017, the Commission announced infringement proceedings against the Czech Republic, Hungary and Poland for failure to implement the legally binding September 2015 Relocation Decision. Hungary and Poland had not relocated anyone while the Czech Republic had relocated a mere 12 asylum applicants from Greece. Political changes in 2017 EU member states seem likely to have ramifications for solidarity. When announcing the priorities for the Austrian government's Council Presidency in the second half of 2017, Chancellor Sebastian Kurz said that: 'Our aim is very clear – that in Europe there should not only be a dispute over redistribution (of refugees) but also at last a shift of focus towards securing external borders' (*Euractiv*, 2018).

3. The strengthening of the common asylum policy with a key sticking point being reform of the Dublin regulation that attributes responsibility for an asylum application to the EU country of first entry. The Dublin system led to disproportionate pressure on southern member states, particularly Greece and Italy that were the first countries of entry for many asylum seekers. The relocation system was an *ad hoc* response while the Commission-instigated reform of the Common European Asylum System was seen to offer scope for more profound change. At the very least, glaring problems with the existing system needed to be addressed. Rulings from the European Court of Human Rights and EU Court of Justice meant that asylum applicants could not be safely returned to Greece because of protection deficiencies (Beirens, 2018, p. 11). For those seeking asylum, procedures for registering and processing claims, as well as recognition rates vary widely between member states. This contributes to 'secondary movements' as asylum applicants attempt to move from one EU state to another (Beirens, 2018). Secondary movements have been a central component of the crisis with knock-on effects for EU free movement and the Schengen area because of a 'reverse domino effect' with new fencing and border controls introduced within the Schengen area to stop onwards movement. The Commission reform package contained seven elements, including the creation of a European Asylum Agency upon which agreement was reached in June 2017. The most important and most difficult was reform of the Dublin system, upon which little progress was made.

4. A new policy on legal migration, which the Commission in the EAM linked to the future economic needs of the EU given demographic decline in Europe. The EU Blue Card targeted at migration into high skilled employment, introduced in 2009, was significantly limited in its effects. Member states adopted very different approaches to its implementation. For example, salary thresholds ranged from €13,000 to €68,000, conditions for labour market testing varied as too did the permit's duration (ranging from 1 to 4 years). Even a revised scheme, as proposed by the Commission, would remain subject to member state controls over admissions (Cerna, 2018).

III. 'Future Proof' Policy

There has been a self-conscious desire on the part of the EU institutions to think beyond the crisis and 'future proof' migration and asylum policies. Future proof policies, according to the Commission (CEC, 2017a, p. 5) should be: 'built on strong foundations and clear values: a more effective and fairer approach based on solidarity and responsibility'. In December 2017, European Commission President Juncker called for a 'move away from crisis mode [because] migration will remain a challenge for a generation of Europeans. Europe urgently needs to equip itself with future-proof means of managing migration responsibly and fairly'. In its contribution to the EU Leaders' thematic debate on a way forward on the external and internal dimensions of migration policy, the Commission identified two key aspects of a future-proof policy: developing a stable and integrated EU approach to migration and asylum; and, ensuring that future-proofed policies are informed by values of solidarity and responsibility while inspiring trust and confidence (CEC, 2017a). Future-proof policy is also based on an understanding of the likely future dynamics of migration and mobility both within and from outside the EU. In its 2017 review of delivery of the European Agenda on Migration the Commission noted that:

> 'In the last two years, Europe experienced the largest number of arrivals of refugees and migrants since the end of the Second World War. The Syrian crisis played an important part in generating this record number, as did conflicts, instability and poverty in many parts of the world. Migration, asylum and border management systems were put under huge pressure. The Union and its Member States were not sufficiently prepared to respond effectively. The scale of the crisis had a powerful impact across the EU. The integrity of both the Common European Asylum System and of the Schengen area of free movement for European citizens was put into question' (CEC, 2017b, p. 2).

This Commission statement helps to illustrate the point that EU migration governance is not solely a response or reaction to flows of migrants and asylum seekers because there is also an understanding of the reasons why people move to the EU that informs subsequent EU actions. The above quote represents migration as an act of desperation driven by poverty, conflict and instability. It is, of course, true that those who entered the EU by boat across the Mediterranean were fleeing desperate circumstances. In 2017, however, most migrants to European countries moved via regular channels for employment, to join family or to study, motivated by hope, aspiration and ambition. The organization of migration governance itself and understandings of migration therein (the idea that migration is an act of desperation induced by crisis) helps to define the challenges, shape responses and influence 'future proof' governance.

IV. Attitudes and Mobilizations

Migration governance is more than a technical question because it clearly affects the allocation of resources and values within and between states and thus possesses the potential to be intensely political. Migration was a highly salient factor in European elections in 2017, including the strong first round vote in the April 2017 French presidential elections for Marine Le Pen, and the re-entry of the far-right Freedom Party into the governing Austrian coalition in December 2017. Opposition to immigration aligns with euroscepticism and has been identified as a potentially persistent 'transnational' cleavage in European politics 'grounded in educational opportunities that have persistent effects over a person's life, and which are conveyed to offspring' (Hooghe and Marks, 2018, p. 127). Through schemes such as relocation of asylum-seekers, the EU has wider political effects on the allocation of resources and values between member states. Efforts to externalize controls can have important effects on the allocation of resources and values beyond the confines of the EU system.

Increased support for anti-immigration political parties could give the impression that there has been a surge in anti-immigration sentiment in Europe induced by the crisis and that this explains the increased support for populist and anti-immigration political parties. Figure 1 shows that, of the 14 countries that were investigated by the European Social Survey between 2002 and 2016, 10 became slightly more favourable. This certainly did not mean embracing an open-door approach. In most countries, people were only willing to accept 'few' immigrants, so this should not be seen as indicating widespread support for increased immigration. Strikingly, between 2014 and 2016 – the peak of the 'crisis' – attitudes remained stable and, if anything, became more favourable. Of the 14 countries, only in Austria and Poland did views become more negative over this period (Dennison and Geddes, 2017).

Figure 1: Mean Willingness to Accept Immigrants 'from Poorer Countries Outside of Europe'.

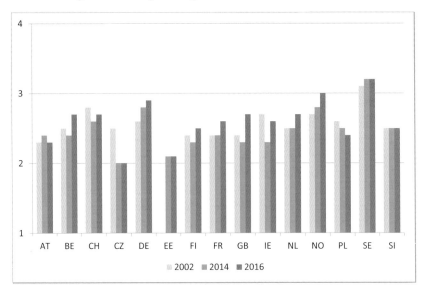

Notes: 1=accept none; 2=few; 3=some; 4=many.
Source: European Social Survey 2002, 2014, 2016.

High levels of issue salience explain why there has been increased support for populist and radical right parties. Eurobarometer data in Figure 2 show how there was a significant spike after 2014 in the salience of the migration issue. In the Netherlands, while salience

Figure 2: What Do You Think Are the Two Most Important Issues Affecting Your Country? Percentage saying 'Immigration'.

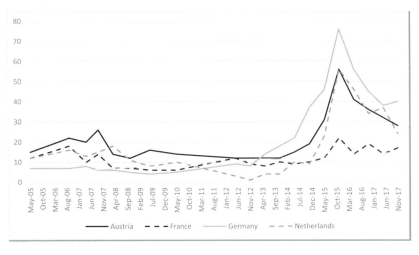

Source: Eurobarometer, 2005–17.

dipped in 2017 before the elections (which may help explain the failure of Geert Wilder's Freedom Party to break through), it still remained historically high when looked at since 2005. As for France, opposition to immigration has always been central to the electoral appeal of the Front National (Betz, 2018).

Increased salience preceded relatively strong performance by anti-immigration parties in Germany, Austria and the Netherlands. While Figure 1 suggests the crisis had little obvious impact on Europeans' attitudes to immigration generally, widespread media coverage of people making dangerous sea crossings to move to Europe coupled with apparently chaotic and disorderly onwards movement could raise concern amongst people with conservative value orientations that favour security, order and societal conformity. If so, then, rather than provoking a general turn against immigration, the crisis could have triggered pre-existing latent attitudes amongst the one-third to one-half of each national population with such conservative value orientations.

More widespread, however, is the negative assessment by Europeans of their national governments and, in particular, of the EU. Figure 3 shows that in 10 EU member states, every country except the UK, perceives the EU to have handled the refugee crisis worse than their national government. Only the Hungarian, Polish and Serbian governments are perceived to have handled the crisis relatively well by their citizens, which, given the content of their actions, is unlikely to be a positive signal for those who advocate a greater focus on international protection. Even in Germany, the carefully accrued political

Figure 3: 'Do You Agree That Your National Government/The European Union Has Responded Well To the Refugee Crisis?'

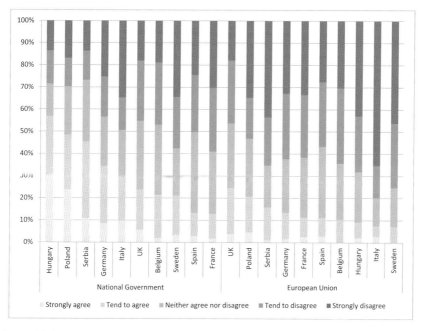

Source: Ipsos Global Tracker 2017.

capital of Chancellor Merkel and her one-time slogan of *wir schaffen das* (we can do this) was eroded by negative the reaction to increased refugee flows that contributed to a 12.6 per cent vote share for the AfD at the 2017 federal elections, which more than doubled its previous performance.

Attitudes to immigration in Europe have remained relatively stable in recent years and, indeed, have actually become slightly less negative in most countries, even during the deeper political and institutional crisis at national and EU levels exposed by the migration crisis. This suggests that the increased recent electoral success of radical right parties such as the AfD can be explained by increased issue salience. As Figure 2 showed, immigration is now considered far more important, only partially subsiding again in 2017. An emphasis on salience would suggest that, rather than converting people to anti-migration positions, an effect of the crisis was to activate latent anti-immigration beliefs amongst those with conservative value orientations. This, coupled with the near universal belief that the EU and many European national governments have handled the situation poorly – to the dissatisfaction of both those on the left and right – has led to significant changes in European party systems.

Conclusions

Four dimensions of potential change in EU migration governance were identified. First, was change in understanding of the underlying drivers of migration. Here we saw the continuation in 2017 of longer standing concern about large-scale migration flows to the EU dating back to the end of the Cold War and its impact at that time on the development of the Maastricht Treaty. While the focus on potentially large migration flows (whether well-founded or not) might not be new, the emphasis has changed with evidence that persistent and high migratory pressures on the EU's external borders has become what the Commission itself has referred to as a 'new normal' (CEC, 2016). Second, policy change is marked either by the density of outputs or their focus. On the former count, it is the case that there is an increasingly more complex web of EU outputs interacting with the immigration and asylum systems of the member states. On the latter count, there has been a consistent focus on external borders and measures on irregular migration and asylum that dates back to at least the late 1990s. In 2017, there was, if anything, a hardening of this focus rather than change. Third, change in the participants in EU migration governance. Again, we can see a much more densely populated field with, for example, almost all Directorate Generals within the European Commission now devoting staff and resources to migration issues. The European External Action Service and the Commission's Development DG (DEVCO) are closely involved with responses to migration, although the High-Level Working Group on Migration, established back in 1999 was already designed to promote closer co-operation between these branches of national governments and the EU administration. The crisis also led to a greater role for international organizations such as UNHCR and IOM and, connected to the crisis in Europe, wider international developments in the form of the negotiation of 'Global Compacts' on migration and asylum within the United Nations system and due to be agreed in 2018. Finally, and an area where change has been particularly profound, are the politics of migration governance. Migration has been a high salience issue in many EU member states and seems likely to remain a key concern. The Visegrad group of member states (Czech Republic,

Hungary, Poland and Slovakia) has found a new ally in an Austrian government containing the far-right Freedom Party. Attitudes to immigration and European integration are also seen to have coalesced into a new 'transnational' cleavage with potentially powerful structuring effects on European party politics.

References

Alpes, M.J., Tunaboylu, S., Ulusoy, O. and Hassan, S. (2017) *Post-Deportation Risks Under the EU-Turkey Statement: What Happens after Readmission to Turkey?* Policy Brief 2017/30, Migration Policy Centre (Florence: European University Institute).

Beirens, H. (2018) *Cracked Foundations, Uncertain Future: Structural Weaknesses in the Common European Asylum System* (Brussels: Migration Policy Institute Europe).

Betz, H.-G. (2018) 'The New National Front: Still a Master Case?' In Fossum, J.-E., Kastoryano, R. and Siim, B. (eds) *Diversity and Contestations over Nationalism in Europe and Canada* (London: Palgrave Macmillan) pp), pp. 313–36.

Cerna, L. (2018) 'European High-skilled Migration Policy'. In Czaika, M. (ed.) *High Skilled Migration: Drivers and Policies* (Oxford: Oxford University Press), pp. 87–107.

CEC (2015) 'A European Agenda on Migration', COM (2015) 240 final, 13 May.

CEC (2016) 'On Establishing a New Partnership Framework with Third Countries under the European Agenda on Migration', COM (2016) 385 final, 7 June.

CEC (2017a) 'Commission Contribution to the EU Leaders' Thematic Debate on a Way Forward on the External and the Internal Dimension of Migration Policy', COM (2017) 820 final, 7 December.

CEC (2017b) 'On the Delivery of the European Agenda on Migration', COM (2017) 558 final, 27 September.

CEC (2018) 'Member States Support to Emergency Relocation Mechanism' (as of 26 March 2018). Available online at: https://ec.europa.eu/home-affairs/sites/homeaffairs/files/what-we-do/policies/european-agenda-migration/press-material/docs/state_of_play_-_relocation_en.pdf, accessed 16 April 2018.

Council of the EU (2016) EU-Turkey Statement, Press Release 144/16, 18 March.

Dempster, H. and Hargrave, K. (2017) *Understanding Publica Attitudes Towards Refugees and Migrants*, Working Paper 512 (London: Overseas Development Institute).

Dennison, J and A. Geddes (2017) 'Op-Ed: Are Europeans Turning against Asylum Seekers and Refugees?' European Council on Refugees and Exiles Bulletin, 17 November.

Euractiv (2018) 'Austria Plans To Put Immigration and Borders at Heart of EU Presidency', Euractiv, 9 March. Available online at: https://www.euractiv.com/section/justice-home-affairs/news/austria-plans-to-put-immigration-and-borders-at-heart-of-eu-presidency/,

European Political Strategy Centre (2015) Legal Migration in the EU: From Stop-Gap Solutions to a Future-Proof Policy, EPSC Strategic Notes, No. 2, April.

Eurostat (2018) *Asylum and Managed Migration Statistics* (Brussels: Eurostat) Available online at: http://ec.europa.eu/eurostat/web/asylum-and-managed-migration/data/database.

FAO (2017) *Rural Africa in Motion: Dynamics (Pembroke, Ont.) and Drivers of Migration South of the Sahara* (Rome: Food and Agricultural Organisation of the United Nations).

Garlick, M. (2006) 'The EU Discussions on Extraterritorial Processing: Solution or Conundrum?' *International Journal of Refugee Law*, Vol. 18, No. 3–4, pp. 601–29.

Geddes, A. (2007) *Immigration and European Integration: Beyond Fortress Europe?* (Manchester: Manchester University Press).

Godenau, D. and López-Sala, A. (2016) 'Multi-layered Migration Deterrence and Technology in Spanish Maritime Border Management'. *Journal of Borderlands Studies*, Vol. 31, No. 2, pp. 151–69.

Guiraudon, V. (2017) 'The 2015 Refugee Crisis Was Not a Turning Point: Explaining Policy Inertia in EU Border Control'. *European Political Science*, Vol. 17, No. 1, pp. 151–60.

Hooghe, L. and Marks, G. (2018) 'Cleavage Theory Meets Europe's Crises: Lipset, Rokkan, and the Transnational Cleavage'. *Journal of European Public Policy*, Vol. 25, No. 1, pp. 109–35.

Lavenex, S. (1999) *Safe Third Countries: Extending the EU Asylum and Immigration Policies to Central and Eastern Europe* (Budapest: Central European University Press).

Ministero dell'Interno (2017) *Dati Asilo 2016–17* (Rome: Ministero dell' Interno) Available online at: http://www.libertaciviliimmigrazione.dlci.interno.gov.it/sites/default/files/allegati/dati_asilo_2017_.pdf.

Oxfam (2017) *An Emergency for Whom? The EU Emergency Trust Fund for Africa* (Oxford: Oxfam).

UNHCR (2018) Operational Portal Refugee Situations: Mediterranean Situation (Geneva: UNHCR). Available online at: http://data2.unhcr.org/en/situations/mediterranean.

Wittenberg, L. (2017) *Managing Mixed Migration: The Central Mediterranean Route to Europe*, Desperate Migration Series No. 3 (New York: International Peace Institute).

Zhang, S., Sanchez, G. and Achilli, L. (2018) 'Crimes of Solidarity in Mobility: Alternative Views on Migrant Smuggling'. *The Annals of the American Academy of Political and Social Science*, Vol. 676, No. 1, pp. 6–15.

JCMS 2018 Volume 56. Annual Review pp. 131–141   DOI: 10.1111/jcms.12752

Towards a European Security and Defence Union: Was 2017 a Watershed?

NATHALIE TOCCI
Istituto Affari Internazionali

Introduction

The year 2017 has been a remarkable one for European security and defence. The work began with the EU Global Strategy (EUGS), presented by High Representative and Vice President (HRVP) Federica Mogherini in June 2016, a mere 48 hours after the UK vote to leave the European Union (EU HRVP, 2016a). At that time, all talk was about a potential disintegrative domino effect across the Union (Lichfield, 2016). Against the current, right when the Union was living through its deepest existential crisis, the HRVP pushed ahead with the EUGS. Only a few months later, the Council welcomed an ambitious Security and Defence Implementation Plan, which aimed to translate the security and defence dimension of the EUGS into reality (EU HRVP, 2016b). To do so, a new Level of Ambition and 13 tasks were identified in November 2016, endorsed politically by the European Council a month later (European Council, 2016).

The year 2017 was entirely devoted to the implementation of these tasks, leading to significant activism in European security and defence. Talk about a 'European Security and Defence Union' and a 'Europe of Defence' became louder as the months went by (Lazarou, 2016), culminating in declarations of a 'new EU' as the year came to an end (EEAS, 2017). All this took place while the Union began grappling with Brexit and lived through a succession of key national elections in Austria, the Netherlands, France and Germany, in which the spectre of eurosceptic populism loomed large. While the Union kept struggling politically, with precious little progress made on internal policy areas of European integration such as the eurozone or the EU asylum system, security and defence, traditionally the ugly duckling of European integration, began blossoming.

In what follows, this essay discusses the why, the what and the what next for this remarkable year in European security and defence. Why, as some put it, has the EU's 'sleeping beauty' (Selmayr, 2017) awakened? What concretely does a European Security and Defence Union mean? And what hurdles must be overcome to ensure that 2017 will not be remembered as another false dawn for European security and defence?

I. Why do we need a European Security and Defence Union?

Three structural trends coupled with three enabling factors explain the notable activism on European security and defence over the last year.

Structural Factors: Europe in a Turbulent Multipolar World

First, the US security umbrella provided through NATO cannot be indefinitely taken for granted. An assertive Russia notwithstanding, the Cold War ended almost three decades ago, while globally power has been shifting to multiple centres, as well as flowing between them (Grevi, 2009). Although the US is increasing its military presence in Europe, Washington will neither have the will nor the capacity to look after Europe nor in fact be the 'global policeman' in the years ahead (Peña, 2017). Some applaud, others mourn, this structural shift. But no one can convincingly deny it. This means that Europeans need to assume greater responsibility for their own security. Political leaders increasingly recognize this (Taylor, 2017). Under the Obama administrations, Washington began sending clear messages across to the Atlantic but to little avail (Traynor, 2011). The reliability of the transatlantic partnership in those years coupled with the all-consuming eurozone crisis led European leaders to bury their heads in the sand on defence. With the election of Donald Trump to the White House, a long-standing sceptic that America's system of alliances truly serve US interests (Trump, 1987), the sheer unpredictability of the American security guarantee to Europe woke Europeans from their torpor. In other words, the days in which Europeans exclusively took care of soft security while sheltering under the transatlantic hard security umbrella are fast fading. Not only can and must the EU enable and enhance the ability of Europeans to achieve strategic autonomy through a European Security and Defence union, but a strong transatlantic bond in the twenty-first century arguably rests on this foundation (EU HRVP, 2016a). In other words, a European Security and Defence Union is not only not incompatible with, but is also conducive to the reinforcement of a European pillar within NATO.

Second, the need for Europeans to assume greater responsibility in the fields of security and defence becomes all the more important given the sharp increase in real and perceived insecurity across the Union and beyond. Robert Kagan (2003) once (in) famously said that Americans are from Mars, while Europeans are from Venus, the latter lulled by decades of peace on the continent achieved through European integration and the US security umbrella. While deliberately provocative and over-simplistic, there was more than a grain of truth in the statement. Today no longer. After decades of peace in Europe, the strategic environment in which the Union navigates has visibly deteriorated and Europe is directly affected by the fall-out. To the east, the EU faces an assertive Russia, intent on reaffirming its sphere of influence by exploiting the security, economic, political and energy-related vulnerabilities of the Eastern Partnership countries (Youngs, 2017). Across the Mediterranean, the spread of ungoverned spaces and conflict has enabled terrorists and criminals to thrive, while regional rivalries are escalating in the Middle East and East Asia. Globally, there has been a dramatic rise in civilian victims and refugees: more than 65 million people were displaced by early 2017 and the number is steadily climbing. Moreover, climate change and resource scarcity, coupled with demographic growth and state fragility, promise more turbulence, conflict and displacement in the years ahead. It is no surprise that in this context, European public opinion is increasingly concerned about security. Opinion polls point to the fact that security has become the number one concern for most Europeans (European Commission, 2017). The causes of insecurity differ between member states, with countries in central and eastern Europe worried about Russia, while countries in western and southern Europe fear mainly terrorism. But causes aside, Europeans agree that security is one of their top priorities.

Third, in a twenty-first century world of continental-sized powers, all EU member states, including the largest ones, are small-to-medium-sized countries globally, as well as highly interdependent. The financial and technological implication of this is that Europeans can only assume responsibility on security and defence by acting together. Collectively, member states spend approximately 200 billion euros per year on defence, making the EU – even without the UK –the second largest military spender worldwide. Yet wasteful duplications – 80 per cent of investment is still spent nationally whereas up to 30 per cent could be saved by pooling procurement – the fragmentation of European defence markets, insufficient interoperability, and lack of co-ordination all seriously hamper the 'value for money' that Europeans get on defence. European security and European taxpayers simply cannot afford this any longer. Added to this, the information technology revolution implies that effective European security and defence require systematic co-operation on research and development. Hence, while the downturn in European defence spending during the economic crisis has been reversed, the road towards Europe's strategic autonomy requires spending better, which in turn means spending together (Munich Security Conference, 2017). Interestingly, European public opinion appreciates this. Large majorities in all member states would like to see 'more Europe' in security and defence, seemingly aware that in a space in which goods, services, money and people move freely, security can neither be compartmentalized nor guaranteed by member states acting alone (Stokes et al., 2016). In a world in which the US security guarantee becomes less predictable and Europeans need to assume greater responsibilities faced with an increasingly crisis-prone world, they can only do so collectively.

Enabling Factors: A Political Commission, Brexit and the Franco-German Engine

To these three structural trends, three further enabling factors should be added: the role of the European Commission, Brexit and the Franco-German engine of integration.

Traditionally, the European Commission was unwilling to touch defence issues. The 'D' word was somewhat of a dirty word in the *Berlaymont*. The limits set by the EU Treaties to fund defence from the EU budget made the Commission, as guardian of the Treaties, doubly sceptical. This began to change under Commission President Barroso, but acquired a new momentum under the Juncker Commission. Specifically, with the work carried out on the EUGS and the full use of the double-hatted role of the High Representative as also Vice President of the European Commission, the European Commission is now fully committed to becoming a security and defence player. Led by President Juncker and his special adviser Michel Barnier, the Commission began exploring how to facilitate and provide incentives for Europeans to do more together in this field. In November 2016, it presented a European Defence Action Plan, outlining a set of financial measures to induce member states to move towards greater defence co-operation. The most concrete element in this Plan is the launch of a defence research and development programme, in which the Commission will start funding collaborative defence research (much like it already does in non-defence research under Horizon 2020) as well as industrial capability development projects. Following legislative proposals in July 2017, the Council made its first concrete step towards enacting a European Defence Fund by agreeing in December 2017 on a General Approach to the Commission's proposal for a regulation on the European Defence Industrial Development Programme (EDIDP). In so far as defence R&D is amongst the areas in which Europeans spend the least within their defence budgets and certainly do not spend together, the EDIDP is an important step forward. The Commission's commitment to put concrete chips on the defence table has represented a key contribution, potentially even a game changer, towards a European security and defence union.

The tortured British exit journey from the European Union is a second enabling factor for European security and defence. Whereas the UK had been at the forefront of the push towards what eventually became the Common Security and Defence Policy in the years following the Franco-British 1998 St Malò Declaration, after the Conservative Party's return to power in 2010, London became lukewarm if not outright sceptical of the idea of deeper European defence co-operation. The concern, which visibly rose as uroscepticism escalated under Tory rule, was that stepping up European security and defence would be to the detriment of the Atlantic Alliance. Hence, those in continental Europe who believed instead that the Union should enhance its integration efforts, including in the sphere of defence, saw a silver lining in the outcome of the 23 June 2016 British referendum. Now that the British foot was off the brake of EU security and defence, the rest could get on with the business. Despite the fact that (or perhaps because) the UK's departure would generate a gap in military capabilities, the UK referendum led to greater unity of purpose on the continent to propel the European security and defence to a new level. On top, signaling European unity after the UK referendum became an overarching political priority. Faced with deep intra-EU divisions over the eurozone and migration, security and defence became the obvious candidate to demonstrate such unity of purpose. No wonder that it was thus put high on the list of priorities which emerged from the informal Bratislava summit of September 2017 held by the 27 on the future of the EU.

Finally, the major push in 2017 on European security and defence would not have been possible without the restart of the Franco-German engine. When it comes to defence, the restart of the engine took place in an unexpected order. Traditionally, Paris rather than Berlin has always been more sanguine about European defence, as post World War II Germany struggled to reconcile itself with defence policy, and specifically with expeditionary demanding missions abroad. Yet as Germany's leadership role in the Union grew (Paterson, 2011), and the three above mentioned structural factors could no longer be denied, Berlin took the initiative first. No sooner had the EUGS been published, back-to-back with the 2016 German Defence White Paper (German Federal Ministry of Defence, 2016), than Germany adamantly began pushing forward European defence. France, during the last months of Francois Hollande's presidency, reluctantly followed (Ayrault and Steinmeier, 2016; von der Leyen and Le Drian, 2016). It was only after the election of Emmanuel Macron to the Elysée that the Franco-German engine seriously restarted, enabling the stride forward on European security and defence.

II. What is the European Security and Defence Union? To think, to buy and to act together

If there has been a stride forward, what precisely does it consist of? What concretely does or can a European Security and Defence Union mean?[1] The European Security and Defence Union can be synthesized into three interrelated pillars. 2017 was the year in which the necessary mechanisms and instruments were established to erect these pillars on which European security and defence can eventually rest.

First, a European Security and Defence Union means that Europeans will jointly research and develop defence capabilities together: member states would collaboratively conduct defence research and development, fostering a cutting-edge defence technological and industrial base. The launch of a Preparatory Action for Defence Research in 2017, followed by the EDIDP regulation, and more broadly the ambition to launch a €5.5 billion European Defence Fund in the framework of the next Multiannual Financial Framework will add unprecedented incentives for Europeans to co-operatively conduct defence R&D. The sceptic may object that €5.5 billion in an overall context in which Europeans spend over €200 billion on defence is rather insignificant. Yet insofar as the European Defence Fund will only finance collaborative projects rather than national R&D initiatives, it will supplement and amplify national investments in defence research in the development of prototypes and in the acquisition of defence equipment and technology, and provide a key incentive to a more collaborative approach by member states.

Second, a European Security and Defence Union means that Europeans will jointly build and buy defence capabilities to ensure that the Union collectively acquires and maintains full spectrum capacities. In 2017 the Union launched its trial run for a Coordinated Annual Review on Defence (CARD) to promote transparency and co-ordination in national defence spending plans. This mechanism is meant to facilitate regular and systematic information sharing between member states on their respective defence planning, thus providing the necessary advance information to enable joint capability development and procurement. Alongside CARD, in November 2017, 25 member states notified the HRVP of their intention to activate the Permanent Structured Cooperation (PESCO), an article of the Treaty on European Union left dormant until then, which allows a group of willing and able member states to make more binding commitments to one another with a view to the most demanding missions. PESCO foresees the development of joint capabilities, where possible supported by the European Defence Fund, with proposals for instance to develop a single European armored vehicle as one of PESCO's potentially most far-reaching projects identified so far.

Finally, a European Security and Defence Union should allow member states to act together, jointly deploying forces and capabilities. In June 2017, the Union established its first-ever permanent European military command centre, an important step in this direction. While shying away from calling it a Headquarter, the EU has set up a permanent so-called military planning and conduct capability (MPCC) for its non-executive military missions such as those currently ongoing in the Central African Republic, Mali and Somalia. For the first time, this has allowed a streamlined command and control line from

---

[1]President Juncker has called for a European Defence Union by 2025. I would propose here to use the wider concept of a European Security and Defence Union to encompass more clearly the civilian dimension of CSDP and the security aspects of CFSP, in line with the vision of the EU as a comprehensive global actor.

the political level down to missions in the field. Before the end of 2018, the MPCC will be reviewed by the Council with an aim to expanding its mandate to cover the EU's military operations too. The point here in fact has not been that of creating new and heavy bureaucratic structures but rather of filling a gap in command and control thus enabling more effective and efficient action. In any case, even a more ambitious EU military headquarter would remain of entirely different dimensions compared to NATO's SHAPE in terms of mandate and size. Alongside this, PESCO has in store several operational projects, such as a medical command, a logistics hub, a disaster relief package, a training certification centre, an energy operational function, a secure military communications system, or a military mobility project, amongst others. A last aspect connected to action concerns EU-NATO co-operation. Disproving those who believed that developing European defence would be to the detriment of NATO, 2016–17 proved precisely the opposite. For the first time in history and precisely as the EU was putting in place all the above-mentioned tools and mechanisms, the EU and NATO agreed first on a list of 42 collaborative action points in November 2016 and then on a further 34 measures in November 2017. The areas of co-operation span from hybrid threats and strategic communications to maritime security and capacity building, and are all aimed at increasing both the EU and NATO's effectiveness of action.

III. What Next: How to Avoid Another False Dawn in European Security and Defence?

With the establishment of a permanent European military command centre, the launching of the co-ordinated annual review on defence, the first steps on the European Defence Fund, the launching of a permanent structured co-operation, and the unprecedented EU-NATO co-operation, the EU has not reached the finishing line of a Security and Defence Union: it has rather reached the starting point of this new adventure of the European project for an ever closer Union. It has established all the tools and mechanisms to think, buy and act together on defence, but realizing coherently and ambitiously this potential is no foregone conclusion. The building blocks of a security and defence union are in place. While completing them, the task ahead is to stack them in the right way, at the right speed, and with the right ambition to build a solid castle. To do so, three sets of challenges must be met. If, and only if these challenges are overcome, the fourth and most daunting quest lies ahead.

Credibility

Early debates about PESCO in 2017 revolved around the balance between ambition and inclusivity. The more inclusive PESCO would be the less ambitious it was likely to become was the zero-sum reasoning by some (Marrone *et al.*, 2017). Germany, at the helm of the initial push on PESCO, made no secret of its preference for inclusivity, even if this were to come at the cost of ambition. What mattered was to get started with the process of deepening defence co-operation within the Union framework, and to do so in a manner that was the least divisive possible. Avoiding divisions at such a fragile moment in the history of European integration was imperative for Berlin. France was deeply sceptical – as were Italy and Spain to a lesser extent – arguing that PESCO was a one-shot game, the best chance provided by the Treaty to make a leap forward on defence through a core group or avant-garde, and its ambition should not be diluted for the sake of inclusion. This scepticism – alongside the presidential campaign in France – largely explained Paris' foot dragging on PESCO in the early months of 2017. With Macron's election, the tune quickly changed, and France not only became a promoter of PESCO but also the member state most intent on ensuring its ambitious realization. A joint Franco-German paper, immediately joined by Italy and Spain, and then supported by the Netherlands, Finland, Belgium and the Czech Republic, outlined the commitments which an ambitious PESCO should aim for in line with the provisions in the Treaty. Comparing the July 2017 '4+4' paper – by what could be seen as the vanguard of member states – and the notification signed by 25 member states in December 2017, what emerges clearly is that there was only a minimal dilution of ambition despite the inclusion of most member states (Council of Ministers, 2017). The legally binding commitments the 25 PESCO members signed up to are ambitious indeed, be it in terms of defence investment or of defence co-operation, especially considering the long-held resistance by many if not all member states to a binding framework in favour of a purely voluntary approach.

At least on paper therefore, the EU has apparently squared the circle of ambition and inclusivity. 25 member states joined PESCO, and therefore signed up to the ambitious commitments laid out in their common notification, and ensuing Council Decision. PESCO members have already translated these commitments into first national implementation plans, and the Council (with only PESCO members voting) will assess yearly their progress in meeting these commitments based on a report by the High Representative – with the ultimate sanction of suspending, through a qualified majority, the membership of a PESCO member that does not live up to its obligations. The success of PESCO, and therefore of a closer Union in security and defence, lies in a credible verification and incentive mechanism to ensure that member states live up to the commitments they have signed. And if they do not, a credible PESCO should be able to resort to excluding the non-compliant Member State (s). At stake is the solidarity between PESCO members and the credibility of European defence as a whole, which requires that each member is punching its weight and making an equivalent effort towards a shared goal.

Coherence

The European Council and the Council of Ministers, the Commission, the European External Action Service, and the European Defence Agency have all played their part in reaching the starting line of a European Security and Defence Union. Looking ahead, guaranteeing coherence between these new instruments, mechanisms and institutions (notably PESCO, CARD and the European Defence Fund), as well as between them and other initiatives – for instance the Security Union concerned with internal security under Commissioner Julian King – will be both important and challenging given the traditional institutional turf wars in Brussels.

Equally important is the quest for co-ordination between the EU's initiatives on security and defence and the security and defence partnerships with third parties. As mentioned, EU–NATO co-operation has been moving at full speed, and some of the new forms of co-operation inaugurated over the last year are such precisely because of the internal steps the EU has taken. For instance, included in the agreed list of common actions between the EU and NATO is defence capability planning, given the need to make the outcomes and timelines between NATO's defence planning process and the EU process, including the EU's newly launched CARD, as coherent as possible. However, beyond NATO more needs to be done. The EU's co-operation with partners such as the United Nations, the African Union as well as third states such as Norway and, after 2019, the United Kingdom, will need to be rethought and eventually revamped to ensure that the EU's security and defence efforts punch their full weight. A debate which has only just started regards the role of third countries in frameworks such as PESCO, and particularly the possibility for third countries to participate in specific PESCO projects be these operational or capability oriented without participating in PESCO as such.

More than a Paper Tiger

The launch of PESCO, while applauded by many notably within the Brussels bubble (Fiott *et al.*, 2017), was greeted by deep scepticism by some outside (Witney, 2017). How could a PESCO at 25, with eurosceptic member states such as Poland or Hungary, as well as defence-light member states such as Ireland or Austria deliver in practice? Given that within PESCO, unanimity would remain the rule – although for the establishment of PESCO technically only a qualified majority was necessary – why should PESCO end up being more ambitious than the Common Security and Defence Policy has been to date? If modest achievements were made in the Common Security and Defence Policy at 27 (barring Denmark in view of its opt-out), why should anyone expect anything fundamentally different to emerge at 25? Was the United Kingdom really the only brake on European defence? These questions point to a deeper fundamental truth about European defence: the different national threat perceptions of western, southern and eastern member states. In 2016, in the wake of the Global Strategy, there was a clear trade-off between those who want to focus on external deployments and those who emphasize the need to redirect attention to improving the EU's own security more directly.

The onus is on the Union to prove sceptics wrong. This will require that momentum is kept up, even as the memory of the UK referendum fades and the Trump administration's scepticism towards European defence picks up, demonstrating that all the legal, institutional and financial mechanisms established indeed serve the purpose of delivering on more and better actions that strengthen European security and defence. PESCO should shore up the collective political will to undertake military operations when the situation demands. Beyond the EU's current six military missions and operations, this means addressing the tragic case of the EU Battlegroups, born a decade ago and never deployed due to financial and political obstacles. It also regards the development of European defence capabilities, training, interoperability and deployability: ensuring that concrete progress is made on the first set of projects selected by PESCO members. Although many of these projects will take years and not months to deliver, work needs to start apace on all fronts to demonstrate that the European Security and Defence Union in the making is no paper tiger.

What if it Works?

Meeting the challenges of credibility, coherence and action is no small feat, and the history of European integration in this field provides ample cause for scepticism. The problems which have plagued European defence for years if not decades have certainly not vanished overnight. Yet there is a real possibility that the unprecedented alignment of the stars described above – from the proliferation of crises and an unpredictable American ally, to Brexit, the Franco-German engine and the role of Commission – is sufficient to turn the tide in this unwritten chapter of European integration.

If this happens, and a decade or so from now Europeans will think, buy and act together on defence, then the purely intergovernmental basis of their common endeavours will urgently need to be reconsidered. Were it not, then a systemic risk would loom large, one typical of the recent troubled history of European integration. Taking the eurozone as a point of comparison, at the turn of the century Europeans took a huge step forward through the monetary union. But they stopped half way, unable and unwilling to resolve the political obstacles that prevented them from completing a fiscal union too. In fair weather the half-built house stood and delivered to European citizens. When the global financial crisis hit however, the incomplete edifice risked collapsing. Likewise, if a European Security and Defence Union sees light of day in the decade ahead but the allocation of competences – or at the very least the insertion of qualified majority decision-making – does not follow, then the half-built edifice would risk crashing down if tested by a major crisis or war. Just imagine if Allison's (2017) spectre were to materialize, with a war erupting between the US and China in the years ahead, dragging Europe in at a time in which sovereignty in defence matters is still national while capabilities are increasingly European. Raising this question in official circles today is unwise, scaring leaders from taking the big and small steps made over the last two years. Ultimately, politics is the art of the possible, and what is possible not always follows the theoretically correct content and sequencing of action. However, raising and debating this question in the wider academic and policy community is essential, to speed the consequent political decisions to ensure that the edifice of a European Security and Defence Union does not remain hanging indefinitely in mid-air.

Conclusion

After centuries of warfare, European integration has brought unprecedented security, prosperity and unity to the continent. Notwithstanding the manifold crises the Union has lived through in recent years, this remains an irrefutable fact. European defence integration was meant to be one of the founding stones of the European project, but this foundered in 1954 with the French rejection of their own Pleven Plan establishing the European Defence Community. For decades, defence remained the area in which national sovereignty was most jealously guarded and thus where the European project struggled to gain traction. The underperformance in defence has been a long-standing *European* problem, which has hampered not only the EU but the European pillar in NATO too.

In today's deteriorated and radically transformed strategic environment, this is no longer sustainable. The European project cannot be built only on security and defence. But its success in the twenty-first century will likely also depend on it. In 2017 Europeans set the foundations of a European Security and Defence Union. But this is only the beginning of a steep and bumpy road. Time will tell whether the unprecedented structural and enabling factors that have brought the Union to this point are strong enough to generate the necessary European political will to overcome the insidious challenges lying ahead.

Acting credibly and coherently will be the litmus test of a European Security and Defence Union. If and when this test is passed, the sharing of national sovereignty in the field of defence will become the tallest and yet most imperative order to meet.

References

Allison, G. (2017) *Destined for War. Can America and China Escape Thucydides' Trap?* (Boston and New York: Houghton Mifflin Harcourt, Boston and New York).

Ayrault, J.-M. and Steinmeier, F.-W. (2016) 'A Strong Europe in a World of Uncertainties', Federal Foreign Office, Germany, 27 June. Available online at: https://www.auswaertiges-amt.de/en/aussenpolitik/europa/160624-bm-am-fra-st/281702.

Council of Ministers of the European Union (2017) 'Notification on Permanent Structured Co-operation (PESCO), November. Available online at: https://www.consilium.europa.eu/media/31511/171113-pesco-notification.pdf.

European Commission (2017) 'Reflection Paper on the Future of European Defence' (COM (2017)315, 7 June, Available online at: https://eur-lex.europa.eu/legal-content/en/TXT/?uri=celex:52017DC0315.

European Council (2016) 'Presidency Conclusions', 15 December. Available online at: http://www.consilium.europa.eu/media/21929/15-euco-conclusions-final.pdf.

European External Action Service (2017) 'Time for the EU to be Bold', Brussels, 14 December. Available online at: https://eeas.europa.eu/headquarters/headQuarters-homepage/37504.

EU High Representative and Vice President (2016a) 'Shared Vision, Common Action: A Stronger Europe. A Global Strategy for the EU's Foreign and Security Policy', 28 June. Available online at: https://europa.eu/globalstrategy/en/node/339.

EU High Representative and Vice President (2016b) 'Implementation Plan on Security and Defence', 14 November. Available online at: https://europa.eu/globalstrategy/en/node/459.

Fiott, D., Missiroli, A. and Tardy, T. (2017) 'Permanent Structured Cooperation: What's in a name?' *Chaillot Papers*, No. 142. Available online at: https://www.iss.europa.eu/node/2177.

German Federal Ministry of Defence (2016) *White Paper 2016 on Security Policy and the Future of the Bundeswehr* (Berlin: Federal Ministry of Defence, Germany). Available online at: https://issat.dcaf.ch/download/111704/2027268/2016WhitePaper.pdf.

Grevi, G. (2009) 'The Interpolar World. A New Scenario', *EUISS Occasional Papers*, No. 79. Available online at: https://www.iss.europa.eu/node/602.

Kagan, R. (2003) *Of Paradise and Power. America and Europe in the New World Order* (New York: Knopf).

Lazarou, E. (2016) 'Europe of Defence? Views on the Future of Defence Cooperation'. *EPRS Briefings*, July. Available online at: http://www.europarl.europa.eu/thinktank/en/document.html?reference=EPRS_BRI(2016)586607.

Lichfield, J. (2016) 'Brexit could Lead to 'Domino Effect' in Europe as Far-Right Celebrates Referendum Result', *Independent,* 24 June. Available online at: http://www.independent.co.uk/news/world/europe/brexit-could-lead-to domino effect-in-europe-as-far-right-celebrates-referendum-result-a7101391.html.

Marrone, A., Pirozzi, N. and Sartori, P. (2017) 'PESCO: An Ace in the Hand of European Defence'. *EU 60 Papers*, No. 9, March. Available online at: http://www.iai.it/sites/default/files/eu60_9.pdf.

Munich Security Conference (2017) *More European, More Connected, and More Capable. Building the European Armed Forces of the Future* (Munich Security Conference Foundation).

Available online at: https://www.securityconference.de/en/discussion/european-defence-report.

Paterson, W. (2011) 'The Reluctant Hegemon? Germany Moves Centre Stage in the European Union'. *JCMS*, Vol. 49, Annual Review, pp. 57–75.

Peña, C.V. (2017) 'Should America be the World's Policeman?' *The American Conservative*, 6 February. Available online at: http://www.theamericanconservative.com/articles/should-america-be-the-worlds-policeman.

Selmayr, M. (2017) 'She is Awake'. Twitter post, 13 November. Available online at: https://twitter.com/martinselmayr/status/930057627324862466.

Stokes, B., Wike, R. and Poushter, J. (2016) 'Europeans Face the World Divided'. *Pew Research Center Reports*, 13 June. Available online at: http://pewrsr.ch/1WIdvUf.

Taylor, P. (2017) 'Merkel's Thunderbolt is a Starting Gun for European defense drive', *Politico,* 6 January. Available online at: https://www.politico.eu/article/angela-merkel-nato-g7-donald-trump-germany-us-thunderbolt-is-starting-gun-for-european-defense-drive.

Traynor, I. (2011) 'US Defence Chief Blasts Europe over NATO', *The Guardian*, 10 June. Available online at: https://www.theguardian.com/world/2011/jun/10/nato-dismal-future-pentagon-chief.

Trump, D. (1987) 'Trump's $95,000 1987 Ad in the New York Times on Foreign Policy', *New York Times*. Available online at: https://www.reddit.com/r/The_Donald/comments/4521em.

von der Leyen, U. and Le Drian, J.-Y. (2016) 'Revitalizing CSDP. Towards a Comprehensive, Realistic and Credible Defence in the EU', 11 September, pp. 71–6. Available online at: http://www.senato.it/service/PDF/PDFServer/BGT/00990802.pdf.

Witney, N. (2017) 'EU defence Efforts Miss the Open Goal Again', *ECFR Commentaries*, 15 November. Available online at: http://www.ecfr.eu/article/commentary_eu_defence_efforts_miss_the_open_goal_again.

Youngs, R. (2017) *Europe's Eastern Crisis. The Geopolitics of Asymmetry* (Cambridge: Cambridge University Press).

JCMS 2018 Volume 56. Annual Review pp. 142–151

DOI: 10.1111/jcms.12767

Small States as Agenda-setters? The Council Presidencies of Malta and Estonia

DIANA PANKE and JULIA GUROL
Albert-Ludwigs-Universität Freiburg

Introduction

Comparing the 28 EU member states to all of today's sovereign countries, it becomes apparent that the former have much in common. They all share macro-geographical location, they are all democracies with liberal market economies, and all formally subscribe to human rights and good governance principles. Zooming into the EU reveals that the 28 EU member states also differ in several respects. Most notably, the size of their population, which ranges from 82.5 million (Germany) to 460,297 (Malta) (Eurostat, 2018a) and the size of their economies differs as well (strongest is Germany with a gross domestic product (GDP) of €3,263,350 million in 2017, the weakest being Malta with a GDP of €11,126 million in 2017) (Eurostat, 2018b). In other words: while some EU member states are relatively big in population and economy, others are considerably smaller on both counts. This contribution sheds light on how smaller EU member states act as Council Presidents and addresses the following questions: Is the Council Presidency a window of opportunity for smaller states to pursue national niche interests? Which and how many priorities did Malta and Estonia pursue whilst serving as Council Presidents? What do the Maltese and the Estonian Council Presidencies have in common and how do they differ (Hosli, 1995)?

In answering these questions, the contribution adds to the literature on small states in the European Union, which predominantly examines how small states operate in the Council of Ministers (Bjoerkdahl, 2008; Goetschel, 1998; Hanf and Soetendorp, 1998; Hosli, 1995; Magnette and Nicolaidis, 2005; Panke, 2011, 2012a; Schure and Verdun, 2008; Sepos, 2005; Thorhallsson, 2006a), but less often sheds light on the opportunities that the rotating office of the Council Presidency presents (exceptions include Panke, 2010). Accordingly, the contribution reviews insights from research on small states and develops two propositions. First, it expects that the number of issues a state is likely to pursue as Council Presidency is more limited, the smaller the state in question is. Second, it expects that the more selective states are on the topics they pursue, the more likely they are to have a lasting and prominent impact on EU policies. The subsequent part of the contribution empirically investigates these propositions by official documents and news reports. This reveals that both countries focus on a limited number of priorities during the Council Presidency, but Malta – despite being smaller than Estonia – was less selective in what they pursued. Malta focused on six priorities, which were not subsumed under one common theme. Estonia by contrast focused on digitalization as one of four priorities and streamlined this core theme in the other three areas of interest. The difference in the prioritization approaches was not without consequences: Estonia attained

'Digital Presidency' (Teffer, 2017) and succeeded in setting the EU agenda accordingly. Malta also had achievements, but they were not fundamental in character (for example, not reforming the Dublin system) and were scattered over a broad array of different policy areas. Thus, the Council Presidency is a window of opportunity for officeholders, whereby small states can make the most of it when they are highly selective and concentrate their efforts on one core theme with a high innovation potential.

I. Small States in the EU – Challenges and Strategies

Size is a social construction, and there is no one and only correct definition and measurement of what constitutes small (Goetschel, 1998; Hey, 2003; Ingebritsen *et al.*, 2006; Panke, 2010; Rothstein, 1963). Since size can ultimately have a series of real-work effects (Hosli, 1995; Panke, 2011; Panke, 2012a; Schure and Verdun, 2008; Steinmetz and Wivel, 2010; Vital, 1971), it is worth investigating. We start to do so by defining that what constitutes big and small is context dependent. Within the EU, it is not so crucial that some states have nuclear weapons while others do not possess such weapons. It is likewise not important how much the states differ in the size of their armed forces. In order to understand how the EU operates in its day-to-day practices and how the medium-term political agenda of the EU is set, a different measurement for size is needed. Formally, all EU member states are equal, as each has one vote in Intergovernmental Conferences in which the EU primary law is changed. Additionally, each EU member state has one vote in the Council of Ministers based on the double majority principle applied during the ordinary legislative procedure (Cini and Pèrez-Solòrzano Borragàn, 2015; Panke and Haubrich Seco, 2016). Yet, the states differ in two respects: first, population ranges from 460,297 in Malta to 82.5 million in Germany which is decisive for the application of the double majority principle in the Council of Ministers, since not only do at least 55 per cent of member states need to agree in order to pass a directive or a regulation, but they also need to represent at least 65 per cent of the EU population. Second, the financial capacities differ considerably between the 28 EU member states and with them, the size of their respective foreign and line ministries and the number of experts available to work on EU issues both in the respective capitals and in the permanent representations in Brussels (Panke, 2010; Panke, 2012a; Thorhallsson, 2006b). This contribution investigates the operation of the Council Presidency. Accordingly, differences in financial capacities and – linked to that – the size of the ministries and permanent representation are likely to be more important than differences in population size.

Small states with limited financial capacities and corresponding limited human resources based on slimmer ministries and embassies face challenges in multilevel governance systems, such as the EU. In multilevel governance systems, policy cycles take place on the state and the regional or international level of the system (Panke and Haubrich Seco, 2016). This places a high demand on the capacities of actors, especially if the number of policy proposals on negotiation tables is high. In the European Union's ordinary legislative procedure, each proposal for a directive or regulation is drafted by the European Commission as the executive branch and negotiated and passed by the European Parliament together with the Council of Ministers, which form the legislative branch. In order to actively participate in the Council of Ministers and shape EU policy outcomes, national delegates need to be present in the working group, COREPER and ministerial meetings and need to know the position of their respective countries (Panke, 2010, 2012a). Given the broad array of items on the negotiation agenda in the Council of Ministers, small EU member states grapple with the challenges of actively participating in all issues. Slim ministries back home can run into capacity shortages and face situations in which they won't be able to develop national positions and negotiation instructions (with the proposal for changes, speaking points, red lines and well-backed up reasons for all of them) for all issues on the negotiation agenda. Without such positions, smaller EU member states tend to be silent on some topics or only participate actively in the negotiations at later stages in case instructions arrive with a delay. In addition, smaller states with limited numbers of attachés and diplomats posted in Brussels are more likely than bigger member states to encounter situations in which they do not have enough manpower to physically attend all the negotiation meetings that are ongoing in parallel in the EU (Panke, 2010, 2012a). Both, delayed or missing instructions from the capitals as well as insufficient manpower available in Brussels, negatively affect the chances of smaller EU member states to exert influence over the content of EU policy and leave national imprints on EU law (Panke, 2010, 2012a).

Given these challenges, smaller member states have developed counter-strategies that can help cope with the fact that they tend to have smaller budgets and slimmer ministries and delegations than larger EU member states. Two of these strategies are selective engagement (prioritization) and using windows of opportunity to promote their own interests.

Rather than covering all themes with relevance to the EU and preparing in detail for all issues on the EU's agenda, smaller states increase their chances of exerting an impact on policy outcomes if they pick and choose. Being selective and engaging in systematic prioritization allows them to save scarce resources on less essential themes and redirect them to issues of high priority (Bunse, 2009; Laffan, 2006; Magnúsdóttir, 2010; Tiilikainen, 2006). Accordingly, for its prioritized issues, it is less likely that a smaller state will lack the human resources to attend all negotiation meetings in Brussels and it is also less likely that its delegation in Brussels does not obtain instructions from the capital back home (Panke, 2010, 2012b). In addition, smaller states can concentrate their diplomatic resources in Brussels on their high priority issues, and systematically engage in lobbying and coalition-building exercises to increase their chances of being successful in the Council negotiations. The more limited the capacities a state has available, the more critical a selective approach to EU policy-making becomes. Thus, the smaller the state in question, the lower the number of issues it is likely to pursue in general and as Council Presidency.

Second, larger states have more extensive diplomatic networks in Brussels to other delegations, the EP and the Commission than smaller states allowing them to use these resources to promote national interests in the day-to-day operation of the EU. Thus the Council Presidency provides a window of opportunity especially for smaller states with less political clout (Magnúsdóttir, 2010; Panke, 2012b). The office rotates every six months amongst the 28 EU member states – irrespective of their size. The state holding the Council Presidency has the competency to influence the political agenda of the EU (Elgström, 2003; Quaglia and Moxon-Browne, 2006; Schalk et al., 2007; Tallberg, 2003). Hence, smaller states can use this office as a means to provide impulses for the development of the EU that reflect national priorities – even if they represent a country's niche interests. Thereby, smaller states are more likely to be successful in having a lasting and prominent impact on EU policies the more selective they are on the topics they pursue.

Table 1: GDP EU Member States in 2017

Country	GDP in million €, 2017	Country	GDP in million €, 2017
Austria	369,685.9	Italy	1,716,934.7
Belgium	437,204.1	Latvia	26,856.6
Bulgaria	50,430.6	Lithuania	41,857.0
Croatia	48,676.9	Luxembourg	55,377.6
Cyprus	19,213.8^P	Malta	11,126.0
Czech Republic	192,016.6	Netherlands	733,168.0^P
Denmark	288,373.5	Poland	465,604.9
Estonia	23,002.3	Portugal	193,072.0^e
Finland	223,522.0	Romania	187,868.3^P
France	2,291,705.0^P	Slovakia	84,985.2
Germany	3,263,350.0	Slovenia	43,278.1
Greece	177,735.3^P	Spain	1,163,662.0^P
Hungary	123,494.6	Sweden	477,383.0
Ireland	296,151.8	United Kingdom	2,324,293.1

Note: ^{P} = provisional, ^{e} = estimated.

Using GDP as a proxy for how much finance and manpower states have at their availability to tackle the tasks assigned with holding the Council Presidency, some states are considerably smaller than others (see Table 1). Together the EU member states' GDP was €15,330,010.9 million in 2017, and the country average was €547,501.014 million. Estonia and Malta have below average GDPs and can, therefore, be regarded as smaller EU member states.

On this basis, the remainder of the contribution investigates two aspects:

(1) Malta is smaller than Estonia. Does the size difference between Estonia and Malta play out empirically? Is Malta engaging more heavily in the prioritization of topics than Estonia?
(2) In the EU-28 context, both states are relatively small. Thus, did Estonia and Malta use the office of the Council Presidency to promote selected niche interests in the EU?

II. Empirical Analysis: Estonia and Malta as Council Presidencies

Malta held the Council Presidency from 1 January to the 30 June 2017. In its Presidency Programme, named rEUnion, Malta introduced six priorities around which its Council leadership was based. These were (1) reaching agreements on migration and asylum, (2) addressing instability in the Mediterranean and the near abroad, (3) improving the Digital Single Market, (4) building an inclusive society, (5) implementing border security measures including maritime security, and (6) ensuring the sustainability of the ocean and promoting growth in areas such as maritime tourism and sea freight (Programme of the Maltese Presidency of the Council of the European Union, 2017, p. 7). For every one of the six priorities, the Maltese Presidency outlined several more specific themes. First, Malta intended reforming the EU's asylum rules as well as the Dublin system as such. In its second priority, Malta emphasized instability in the EU's Southern neighbourhood, especially Libya. In addition, Malta pushed for facilitating trade within the EU by 'tearing down the digital fences' ('Programme of the Maltese Presidency of the Council of the European Union', 2017, p. 7). As part of its fourth priority, Malta intended to tackle gender violence and social exclusion, whilst creating equal opportunities for people of all sexual orientations. Within the priority 'border security measures' Malta emphasized the establishment of an Entry/Exit System as well as the development of a European Travel Information and Authorization System. As part of the sixth priority, the Maltese Presidency wanted to promote a cleaner and more environmental friendly usage of maritime resources and revise the European Maritime Transport Strategy 2018.

Estonia succeeded Malta as Council Presidency and took office on 1 July 2017. Originally Estonia had been due to serve as Council Presidency for the first half of 2018, but stepped up and took office six months earlier than planned as the United Kingdom decided to leave the EU. During its Presidency, Estonia focused on four priorities. Apart from mainstreaming the theme of digitalization in all policy areas, digitalization additionally formed a priority of its own. The four Estonian priorities were (1) innovation in economy, (2) safety and security issues, (3) digitalization and a free movement of data, as well as (4) inclusiveness and sustainability ('Programme of the Estonian Presidency of the Council of the European Union', 2017). These priorities included several items which each related to digitalization. For instance, in the realm of safety and security, they emphasized the role of information technology both for border security and border control and for combatting terrorism and organized crime. Also, the Presidency stressed the need for the development of a digital society in all areas of life, such as cross-border e-commerce, e-services, e-health, e-justice and e-privacy, and promoted the notions of a smart economy and e-government. The fourth priority, inclusiveness and sustainability, covered a series of themes including the role of IT in the economy and the environment, the implementation of the Paris Agreement, and ideas towards strengthened equal opportunities in Europe.

Although both states are relatively small in the EU-context, Estonia is larger than Malta. Accordingly, we would expect that the latter engaged more strongly in prioritizing than the former and pursued a lower number of priorities during its Council Presidency.

While Malta identified six priorities, Estonia only four (and all relating to the theme of digitalization). In addition to the six priorities, Malta identified topics of relevance in each policy area (Foreign Affairs; Economic and Financial Affairs; Justice and Home Affairs; Employment, Social Policy, Health and Consumer Affairs; Competitiveness; Transport, Telecommunication and Energy; Agriculture and Fisheries; Environment; as well as Education, Youth, Culture and Sport) and outlined how it will use its Presidency to further developments in the respective areas ('Programme of the Maltese Presidency of the Council of the European Union', 2017, p. 3). Estonia's Council Presidency Programme also incorporates additional issues of importance. Yet, it does not cover each policy area separately but instead subsumes the topics of relevance under its four outlined priorities, which are subject to IT-mainstreaming.

Thus, Estonia engages more strongly and more systematically in setting a limited number of priorities, while Malta has a more encompassing and more comprehensive approach to its Presidency. Looking at GDP as a proxy for a country's financial capacities, Estonia has twice as many resources as Malta. Accordingly, the fact that

Estonia is more selective in its engagement than Malta is not in line with the expectation developed above, according to which smaller states concentrate their scarce financial and human resources on a lower number of priorities that they pursue during their Council Presidency.

Malta and Estonia faced similar geopolitical situations in 2017. This included the Brexit debate, growing terrorism, the ongoing migration crises, the unstable security situation in the EU's Southern neighbourhood, transatlantic uncertainties and increasing populism (Bendel and Magnúsdóttir, 2017). Accordingly, one of the most significant challenges to both Presidencies was marshalling the EU's approach towards the Brexit negotiations on the withdrawal of the United Kingdom from the EU in accordance with the EU Council guidelines ('Programme of the Estonian Presidency of the Council of the European Union', 2017). Although no formal Brexit-related agreement could be reached during its Council Presidency, Malta managed to create unity among the remaining EU27 (*Politico*, 2017b). Similarly, Estonia stressed the importance of adapting to a Union of 27 'as swiftly as possible' ('Programme of the Estonian Presidency of the Council of the European Union', 2017). Despite the high workload associated with this and the other ongoing issues, both Estonia and Malta also used the office of the Council Presidency to promote their prioritized interests in the EU.

Both small states not only formulated priorities but also acted upon them. In the case of Malta, this was reforming the EU's approach to migration and asylum, as well as several other issues that were given considerable weight such as maritime security and fisheries (*Politico*, 2017b). In contrast, Estonia placed its primary emphasis on one topic: digitalization, which was not only one of the four priorities but also a cross-cutting issue in the other three priorities (*Politico*, 2017a).

Located less than 300 km from the Northern Africa coast, Malta is a popular transit country on the refugee route from Northern Africa to Europe (Migration Policy Centre, 2018). Therefore, it is an essential national interest to implement border security measures, reach agreements on migration and address instability in the South and the Mediterranean. Together with Italy, Malta had already called upon the other EU member states for support to share the responsibility of the refugee crisis and, during its Presidency, Malta managed to raise this issue to the top of the political agenda. The Valletta Informal Council passed a Malta Declaration, with emphasis on the island's external borders and concrete measures to handle immigration. This declaration was assisted by further dossiers on border management and control and introduced a specific entry-exit system for the detection of migrants with links to terrorism and organized crime (Agius, 2017). Furthermore, the Maltese Presidency was able to push a political agreement on the establishment of a joint EU Agency for Asylum (European Council, 2017). These successes were due to the agenda-setting activities of Malta as well as the geopolitical developments and the associated high issue salience across the EU (Dinan *et al.*, 2017; Scipioni, 2017). Despite these achievements, Malta did not bring about comprehensive and fundamental reform of the Dublin system and also did not facilitate a consensus amongst the 28 EU member states with respect to the underlying normative and political issues.

Estonia, on the other hand, had one core priority: digitalization (Teffer, 2017). More specifically, it promoted digitalization and the usage of IT in the political, the economic and the social sphere. One of the main reasons behind Estonia's rise as a digital leader is that the country managed to build trust in technology amongst its citizens. Not in the least due to the accessibility of data by the individuals concerned, the transparency of data usage, and the high standards of data security (Auväärt and Kaska, 2017). This contrasts with many other countries, such as Great Britain and Germany, where similar digital transformation attempts remain difficult (Kollmann and Schmidt, 2016). Estonia has been a frontrunner in digitalization for some time already (Björklund, 2016). The process started in the 1990s when the Estonian government introduced computers at school and digitalized processes such as elections or the registration of companies (Lorenz *et al.*, 2016). Estonian reputation as being a digital leader is reflected in NATO's decision to move its cyber-security headquarters to Tallinn. Being the leading digital country of Europe, research and innovation in the IT and digitalization realm played a vital role in its political programme. Thus, it is not surprising that Estonia used the Council Presidency as a means to bringing digitalization and technological development to the forefront of the EU's agenda in the form of digital policy, digital events and digital legacy. Estonia's digital priorities went beyond the Digital Single Market 'for the purpose of achieving economic success and the well-being of citizens' ('Programme of the Estonian Presidency of the Council of the European Union', 2017) and included themes such as e-residency, e-commerce, e-services, e-health and e-privacy. In order to further promote its interest, Estonia invested their own capacities in order to organize several conferences and workshops, such as the Digital Summit in September 2017 in Tallinn to discuss visions for the digital future of Europe or the conference on Health in the Digital Society in Tallinn in October 2017. Amongst the most remarkable successes in this policy area, is the 'Tallinn Declaration on eGovernment' that outlines pathways of future development towards a free movement of services and data between member states. Besides that, the Economic and Financial Affairs Council reached an agreement on the updating of the e-commerce VAT package in December 2017. This includes simplifying measures for intra-EU sales of e-services as of 2019 and facilitating cross-border trade as of 2021 (European Commission, 2017). In addition, the Estonian Presidency successfully pushed for the conclusion of negotiations and the passing of the corresponding legal acts on geo-blocking which concerns limitations of online access based on the location of users and parcel delivery across borders facilitating online shopping (Teffer, 2017). Furthermore, Estonia concluded an agreement for starting negotiations with the European Parliament about regulation on the free movement of non-personal data and initiated a plan to regulate geo-blocking and facilitate e-commerce (Estonian Presidency of the Council of the European Union, 2017). Overall, the Estonian Presidency brought innovative digital topics to the EU's agenda and also triggered discussions on additional digital issues among other EU member states' governments (*Politico*, 2017a). In addition, legislative initiatives, such as a directive on copyright in the digital market, a regulation on e-privacy, or a regulation on digital media, are still underway (Stupp, 2018).

In sum, as expected, both small countries used the Council Presidency to promote specific national interests. Yet, the countries differ with respect to the extent to which the Council Presidency could amplify their reputations as policy leaders and as forces for reform in the EU. While Estonia sharpened its profile as a digital leader and was successful in proving the impetus for political change in the EU in this area, Malta's record is less pronounced. The Maltese Presidency did not trigger a fundamental re-thinking in the migration and asylum field, and comprehensive reform of the EU's migration and asylum system is difficult and not yet in sight. In addition to placing emphasis on a policy area in which fundamental reform is needed but political consensus on whether and how is lacking, Malta did not promote one flagship project as such but pursued other policy issues with almost equal emphasis. For instance, in the realms of maritime issues and fishery, Malta managed to organize support for a 'North Sea Multiannual Plan; the Sustainable Management of External Fishing Fleets; the MedFish4Ever declaration to save Mediterranean fish stocks; and rules on the characteristics of fishing vessels' (*Politico*, 2017b). As a result of limited prioritization and focus on policy areas in which reform was politically difficult, both the extent of policy innovation and the depth and scope of the reforms triggered by Malta lag behind Estonia. While the latter made a name for itself as a beacon of digitalization, Malta did not brand itself in any particular way.

Conclusions

In the EU28, both Malta and Estonia are smaller EU member states. Therefore, they have fewer capacities and less political influence in the day-to-day operations of the EU. Thus, the office of the EU Council Presidency provides a window of opportunity for these small states to amplify their voices and provide an impetus for reform in the EU in line with their core interests.

Comparing Malta with Estonia, it becomes apparent that the former engages less intensely in setting priorities to pursue in their Council Presidency than the latter. While Malta had six different priorities, Estonia focused on four, which were all more or less related to the theme of digitalization. Although being smaller and having fewer resources, Malta was not as selective as Estonia. This contribution argued that this difference in their approach to the office of the Presidency had consequences. Estonia could sharpen their reputation as being Europe's digital leader and managed to leave an imprint on the EU in this respect. Compared to that, Malta's impact was less pronounced. Malta reached several accomplishments in the area of migration and asylum as well as in its other priorities. Yet, there is no single achievement that sticks out as being fundamental in character or representing a high level of novelty and innovation.

Hence, the empirical analysis of the Council Presidency of these two smaller EU member states supports the insight from the more general small state literature that selective engagement and a high level of prioritization is an important factor for small state success in regional and international organizations. Concentrating efforts on a limited number of issues and selecting the issues carefully is key for smaller states to become influential political force – despite operating with more limited capacities than larger states.

References

Agius, P. (2017) 'A Look Back at Malta's Presidency', *Times of Malta*, 2 July.

Auväärt, G. and Kaska, K. (2017) 'Ensuring the Digital Way of Life in E-Estonia'. Available online at: https://e-estonia.com/digital-way-life-e-estonia/. Last accessed: 18 January 2018.

Bendel, J. and Magnúsdóttir, G.L. (2017) 'Opportunities and Challenges of a Small State Presidency: The Estonian Council Presidency 2017'. *Administrative Culture*, Vol. 18, No. 1, pp. 17–52.

Bjoerkdahl, A. (2008) 'Norm Advocacy: A Small State Strategy to Influence the EU'. *Journal of European Public Policy*, Vol. 15, No. 1, pp. 135–54.

Björklund, F. (2016) 'E-Government and Moral Citizenship: The Case of Estonia'. *Citizenship studies*, Vol. 20, pp. 914–31.

Bunse, S. (2009) *Small States and EU Governance Leadership through the Council Presidency* (Basingstoke: Palgrave Macmillan).

Cini, M. and Pèrez-Solòrzano Borragàn, N. (2015) *European Union Politics* (Oxford: Oxford University Press).

Dinan, D., Nugent, N. and Paterson, W.E. (2017) *The European Union in Crisis* (New York: Springer).

Elgström, O. (2003) *European Union Council Presidencies. A Comparative Perspective* (London: Routledge).

Estonian Presidency of the Council of the European Union (2017) 'The Preliminary Results of the Estonian Presidency of the Council of the European Union as of 21 December 2017' (03.01.2018). Available online at: https://e-estonia.com/digital-way-life-e-estonia/. Last accessed: 18 January 2018.

European Commission (2017) 'VAT: Commission Welcomes Agreement on Simpler and More Efficient Rules for Businesses That Sell Goods Online (IP/17/4404)' (5 December 2017).

European Council (2017) 'EU Agency for Asylum: Presidency and European Parliament Reach a Broad Political Agreement (431/17)' (Brussels).

Eurostat (2018a) 'Population on 1 January'. Available online at: http://ec.europa.eu/eurostat/tgm/table.do?tab=table&plugin=1&language=en&pcode=tps00001. Last accessed: 18 June 2018.

Eurostat (2018b) 'Gross Domestic Product at Market Prices'. Available online at: ec.europa.eu/eurostat/tgm/refreshTableAction.do?tab=table&plugin=1&pcode=tec00001&language=en. Last accessed: 18 June 2018.

Goetschel, L. (1998) *Small States Inside and Outside the European Union: Interests and Policies* (Boston, MA: Kluver Academic Publishers).

Hanf, K. and Soetendorp, B. (1998) *Adapting to European Integration: Small States and the European Union* (London: Longman).

Hey, J.A.K. (2003) *Small States in World Politics: Explaining Foreign Policy Behavior* (Boulder, CO: Lynne Rienner Publishers).

Hosli, M.O. (1995) 'The Balance between Small and Large: Effects of a Double-Majority System on Voting Power in the European Union'. *International Studies Quarterly*, Vol. 39, pp. 351–70.

Ingebritsen, C., Neumann, I.B., Gstoehl, S. and Beyer, J. (2006) *Small States in International Relations* (Seattle, WA: University of Washington Press).

Kollmann, T. and Schmidt, H. (2016) *Deutschland 4.0* (Wiesbaden: Springer Fachmedien Wiesbaden).

Laffan, B. (2006) 'Managing Europe from Home in Dublin, Athens and Helsinki: A Comparative Analysis'. *West European Politics*, Vol. 29, pp. 687–708.

Lorenz, B., Kikkas, K. and Laanpere, M. (2016) 'Digital Turn in the Schools of Estonia: Obstacles and Solutions'. In Zaphiris, P. and Ioannou, A. (eds) *Learning and Collaboration Technologies* (Cham: Springer International Publishing), pp. 722–31.

Magnette, P. and Nicolaidis, K. (2005) 'Coping with the Lilliput Syndrome: Large vs Small States in the European Convention'. *European Public Law*, Vol. 11, pp. 83–102.

Magnúsdóttir, G.L. (2010) *Small States' Power Resources in EU Negotiations: Nordic Eco-Entrepreneurship within the Environmental Policy of the European Union* (Saarbrücken, Germany: LAP Lambert Academic Publishing).

Migration Policy Centre (2018) *Malta* (Florence: Migration Policy Center).

Panke, D. (2010) 'Small States in the European Union: Structural Disadvantages in EU Policy-Making and Counter-Strategies'. *Journal of European Public Policy*, Vol. 17, No. 6, pp. 801–19.

Panke, D. (2011) 'Small States in EU Negotiations. Political Dwarfs or Power-Brokers?' *Cooperation and Conflict*, Vol. 46, No. 2, pp. 123–43.

Panke, D. (2012a) 'Explaining Differences in the Shaping Effectiveness. Why Some States Are More Effective in Making Their Voices Heard in International Negotiations'. *Comparative European Politics*, Vol. 10, No. 1, pp. 111–32.

Panke, D. (2012b) 'Being Small in a Big Union: Punching Above Their Weights? How Small States Prevailed in the Vodka and the Pesticides Cases'. *Cambridge Review of International Affairs*, Vol. 25, No. 3, pp. 329–44.

Panke, D. and Haubrich Seco, M. (2016) 'EU and Supranational Governance'. In Torfing, J. and Ansell, C. (eds) *Handbook on Theories of Governance* (Cheltenham: Edward Elgar), pp. 499–513.

Politico (2017a) 'Estonia's Presidency: How It Went'. *Politico,* 20 December. Available online at: https://www.politico.eu/article/estonias-presidency-how-it-went/

Politico (2017b) 'Malta's EU Presidency: How It Went'. *Politico,* 30 June. Available online at: https://www.politico.eu/article/maltas-eu-presidency-how-did-it-go/

'Programme of the Estonian Presidency of the Council of the European Union' (2017). Available online at: https://www.eu2017.ee/node/3062.html. Last accessed: 20 June 2018.

'Programme of the Maltese Presidency of the Council of the European Union' (2017). Available online at: https://www.eu2017.mt/en/Documents/NationalProgramme_EN.pdf. Last accessed: 20 June 2018.

Quaglia, L. and Moxon-Browne, E. (2006) 'What Makes a Good EU Presidency? Italy and Ireland Compared'. *JCMS*, Vol. 44, No. 2, pp. 349–68.

Rothstein, R.L. (1963) *Alliances and Small Powers* (New York: Columbia University Press).

Schalk, J., Torenvlied, R., Weesie, J. and Strokman, F. (2007) 'The Power of the Presidency in EU Council Decision-Making'. *European Union Politics*, Vol. 8, No. 2, pp. 229–50.

Schure, P. and Verdun, A. (2008) 'Legislative Bargaining in the European Union: The Divide between Large and Small Member States'. *European Union Politics*, Vol. 9, No. 4, pp. 459–86.

Scipioni, M. (2017) 'Failing Forward in EU Migration Policy? EU Integration after the 2015 Asylum and Migration Crisis'. *Journal of European Public Policy*, Advance online publication.

Sepos, A. (2005) 'Differentiated Integration in the EU: The Position of Small Member States'. *EUI Working Papers*.

Steinmetz, R. and Wivel, A. (2010) *Small States in Europe. Challenges and Opportunities* (Farnham: Ashgate).

Stupp, C. (2018) 'EU Scrambles to Finish Digital Single Market in 2018', *Euractiv,* 12 January.

Tallberg, J. (2003) 'The Agenda-Shaping Powers of the EU Council Presidency'. *Journal of European Public Policy*, Vol. 10, No. 1, pp. 1–19.

Teffer, P. (2017) 'Estonia Completes Two out of Three Priority Digital Bills', *EU Observer*, 14 December.

Thorhallsson, B. (2006a) 'The Role of Small States in the European Union'. In Ingebritsen, C., Neumann, I.B., Gstoehl, S. and Beyer, J. (eds) *Small States in International Relations* (Seattle, WA: University of Washington Press), pp. 218–27.

Thorhallsson, B. (2006b) 'The Size of States in the European Union: Theoretical and Conceptual Perspectives'. *European Integration*, Vol. 28, No. 1, pp. 7–31.

Tiilikainen, T. (2006) 'Finland - An EU Member with a Small State Identity'. *Journal of European Integration*, Vol. 28, No. 1, pp. 73–87.

Vital, D. (1971) *The Survival of Small States: Studies in Small Power/Great Power Conflict* (London: Oxford University Press).

Index

Note: Italicised page references indicate information contained in tables.

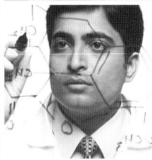